Cultural Dividends

JONATHAN PALMER AND
JOHNNIE BROWN

PAGE PUBLISHING, INC.
Conneaut Lake, PA

First originally published by Page Publishing 2021

ISBN 978-1-6624-5555-1 (pbk)
ISBN 978-1-6624-5556-8 (digital)

Printed in the United States of America

Episode 1

Scene one. Scene one takes place at the engagement party for Haseem and his beautiful fiancée, Nadia; everyone is there for this celebration. Parents and family of both Haseem and Nadia, along with their close friends, Haseem's business partners, and college friends that are his most reliable friends in his life are there to enjoy this special moment with him. Mohan, Peter, and Steven have been there for Haseem for everything, and the bond that they created in college is working out to be great. Mohan's parents, Peter's parents, and Steven's parents are also there for the engagement party, along with some outside friends of theirs. The engagement is held at Haseem's parents' home which is a beautiful mansion with a lovely backyard. The event is being catered, and a DJ is playing a good mix of music. Steven is standing alone and can't help to think about all the good times that they had back in college and how this bond they created has made their investment firm millions way before their goal of turning thirty. He starts to reminisce and narrates their unique story of commitment and what they called the Triple D Effect: "Have the discipline to work hard to achieve your goal, be determined to do whatever it takes to get there, and be dedicated to your dream and let no one stop you from winning."

Scene two. Peter, Mohan, Steven, and Haseem are talking with one another about how things started when they were in college. Everyone is sharing laughs and socializing with one another at the engagement party; the waiters and waitresses are serving food and drinks to everyone.

STEVEN. Haseem, I'm very happy for you even though I think you're a little too young to get tied down, but it's your life, and if you're fine with missing out on all the fun out there. (*Steven makes a funny facial expression on his face, like he doesn't understand why.*)

HASEEM. Hey, listen, I have enjoyed my college years very well. All of you guys know that I was the original playboy of the crew.

Mohan, Peter, and Steven look at one another with a frown on their faces and nod their heads in agreement with what Haseem just said.

PETER. Whatever, I'm not gonna debate on who was the player out of the crew. That is pretty much irrelevant with what we got going on.

MOHAN. Yeah, I agree with Peter, Haseem. The only thing to me that's important to be remembered is, no matter what, the firm is number one and on the same level of your marriage.

Haseem shakes his head in agreement with Mohan and looks at the guys with a serious look on his face.

HASEEM. You guys know I respect the rules that we all agreed to in college. I love Nadia, and she is a sweetheart, but she knows my loyalty and commitment to the firm.

STEVEN. That's right, and I respect that about her. Some woman wouldn't go into a marriage unless they could be only number one. She is a Ryder. No matter how big we build this firm, jealousy and envy can never get in the way of success. We are brothers, and we will always love one another and be there for one another no matter what.

Everyone shakes their head in agreement and take a sip of their drinks while they look around at everyone at the engagement party.

MOHAN. Haseem, we all are happy for you, and we want you to know that we will never violate quality time with you and your family unless it's extremely, extremely important.

PETER. Loyalty and trust is what built our firm. Our firm must stay pure and never stained from betrayal. Just like how I shared my profits from the restaurant in the early stages to get Cultural Dividends going. I love you guys, and greed will never destroy us.

All four men agree with one another and tap their glasses together and have a toast to celebrate the moment.

Scene three. Nadia and her friends are sharing laughs and good times; her friends are not only congratulating her on her engagement but also reminding her that Haseem is rich and his friends like Jamal and Steven are dogs and that she must keep her guard up at all times. They also wouldn't mind getting to know Peter, Mohan, or Steven a little better. Nadia reassures them that she believes in Haseem and that he has proven his love for her. And she accepts and understands the bond and brotherhood that he has with his firm. Nadia is happy and can't wait to start working on raising a family and buying a home also.

NADIA'S FRIEND KIA. Nadia, you definitely picked a good one. Haseem is smart and educated. He is driven and committed to being successful. Plus, he's handsome and comes from a good family that got his back.

Nadia and her friends smile in agreement with what Kia said, and they nod their heads and sip on their drinks.

NADIA'S FRIEND SHAWNA. Just keep your eyes open, girl, because Haseem is a girl magnet and you know that. Let's be honest. He's young and got money, tall and handsome, drives big cars. Yeah, girl, keep your claws dug in on his ass.

Nadia looks over at Haseem with a smile on her face while her girlfriends look at one another with a slight frown on their faces. Nadia watches Haseem for a few seconds and then looks back at her friends.

NADIA. My man is focused on building his future. Our future is his number one concern. All he talks about is business and building his company. He is zoned in on money, not pleasure. But trust me, I know the games men can play. I'm not some dumb Sweet Valley High airhead that's not hip to game. I got my eyes open, but I trust my man, and he got my heart.

NADIA'S FRIEND KIA. Well, good for you, girl. Now when do you plan on hooking us up with some of his baller friends?

Nadia's friends all nod their heads in agreement with big smiles on their faces and give Nadia looks that says, "What is taking so long?" Nadia looks back at her friends and just shakes her head while looking away. She stares at Peter, Mohan, and Steven and then looks back at her girlfriends.

NADIA. Look, knowing Haseem's friends and his business partners the way I do, none of them are looking to settling down in a serious relationship. Unless y'all looking to have a little fun in the fast lane, then that's your decision and your feelings and emotions.

NADIA'S FRIEND SHAWNA. Look, girl, I understand what you saying 'cause I don't have time for games, but if I was to get a few nights with any of them, believe me, their nose will be wide-open.

NADIA. Don't sleep on them, girl. They may not look like they are experienced and hipped to the game, but they on point. And they so focus on their business. They won't put too much attention into finding love, especially Mohan and Peter.

The girls glance back at Haseem and his friends and take a sip of their drinks. Nadia's girlfriends' facial expressions look like they just found out terrible news.

NADIA'S FRIEND KIA. In time, one of them gonna come sniffing up one of our legs, and we'll put it on them so good they ain't gonna know how to handle us.

Nadia and her friends laugh out loud that causes a few people to look over at them; they continue to laugh and shake their head in agreement, causing Haseem and his friends to look over at them.

Scene four. Haseem's parents pull him aside and talk to him about commitment and what it takes to raise a successful family, and it's going to take dedication and commitment to sustain a happy marriage. Haseem's mother is stern on him being faithful to Nadia and not letting money and power get in the way of him being loyal to her. His father reminds him of what he had to endure and go through to not cheat on his mother. Haseem starts to get a little annoyed, but he is loyal to his father and listens to everything he says.

HASEEM's DAD. Well, son, it's a very big step you're about to make. Are you ready to make such a commitment?

HASEEM. Yeah, I'm ready. I already started doing the right thing by cutting off lady friends, not returning their texts or calls.

HASEEM's DAD. Yeah, well, it's a little more to it than that, son. You know, finding love is one thing, but sustaining love and keeping it strong and burning is another. To make it twenty or thirty years in marriage requires hard work and dedication. Now I know how you can be committed to your firm, but can you be committed to keeping your love strong for one woman?

Haseem looks at his father and mother with a curious expression on his face; he shakes his head at his father like he is shocked that his dad is questioning his loyalty.

HASEEM. Dad, trust me, I meet beautiful women almost every day. Almost everywhere I go, I get looks and smiles from women. But I remember what you taught me growing up, and I will never forget it. Women subtract from what you're trying to do and accomplish in life. They can be a distraction and steer you away from achieving your goals. I have applied those teachings to my life and live by that code.

7

Haseem's dad flashes a very big smile on his face; he looks at Haseem with a very proud look on his face. He then looks at his wife with an even bigger smile and shakes his head at her. Haseem's mother looks at her husband with an evil quick stare and then looks at her son.

HASEEM'S MOM. Well, I never agreed with that bullshit. If anything, the right woman builds you up and upgrades you with her support. That is what I want you to understand. Make sure she is willing to support you and keep you driven. Make sure she backs you and is not concerned with materialistic things that you can give her.

Haseem nods his head in agreement with his mother and glances over at Nadia as she is talking with her girlfriends.

HASEEM. You're 100 percent right, Mom, and you know, I definitely ain't gonna let any lady take me for a ride down sucker lane! Nadia isn't like that. She never asked me for anything yet. She is laid-back and humble and not looking for the luxury life.

HASEEM'S MOM. I really don't see that in her either. She really loves you, Haseem, but just make sure your passion of success rubs off on her. Young women lack motivation.

Haseem's mother looks at her son with a serious look on her face; she looks at her husband and takes a deep breath. Haseem looks at his mother, knowing that there is more to come.

HASEEM'S MOM. I will be very upset with you if you let your fast-paced life get in the way of being loyal and faithful. No woman deserves to be cheated on and humiliated. That is probably the worst thing you can do to a married woman, walk on her heart, and crush her trust. She will never fully recover.

Haseem's mom glances at her husband with the corner of her eyes and looks back at her son. Haseem's father looks at his wife and looks away to the partygoers.

HASEEM. Believe me, Mom, I know. You always told me not to marry unless I'm ready, and I am ready. I will not hurt her like that. Nobody will still my heart from her, trust me!

Haseem and his parents smile at each other, and the scene ends.

Scene five. Steven and Peter share a drink together and discuss business. Peter wants to expand his restaurant chain down to Belmar where Steven is from. Steven and Haseem want to hurry up and start cashing in on the medical pot industry and think that the firm is dragging their feet. Peter doesn't mind, but he wants to make sure everything is right before they venture into it, but he also wants Steven to think about letting Mohan handle that business venture.

PETER. I've been thinking really hard about opening up another restaurant down in the South Jersey area. I found some good locations in the Belmar area. The Japanese population has doubled over the years, and there isn't any high-end Japanese restaurants down in that area.

STEVEN. It's a good idea, I think. You said you want to open up a few more locations this year. I was wondering when and where you were gonna make your move.

PETER. Well, you know, it's always about timing in the business world. I didn't wanna overextend our cash flow this early. We got quite a few business opportunities waiting to launch.

STEVEN. Yeah, like me and Haseem, still waiting for approval to get the ball rolling on the medical pot dispensaries. When are we gonna discuss and vote on this thing?

Peter looks at Steven as if Steven is rushing things; his facial expression is in deep thought. He looks around the party and then looks back at Steven. He puts his hand in his pocket and takes a sip of his drink.

PETER. With no disrespect, Steven, I want Mohan and Felize to do some deep research on it first, and I already told Haseem to have his aunt pull a little legal leverage for us. Don't worry, that is already in motion.

STEVEN. You want me to let my people on the board know so we can get easy approval? (*Peter shakes his head as he looks at Steven and takes a long pause and looks around.*)

Peter. Yeah, we definitely gonna need that, but also on another note, I've been looking at your sports bar numbers, and it's doing really well. In the near future, you should think about opening up another one down South Jersey somewhere.

STEVEN. It's crossed my mind already, but the hours and work it takes is more than I expected. I might have to hire some help soon.

Peter smiles at Steven and shakes his head a little while he turns around and looks around the engagement party. Steven looks back at Peter, wondering what he is smiling at.

PETER. It's just funny to me because I knew you were going to start complaining about that sooner or later. It's kind of hard chasing girls and partying with your cousin and balancing business too.

Peter continues to laugh at Steven and grabs him on the shoulder and looks at him. Steven doesn't find things so funny as he isn't really smiling or laughing. The scene ends with Steven taking a sip of his drink and starts to crack a smile himself and turns back to Peter before he walks away.

STEVEN. Whatever, man. I am learning things faster than you think.

Scene six. All the parents get together for a toast and reminisce on how rough it was getting those hardheaded boys to do the right thing and get their education. They also are proud of them establishing a strong bond and turning their firm into a success. They joke about how Haseem is the first one to show maturity by wanting to get married and start a family, and they hope their boys will follow soon.

STEVEN'S MOM. This is a really nice engagement party, and Haseem has picked a beautiful bride to be. Y'all should be very proud of him. Maybe some of his maturity will rub off on Steven.

PETER'S MOTHER. Yes, I am hoping the same for Peter. He is so focused on building his businesses and the firm. I don't know if I will ever have a daughter-in-law or grandchild.

PETER'S FATHER. These boys are young. They're not even thirty yet, and heck, I ain't ready to be babysitting just yet. They got plenty of time to find that special one. It takes time and patience, and I rather Peter not rush love. It will come.

HASEEM'S FATHER. I agree with that all the way. Sometimes I think that our wives are more concerned about being grandmothers and mothers-in-law instead of enjoying the free life that we get to enjoy now.

Mohan's father nods his head in agreement with Haseem's father and looks at his wife with a smile on his face, then looks around to all the wives with his eyebrows raised.

MOHAN'S FATHER. Yes, exactly. All of us have had to sacrifice our lives and our bank accounts for these boys, and we did a lot of talking and preaching to them since they were young about life. It was extremely difficult for all of us to get these blockheads to listen and follow our lead.

STEVEN'S DAD. Especially for us, mainly me. I had to practically drill some sense into Steven head. He kept messing up and hanging with his cousin and friends too much. Transferring him to Rutgers was the best thing for him in a lot of ways. He probably would have never matured and met Mohan, Peter, and Haseem. I'm just glad he is focused and finally dedicated to something, besides the nightlife.

All the parents shake their heads with serious looks on their faces. They all take a couple seconds to ponder over everything that was just talked about.

HASEEM'S MOTHER. We all should be proud of our boys. They have formed a tight bond and built some strong business ventures together. And they have a very bright future together. The sky is the limit for them.

MOHAN'S MOTHER. I just pray that they stick to their plans and not let negativity or people from the outside influence them the wrong way. They are young, and people are going to gravitate to them the more successful they become.

All the parents listen closely to what everyone is saying and display a deep-in-thought look on their faces. They look around at one another and glance over, looking at their sons.

STEVEN'S MOM. We got a long way to go still. These boys are barely in their twenties and haven't begun to experience life yet. We're gonna have to keep them at bay, or they will just sail away on us.

Steven's father interrupts his wife as he puts his arm around her and squeezes her close to him. He looks at her with a big smile and then looks at the other parents.

STEVEN'S FATHER. Ahh, she's just saying that because somebody's getting lonely and sad that little Stevie is too busy for her now. Her little baby is out making moves and Mommy doesn't know what to do with herself.

Steven's mom pushes her husband away with a weak fake smack of his shoulder as she laughs in embarrassment that her husband would say that in front of everyone. She messes with her hair and takes a sip of her drink and smiles it off. Everyone is laughing and smiling at her. All the moms eventually start to come to her defense as they all begin to look at their husbands with a frown on their faces.

PETER'S MOM. There is nothing wrong with keeping your child close to you.

HASEEM'S MOM. That's right. I'd rather be a little overprotective than too loose.

MOHAN'S MOM: We all built a strong love for our boys while you, men, were out doing whatever.

The husbands look around at one another and then look at their wives and start to sip their drinks, with smiles still on their faces. Haseem's father puts his arm around his wife and gives her a hug, and the other husbands start showing affection to their ladies.

Scene seven. Mohan walks over and expresses his joy and happiness with Nadia and her friends and tells her that she is right for Haseem. Nadia's friends joke with Mohan about, one day, he should think about doing the same and flirt with him about how sexy he looks dressed up. Mohan has seen it all when it comes to women and their slick talk and reminds them that he ain't beat and very in tune to the games women play also.

MOHAN. Nadia, I want you to know that I look forward to getting to know you better, and from what I see so far, you're going to make a wonderful wife. Haseem told me that you're his backbone and you support him. That is very important for a man like Haseem.

NADIA. Well, thank you, Mohan. That is very sweet of you. How could I not follow a man like Haseem? His drive and his commitment is very desirable. That is what attracted me to him in the first place.

Mohan listens to Nadia and nods his head very slowly as he reaches his hand out to greet Nadia's friends. Nadia's friends are blushing and sizing Mohan up.

MOHAN. Hello, ladies. I don't believe we ever got to meet. I am Mohan, Haseem's business partner and close, close friend.

NADIA'S FRIEND KIA. I was waiting for one of Haseem's friends to come over and meet the bridesmaids. I mean, so none of us feel awkward at the wedding rehearsals.

NADIA'S FRIEND SHAWNA. Ahh, yeah, how else are we supposed to get familiar with Haseem's closest friends?

Shawna is standing very sexy, with her eyes flirting with Mohan in a very seductive way. Mohan notices her flirting and gives her a flirting look back.

MOHAN. I definitely agree with you on that. I mean, how can any man not wanna come introduce himself to you lovely ladies?

Mohan looks Shawna and Kia up and down with his wandering eyes as he looks at their bodies and then looks back at them with a little tongue wavering outside his lips.

KIA. So when will be a good time for me to learn some of your business save? (*Kia looks Mohan straight in the eyes very sexually and pauses.*) I wanna learn how to make serious moves, and I would love for you to teach me the game. I'll be a good student, trust me.

Nadia looks at her friends with a strong confused look on her face and slightly grins at them while she shakes her head. She then looks back at Mohan and interrupts her flirting friends.

NADIA. So, Mohan, I understand Natalie couldn't make it today. Your mother said she twisted her ankle or something?

SHAWNA. I wouldn't mind twisting his smaller ankle. (*Shawna whispers that to Kia as they are still staring at Mohan as he talks to Nadia.*)

MOHAN. Yeah, she could be a little clumsy sometimes, but she sends her love and told me to tell you congratulations, and she will call you.

Nadia shakes her head as she listens to Mohan and takes another glass of champagne from the waitress walking by.

MOHAN. I want you to let me know, Nadia, if Haseem starts being an asshole down the road. Let us know, and we will set him straight. And if you ever need anything, don't hesitate to let any one of us know. Haseem's schedule can be crazy sometimes, so if an emergency pops up or you're in a bad situation, just call. You're part of our family now, and we welcome you.
KIA. Does that mean us too? I mean, we are her close friends.

Mohan looks at Shawna and Kia with a grin on his face. He takes a second to respond before he hands Shawna his business card.

MOHAN. Yes, if there is anything you need done or need any assistance on something, my door is open to you too. (*Mohan gives them both a look like they are being a little too aggressive toward him, but out of respect, he won't go there.*)

Nadia's friends take his card, and Mohan turns around and starts to walk away. Nadia looks at her friends, shaking her head, while they are busy checking Mohan out as he walks away.

Scene eight. Haseem talks with a few childhood buddies he went to school with. They are trying to get him to help them out on becoming more successful like Haseem and his firm. Haseem drills them on living the right way and staying away from negativity and the nightlife, and the only way to become a success is sticking to the Triple D Effect. But he lets them know that he will always be there and his marriage will not change him.

HASEEM'S FRIEND JAMAL. Well, look at my boy! Damn playa, that's it! No more late nights out with all the women? You better enjoy these last few months before you officially tie that knot 'cause once it's over, it's over!

Haseem looks at Jamal and his friends like they're never gonna change; he grins and gives Jamal a big hug and smacks him on the back. His face is lit up when he is around Jamal. He cares about him so much.

HASEEM. Yeah, the clock is ticking, bro. The curtain is closing for me. (*Haseem grins at Jamal.*) But thanks to you, I would have probably never got the amount of women if I never hung with you. You put me on to some very, very good times.

Jamal looks at his friend and shakes his head in agreement with him. He stares at his boy like he hasn't seen him in years. Other friends of Haseem start to question him about getting legal money and being legit.

HASEEM'S FRIEND RYAN. Yo, Haseem, we tired of living this street life. The game ain't what it used to be. Too many snitches out here, cameras got you under surveillance, and this gangbangin' shit is out of control. It's time to be more organized, bro. It's time to legalize the little money we got.

Haseem looks at his childhood friend with a very compassionate look on his face; he is very sympathetic to what he is saying. He puts his glass down to his waist and starts to explain some things.

HASEEM. Ryan, the hardest thing for a man to do, especially a black man, is to tame his lifestyle down, cut out the nightlife, cut back on chasing the women, and stop buying materialistic things that really have no real value.

Jamal, Ryan, and the rest of his friends listen closely to what Haseem is saying. Their eyes are glued to him. Haseem has noticed that they are seriously paying attention to him and goes more in-depth on things.

HASEEM. See, I learned early in life to live by the Triple D Effect. It's something that our firm lives by.
HASEEM'S FRIEND RYAN. I heard you mention that before. What does that mean again?

HASEEM. It means to have the discipline to work hard to achieve your goal, be determined to do whatever it takes to get there, and be dedicated to live out your dream and let no one stop you from winning.

Haseem's friends look at him in real deep thought; they are all staring at him and nodding their heads.

HASEEM. The future is nothing but a series of probabilities made of decisions that we make right now. These decisions lead to certain events into the future. But every human being has these capabilities that determine their own future. Some are just more in tune than others.

Haseem's friends look at Haseem like he just spoke in a language that they don't understand; they slowly break it down in their minds and look back at Haseem with their eyes wide-open and start to nod their heads really fast in agreement. Haseem looks back at his friends like a teacher looking at his students to make sure they understand before he continues.

HASEEM. Regardless of your living situation, no matter what color you are, you must start by improving your mental. Your thoughts have to be positive. You have to educate yourself on economics and become more business minded. (*Haseem puts his arms in the air and looks at his friends with a grin on his face.*) Find something that has a demand to it and supply it better than your competition.

Haseem looks around to every one of his friends, and they look back at him with a deep look of respect and appreciation.

JAMAL. That is exactly why I love you, bro. You don't mind reaching back and pulling others up with your knowledge, and you always spreading real talk, not that fake irrelevant dumb shit.

You always lead by example, and I'm about to start following your lead, bro.

HASEEM'S FRIEND RYAN. Yo, man, on some real talk, you bagged an official dime piece. Nadia is beautiful, bro. I see why you snatched her up.

Ryan and all of Haseem's friends start to laugh and agree whole-heartedly with what Ryan just said. Haseem looks over to his beautiful fiancée with a smile on his face, then looks back over to his boys as they give him a pat on the back to congratulate him. Jamal grabs a few appetizers from the waiter walking by. His friends follow him, grabbing food like they haven't eaten in days. Haseem shakes his head with a big smile on his face that shows his love for his crazy childhood friends. He then looks back at Nadia and makes his way over to her. She looks back at him and smiles heavily.

Scene nine. Nadia and Haseem share an intimate moment as the night starts to creep in. He kisses her and hugs her and starts to express his feelings toward her. He also wants to make sure she understands his commitment to the firm and the oath between him and his brotherhood. Nadia tells Haseem that that is one of the things she loves the most about him and that she will never get in the way of him reaching his dreams and being the leader of the family. She will stand beside him and let him lead the way.

NADIA. It's good to see you over there sharing laughs with your childhood friends. They really respect you and care so much about you.

HASEEM. Yeah, those guys mean a lot to me. They always had my back growing up. They made sure that I didn't get caught up in none of that street life. Jamal always told me that he saw potential in me and that I was destined to be somebody special. That is why I will never turn my back on him. I will always be there for him, and he has grown so much over the years. He really is trying to turn his life around.

NADIA. Yes, I have noticed that. You are starting to rub off on him.

Haseem squeezes Nadia really tight to him and looks her in the eye. He slowly turns her loose and takes a deep breath. Nadia looks back at him, wondering what is on his mind.

HASEEM. Baby, I just want you to understand that things aren't always going to be peaches and cream in the next few years. We are dedicated to building Cultural Dividends into one of the biggest investment firms in the country. That is gonna require me spending a lot of time working very long hours and spending time away from home. I need to know that you fully understand that.

NADIA. Haseem, I love that about you—your commitment to win, your dedication to be great. You're a leader and a motivated man who will not quit until you reach your goal. That is so attractive to me.

Haseem stares at Nadia in the eye with a look of pride. He grins and gives her a kiss on her lips. Nadia closes her eyes as Haseem steals a quick kiss, then slowly opens them, looking back at Haseem with a happy smile.

HASEEM. I have seen plenty of marriages and relationships turn bad in the first couple of years. Before you came into my life, I was pursued by married woman. If there is ever a time in our marriage that you become lonely or tempted, I want you to keep it real with me. I can't stand sneaky people who keep their feelings concealed.

NADIA. You don't have to worry about that, Haseem. Believe me, when I need my man to spend quality time with me, I will snatch you back away from all that.

HASEEM. Believe me, I know how explicit and controlling you can be. You don't hold back your words, that's for sure.

Haseem starts to laugh a little as he hands Nadia another glass of champagne. He also grabs him another, and he takes a small sip as he looks at Nadia.

HASEEM. I just wanna make sure you understand the oath of our firm and how loyal I am to it. My code of conduct will not change, and I will always move like a solider who operates strategically. Establishing wealth for my family and generations to come is very important to me.

Nadia takes a few steps toward Haseem and looks at him with a very sensual look in her eyes. Haseem's facial expression turns straight face.

NADIA. You are the captain of this ship. Just make sure you can handle this ocean of strong currents, and we good.

Nadia and Haseem share laughs together, and Haseem puts one arm around Nadia with a big smile on his face. He looks around the party and takes another drink of his champagne. Nadia is smiling, but she has a slightly serious look on her face as she looks at Haseem and also looks around the party.

Scene ten. Everyone huddles together for a final toast to conclude the evening. Music starts to play, and friends and family begin to dance. The firm gets together for laughs, and Steven reminisces and narrates early days of their brotherhood. The scene concludes with them reminding one another about their business meeting at one every Monday. Everyone starts to leave and say their goodbyes to everyone, and everyone shares in hugs and smiles as they leave the engagement party.

STEVEN. I'm looking forward to making major moves with you guys. The first few years have gone great, but I personally want to crush those numbers. It's time to double up and end the year off strong!

Flashback to the firm when they were in college. The scene is their dorm, where they are sitting on four folded chairs, looking at one another.

PETER. Man, I believe in you, guys. I see a burning fire in all of you. We got a chance to do something that's rare in this country—to one day build a billion-dollar conglomerate of businesses. Being from different race and color, we will serve as inspiration to kids around the world. We will prove the stereotypes wrong.

MOHAN. We have to trust one another and never let anyone influence us or turn us against one another, to never let women, no matter how much we love them, to separate us. We're not going out like the Beatles.

STEVEN. No matter how successful we become, no matter how much our firm is worth, we will live off a salary that we agree on. That way, we can buy more land and invest into other business opportunities. Smart investments is key to our growth.

HASEEM. Let's make an oath right here right now to never stray away from our dream and our goals and to work hard to live out our dreams of being successful.

All four of them stand up and grab one another's hand and swear to live by the Triple D Effect.

Flashback to present day at the engagement party that is ending. All four men look at one another with a serious but happy expression on their faces. They hold up their champagne glasses and have a toast with one another. "To Cultural Dividends!" They all toast, too, as the scene ends.

Scene eleven. Monday business meeting is the setting, and Peter shares with the firm his plans for the future and what direction he wants the investment firm to go. Everyone chimes in and agrees that it's time to take it to the next level! Music plays in the background as episode one starts to concludes. Peter looks around at everyone with a very serious look on his face. He looks them in the eye and then speaks aggressive to Mohan, Steven, and Haseem. They all look Peter back in the eye with serious facial expressions also.

PETER. It's time to turn it up to the next freaking level. The first few years have been pretty good, but I got bigger plans for us this year. We gonna expand on Steven's sports bar, my restaurant.

We're gonna lock down more shipping and distribution contracts, and we're going to swallow up more commercial land across the country. Mohan, we're going to develop and grow your engineering company with some real estate moguls, and, Haseem, keep doing your thing with your computer software company. I got some connections with that, too, down the road.

All four men look at one another and nod their heads in agreement to what Peter has said.

PETER. Let's get it, fellas. Let's get it.

Episode 2

Scene one. Peter and Felize meet up to look at some commercial property near Belmar. They're discussing if the land is big enough for the type of restaurant that Peter has. Peter is sold on the size and believes that the location is perfect. It's not too far from the boardwalk, and there isn't any upscale Japanese restaurants close within fifty miles. Felize is convinced that the area is good and the Oriental population is climbing in the area also, and he believes he can secure the land for a reasonable price. He tells Peter not to worry because the land has been on the market for over a year, and he has done business with the realtor before and has a good relationship with him. Peter lets Felize know with a stern look to make it happen and to keep him updated by next week. As he starts to ride off, he calls Mohan to let him know the details and to be ready to start the process of engineering and drafting the land for the restaurant.

Peter and Felize are sharing a cup of coffee and looking over the land. They are walking around, looking at the roads close to the land. They are both in agreement about the location.

PETER. So what do you think? I personally think it's a perfect location.

FELIZE. It kind of feels a little isolated to me. Maybe I am just used to North Jersey where it's more congested, not as much trees and open land.

PETER. Yeah, bro, you got to travel more south. That's what make it perfect. What you're used to man, you can always tell.

FELIZE. Open land means wide-open opportunity. Yeah, that is true. According to the numbers, there is a good number of Japanese down here in the area too.

Peter stops walking and looks at Felize with an I-told-you-so face, he then takes a sip of his morning coffee. Felize takes a short pause and looks around at the ground of the land, then looks back at Peter with an "I agree" facial expression.

FELIZE. It's close to the major highways also. Plus, the boardwalk is not too far.

PETER. Exactly now you feeling me. Think about all the foot traffic with it being so close to the boardwalk. And there isn't any upscale or high-end Japanese spots like mine anywhere close either. I think we looking at a winner here, Felize.

Both men look at each other in agreement, and they are both nodding their heads with a big smile on their faces. They both realize for the size of the land that there is plenty of space for parking.

PETER. Do you think we can pull it off?

FELIZE. I don't see why not. It's been on the market for over a year. Plus, I know the realtor pretty good. Me and him go back a little something.

Felize takes a sip of his coffee while he gives Peter a not-to-worry expression on his face as they both look more and more happy.

PETER. In that case, player swing for the fences like you used to in high school. Make it happen I'm sold.

Peter looks at Felize with a very stern look in his eyes. Felize has seen that look before and just nods his head in agreement.

PETER. Keep me updated on things by next week. Work that realtor like a rookie on the mound. Use him and abuse him, bro. (*Peter loves to reference to him and Felize baseball days sometimes. Peter starts walking to his car, dialing Mohan, as he starts to drive off. Felize looks at Peter drive away and also starts messing with his phone.*)

PETER. Hey, you busy?

Mohan is out to lunch with his sister, Natalie. They have just arrived at the restaurant and haven't even been seated yet.

MOHAN. Nah, I'm good. Me and Natalie 'bout to have lunch. What's up?

PETER. Ahh, you're such a good big brother. Look at you. (*Peter laughs for a few seconds.*) The land is perfect. I like it, so I'm gonna need you to start the process of doing what you do best. You know, the engineering and drafting part.

MOHAN. No problem. Just send me the info, and I will jump on it ASAP.

PETER. Cool, I got you and will send it over later today. Fill Steven in with all the details. I'm on my way back to the office.

MOHAN. Aight. I will talk to you later.

Scene two. Steven is getting off to a late start; he had a sleepover with one of his gorgeous lady friends. He is awakened by a call from Mohan, informing him to let his father know about the location for Peter's restaurant so he can go over and survey the land. Steven agrees and tells Mohan that he is already on top of it. He hangs up the phone and walks to the kitchen to start cooking breakfast. While looking in the refrigerator, his gorgeous lady friend walks in and wants a morning treat also.

Steven is lying in the bed when his phone rings. He is knocked out in the bed with his lady friend, the phone rings a few times before Steven pops up and looks for his phone. He wipes his face and answers the phone with a raspy voice.

MOHAN. Let me guess. You're still in the bed. Rough night last night, I guess?

STEVEN. Something like that. Why you calling me so early? What time is it?

MOHAN. It's eleven thirty, man. You must be hungover. You forgot your phone has the time on it. You are off the chain, bro.

Steven, still wiping his half-asleep face while he's on the phone with Mohan, stands up off his bed and starts to walk around like he's looking for something but can't remember what.

STEVEN. What the hell do you want this early? You and Peter with this early shit, you guys got to chill with that.
MOHAN. Look, I just was calling to tell you to let your old man know we need the land for Peter's restaurant looked at ASAP.
STEVEN. Peter told me the other day about it. That's what you woke me up for?
MOHAN. Yeah. We know your late nights can get in the way of your memory. That's why I am reminding you again. We all know you got selective amnesia.

Mohan chuckles a little while he walks around the restaurant's lobby area. His sister, Natalie, is looking at him, wondering who he is talking to.

STEVEN. Mohan, I freaking got it. Go have a fruit salad or read a poetry book.

Steven hangs up the phone and whispers to himself, "What a freaking cornball!" He grabs a pan and puts it on the stove and starts to look in his kitchen cabinets. He still is dazed and struggling to get things right. He opens up the refrigerator and bends over, looking for stuff. He grabs the milk and eggs and puts it on the counter, then reaches back to get the bacon. He closes the fridge with the bacon in his hand when he looks up to find his lady friend is standing right there half naked, with a grin on her face.

STEVEN'S LADY FRIEND. So you start your morning off with milk, I see. Well, I would like some milk also.

Steven grins and looks at her with his eyes popping out of his head; his eyebrows are raised and mouth halfway open.

STEVEN. You can milk this cow as long as you want.

Steven's lady friend walks over to him and starts kissing on him and works her way down to his chest and eventually goes farther down.

Scene three. Mohan and his little sister, Natalie, meet up for lunch. She asks him about Haseem's engagement party and hates that she couldn't be there. Mohan tells her how it was and explains how Haseem's parents went all out for it. He wishes his parents would support him more than they do. He tells Natalie about his struggles dealing with that emotionally but knows that his parents love him. Natalie comforts her brother and reassures him that she believes in him.

NATALIE. Everything okay? You normally don't answer your calls in front of me.
MOHAN. Yeah, it's nothing. Had to talk with Steven about something. What you ordering? I am starving.
NATALIE. I don't know yet. I had a breakfast sandwich early this morning.
MOHAN. So what, you on that I'm-getting-fat-again stuff, I see. Stop trying to be so weight conscious and realize that you always gonna be a thick girl.

Natalie playfully smacks her brother with the menu and smiles at him. Mohan shrugs her attempt off as she hits him with the menu. He is grinning hard too.

NATALIE. So how was Haseem's engagement party? I saw some of the pictures, and everybody looked lit.
MOHAN. It was nice. Haseem's parents really went all out for Haseem. They had good catering, and the food was good. I never really realized how big their backyard is. Hey, is your ankle better?
NATALIE. Yeah, it's better. I still feel a little pain when I'm standing for a long time. Haseem's parents are so nice and down-to-earth.

He's their only child, and you know they gonna make sure he good.

Mohan takes a sip of his lemon water that the waitress brings over and grabs a piece of his butter roll also. He is chewing fast as he kind of gazes off into a slight daze. Natalie, noticing something is on his mind, looks at him while she sends a text out on her phone.

NATALIE. What's on your mind? You drifting into the twilight zone over there.

MOHAN. Nothing really. I'm just thinking about Mom and Dad and how Dad always got to make us follow his lead. We always had to do things his way. Or if we didn't, he wouldn't like it. He was a controlling father to me. I wish he was more understanding like Haseem's father is. They believe in Haseem and back him on his journeys.

NATALIE. Yeah, I feel you on that. Dad is one of those old-school parents who raised us like he was raised. It's part of his culture. He follows the pattern he was shown.

Mohan looks at his sister and agrees with her and looks her back in the eye. Natalie is responding to a text and looks at her brother when the waitress comes over and takes their order. They both order their food and drink on their lemon water.

MOHAN. Nah, I know how Dad is "I kinda get it and understand now that I am older," but it really used to bother me when I was younger. I really struggled with that. He hardly really supported me on any of my aspirations. No matter what I told him what I wanted to be, he would just look at me like I had three heads and tell me that I would make a great doctor one day.

NATALIE. He did the same to me too. I just took a liking to health and medicine when I was younger.

MOHAN. Yeah, I mean he always provided for us and made sure we never went without. You can't ask for perfection from people. He always taught us that.

Mohan and Natalie both look at each other, nodding their heads in remembrance of their father's teachings. They look around the restaurant and both start eating some of the soup that the waitress brought over to their table.

NATALIE. Just know that I see your vision and I believe in you, Mohan. You are an inspiration to me, and I get motivated by learning from you.

Mohan smiles at his sister and looks around for the waitress. He is getting annoyed by how long it's taking for the food to come.

MOHAN. Nah, that's real. That touches me deeply to know that. Stay attentive and observant, little sis. One day, down the road, I will make it pay off for you, believe me.

Natalie looks at her brother with a serious look on her face, and she glances at her soup while she stirs it up. Mohan looks at his little sister with an appreciative facial expression on his face. The waitress brings over some of their food to the table as the scene ends.

Scene four. Haseem is at the office, handling business; he is in the process of reaching a deal with an auto parts company. He wants the owner to commit to the deal for all their whole northeast locations and eventually use his computer software in all his locations around the world. The owner agrees and is willing to test Haseem's software and let him develop a better mobile app that is compatible with the software. Haseem smiles as the owner leaves and texts Felize about the deal and that he wants him to go over it with him.

HASEEM. So as you see, sir, my company has a nice list of clients that are satisfied with my computer software and computer programming services that I have helped them out with. We offer plenty of solutions to help your shipping and distribution, and we can link things all together through the mobile app we will create for you.

AUTO PARTS OWNER. Well, Haseem, I am impressed with your body of work, and looking at the work you have done for similar companies like mine makes me feel confident that you can improve on our computer system. We're desperately looking for improvement because our business is growing rapidly.

HASEEM. Well, sir, we will be able to make big improvements and enhance your whole business operation. Once you see how much better it will be for your drivers, how your customers will be able to interact with management and drivers simultaneously, and it will fix your inventory problems also.

Auto parts owner sits up in the office chair, and looks at the paperwork that Haseem had given him. He realizes that this is the right choice for him and his auto parts company, he raises his eyebrows and nods his head looking at Haseem.

AUTO PARTS OWNER. Well, Haseem, I am liking what I see, and I welcome your business. You got a deal. We will start off with the northeast locations first and will expand to all our locations across the country in the next few months, and if things go well and I like what I see, we will discuss global expansion.

Haseem leans back in his chair and nods his head with a big smile on his face; he looks at the auto parts owner with a very proud look. He pauses for a few and leans forward in his seat as his face turns back to a serious business look.

HASEEM. You will be happy with what I am going to do for you and your company. I will not let you down. I can guarantee that, sir. All I ask is for business referrals so I can get my work out there for other companies to see and recognize.

AUTO PARTS OWNER. I have no problem with that as I know a few business owners who will probably need help as their business grows.

Haseem and the auto parts owner stand up and shake hands and smile at each other. The auto parts owner turns and walks out the office and starts to leave. Haseem walks with him halfway toward the door.

HASEEM. I will send over the contract by the end of the week, and once again, thank you for the opportunity. (*Haseem watches the auto parts owner leave with a proud ecstatic look on his face.*)

Scene five. Peter meets with the manager for the firm truck shipping business company. The manager informs Peter that he got word about a food company that is looking to expand, and they need trucks to carry their loads more Midwest. Peter likes the business proposal and tells the manager to lock the deal down for at least two years and that the firm is willing to start immediately.

PETER'S TRUCK COMPANY MANAGER. I'm glad you finally made time to answer back. I'd been trying to tell you some good news, but you're so freaking busy nowadays.

PETER. My fault on that. It's been hectic lately. I got your messages, and you see, I did respond back. I just haven't been able to get here to talk with you more in-depth about things. So what's the good news?

PETER'S TRUCK COMPANY MANAGER. I got word that this food company up in Maine is looking to expand on their distribution across the Midwest. They're mainly a seafood company, but they're growing very fast. They need a reliable trucking company that will get their loads out there fast and consistent and need loads shipped out six days a week. But this is big, big payday for whoever gets the contract. The good thing for you is, my brother-in-law is friends with his cousin, and I'm confident I can swing the deal for you.

Peter looks a little shocked about the news; he looks at his manager with a surprised look on his face, and he nods his head and leans back in his chair.

PETER. Whoa, that is great news! That's big if you can lock down the deal. You think you can connect the dots?

Peter's trucking company manager looks at Peter with a smile on his face and turns his head to the right and raises his eyebrows.

PETER'S TRUCKING COMPANY MANAGER. Of course, it's no worries on that. I will get to work on securing that contract ASAP.

PETER. As far as drivers and trucks, obviously we're gonna have to deepen up our fleet and find some more reliable drivers. Look to lease some new trucks. If we're gonna be traveling across the Midwest, I want quality, reliable trucks out there on the road.

PETER'S TRUCKING COMPANY MANAGER. I'm already a step ahead of you. Here are some numbers and projected costs. As far as drivers, I got a few good candidates coming in for interviews on Friday.

Peter opens up the folder and looks at the paperwork; his eyes are moving up and down and left to right, his eyebrows raise up a little, and his facial expression is in deep thought.

PETER. Not bad. I will go over this with the guys and get back to you by the end of the week. But I'm trusting in you to lock this deal down. This is a huge payout if we can get this. Don't let me down. Get it done!

Peter gives his manager a very stern look and walks out the office with the folder in his hand while the manager shakes his head and grabs his laptop and flips it open to start doing some work.

Scene six. Steven is at the sports bar that he runs down in Belmar, eating some wings and fries and going over some business on his laptop, when Darren walks in. Darren asks Steven how it went the other night and asks him why he left so early. Steven reminds Darren about his busy schedule and how he's already falling behind on taking care of important things. Darren kinda understands but feels Steven is losing out on all the fun and tells him that he is getting weak for that girl. Steven calmly speaks on how beautiful it was to see his boy Haseem get engaged, but he is far from that because he can't trust women joking.

DARREN. What's up, cuz? Getting some work done, I see.

Darren comes, takes a seat where Steven is sitting, grabs a few wings, and starts eating on them. He tells the waitress to bring him over an order of wings and a Sprite soda. Steven glances at Darren for a split second and looks back at his laptop.

DARREN. So how did it go the other night with the chick you left with?

STEVEN. What do you think happened? I took her back to the crib and smashed, same old story.

DARREN. Yeah, she was on you all night. I peeped her flirting with you. Funny thing is, she didn't know if you had a girl there or wifey. She saw what she wanted and went in hard.

STEVEN. Yeah, she was open. She definitely didn't care if I was in a situation or not. That's what makes me think she loose. Can't get too serious with that type.

Darren looks at Steven like he's shocked by what he just heard. He chews on his wings and takes a weird look at Steven. Steven is writing something in his laptop when he notices Darren looking at him.

DARREN. What do you mean you can't get serious with nothing like that? Serious shouldn't even be on your mind right now in your life, cuz. You're too young to be thinking like that.

STEVEN. Believe me, that isn't on my mind, but I do like a woman to have some class and standards, not to easy. You know how

I am. I like a woman to be intelligent. She got some sense up there. Her convo is pretty much on point. I can tell she's not an airhead.

The waitress brings Darren his soda and wings, and Darren wastes no time on eating them; he grabs one and starts eating it. He then looks back at Steven with a wondering face. Steven isn't paying Darren too much attention as he is into his work.

DARREN. Sounds to me like you're searching for someone to grow with. I mean, ain't nothing wrong with having a special lady on your team, especially if she's bright and smart and she's trying to add on and not subtract.

STEVEN. That's my whole point, Dee. I ain't trying to waste time plucking birds with no intentions on never flying away from their nest. I want a lady with some ambition and drive, motivated and committed to reaching high. Sometimes I get turned off with these girls out here. After I'm done smashing, I don't wanna even be around them.

Darren looks at Steven as if he understands what his cousin is saying. He drinks on his Sprite soda and leans back in his chair and stares at the floor in deep thought. He looks back at Steven and grabs another wing.

DARREN. So where do all this come from? Oh, I get it, Haseem's engagement party, that's it.

STEVEN. Well, that was some of it, but I was feeling this way before the engagement party. But seeing my boy happy and how he found someone, it does make me think about it more. I mean, I think Nadia is a good look for Haseem. She fits the role good for him. Her friends make me kind of question her intentions a little, but Haseem's on point with women.

DARREN. Yeah, Haseem's on point. He ain't no sucker for love. What you doing today? I might go see the Yankees game tonight.

Steven looks up from his laptop and thinks about what Darren just told him. He gives it some thought.

STEVEN. I got to go see my father to get him to look at land for Peter, then after that, I got a few small things to do. I will let you know. I might go with you to the game. (*Darren starts to get up from the table, wiping his face and taking a last sip of his Sprite soda.*)

DARREN. Aight, cuz, I got to go. I'll text you later to see what's up.

Darren walks away from the table and starts to leave. Steven looks at him for a few seconds and goes back to his laptop and writing some things down in his notebook.

Scene seven. Mohan and Haseem attend a baseball game. The firm has a box suite at the Yankees stadium. They're eating and drinking with a few business associates. Mohan is trying to lock down a deal to design homes for a real estate mogul. His engineering business is starting to take off, and if he can land this deal, it could bring in huge revenue. The mogul is impressed with Mohan's work and likes Mohan's professionalism. Haseem is on the phone with Nadia, talking with her about home shopping and watching the game.

HASEEM. The Yankees been doing their thing lately. Hopefully they keep it up because Boston is a much better team this year.

MOHAN. True. It's going to be tough for them this year. Boston is coming up.

Mohan and Haseem looks at the door as the real estate mogul walks in with one of his business partners. Mohan and Haseem stand up to greet them; they walk over and shake their hands.

MOHAN. I'm glad you were able to make it. I know how the traffic is when the Yankees are playing. Please have a sit. Can I get you anything a drink or something to eat?

REAL ESTATE MOGUL. Ahh, yes, I will take some vodka on ice, and let me take a look at the menu.

Mohan brings the real estate mogul over the menu and brings him over his drink; he motions over to the hostess to take over. He then takes a seat and looks at the real estate mogul.

REAL ESTATE MOGUL. So, Mohan, tell me how your company will be able to mesh with mine because we are developing luxury homes at a fast pace. Will you be able to handle the workload? That is really my main concern.

MOHAN. Well, sir, I have a good solid team, and if given enough time and notice on your development plans, there is no doubt that we can't handle the work. As you already know, it's all about communication and timing, and as long as you can give me that, that will be all I need, sir.

REAL ESTATE MOGUL PARTNER. We have looked over your work, and we both like what we see. The only thing is, your company has done more buildings and strip malls and not too many luxury homes.

Mohan listens and gives thought to what was just said; he looks at both men and nods his head. He then leans forward in his chair.

MOHAN. Well, I can understand your concern, but that simply is a matter of what business has come our way. That is what our clients have needed more, and that is exactly why we would love to do work for your company. It will enhance our work portfolio and get our name out there in the housing market. We are capable of getting whatever work you need done, and quality is number one to us.

Real estate mogul ponders over what Mohan has said and gives it deep thought. He takes a sip of his drink and gives the hostess his order. He looks back at his partner and looks back at Mohan and Haseem.

REAL ESTATE MOGUL. I tell you what we will do, Mohan, because of your lack of experience in building luxury homes, but we are still impressed with you and the great work you have done. We will start you off with some work in New Jersey. We are developing some homes there, and we will let your company handle things for us.

Mohan looks at Haseem and then looks back at the real estate mogul and his partner with a very proud look of joy on his face.

MOHAN. Well, I appreciate the opportunity, sir, and I will not let you down. I promise you that. Everything will be exactly to your liking, and don't worry, you will be satisfied with my work.

Haseem gets a phone call and excuses himself from the conversation. It's a call from his fiancée, Nadia.

HASEEM. I'm in a very important business meeting. Is everything okay?
NADIA. I'm sorry. I just wanted to let you know that I scheduled a few appointments with the realtor to look at a few homes.

Haseem walks far away from Mohan and the real estate mogul and starts looking at the game, talking very quietly on the phone. The scene shifts back to Mohan and the real estate mogul.

REAL ESTATE MOGUL. Mohan, I, too, had to start off small. I couldn't get anyone to give me a chance in the beginning. I remember how that felt. It almost destroyed my confidence and desire, but I keep pushing forward. I see potential in you, and I like what I see from your work. You are committed to be great, and that reminds me of me when I started out. That is why I am willing to give you a chance.

The real estate mogul takes a sip of his vodka and looks at Mohan with a slight grin on his face. His partner is also looking at Mohan and sipping on his drink. Mohan is happy, and his facial expression resembles a kid who just received praise from his parents.

MOHAN. Thank you once again, and I am ready to get started as soon as needed.

REAL ESTATE MOGUL. I will have the contract sent over to you in the next few weeks. If you do great work for us and we are satisfied, Mohan, you will have more work than you probably can handle.

The hostess brings over the real estate mogul his order of food. Mohan and the real estate partner look at the food and mouths are wide-open and eyes are bulging out of their head. They both look at each other, and they tell the hostess what they want to eat. Haseem walks back over to the meeting and looks at the real estate mogul's food also.

HASEEM. I'm gonna have to order me something now. That looks good! (*Everybody chuckles a little, and the hostess brings over the vodka bottle to the table.*)

Scene eight. Steven and his father is at the property, looking things over. Peter pulls up with Felize for some coffee and breakfast sandwiches. Steven tells Peter that the land is in a good location and has the parkway close by, so people will be able to find it easy. He tells them he can get started within the next few weeks if they can get the deal done. Felize says not to worry about it as the owner is happy with the offer. Peter smiles and jokes with Steven's dad about trusting the firm's business savvy. Steven tells Peter that he should be in charge of the restaurant since it's right under his nose, right here in Belmar, where he already got the sports bar. Peter agrees but thinks he's gonna hire a manager to run the restaurant to keep the guys' schedule and time more open for other things.

STEVEN. Well, 'bout time you guys showed up. Normally I am the one arriving late. Where is my coffee at? I need a little buzz this morning.

Peter and Felize walks up to Steven and his dad and hand them coffee and shake hands with them. Steven looks at Peter and grabs the bag and takes one of the breakfast sandwiches and looks at his dad. Steven's dad shakes his head no that he doesn't want a sandwich. All four men start drinking their coffee and looking around.

STEVEN'S DAD. Who found this land? You, Peter?

PETER. Nah, it was Felize. He's our real estate guy. He's always on top of new hot spots.

STEVEN'S DAD. Well, he found a pretty good spot. The location is good, and the parkway is down the street. With the boardwalk right down the street, this could be something as long as you don't let the wrong crowd in.

PETER. Well, we plan on being very upscale and selective on dress attire. Our security will make sure the beach thugs stay out.

STEVEN'S DAD. You guys need help with the permits or anything?

PETER. Yeah, we're not that familiar with the town officials down here, so that would be appreciated.

STEVEN. I got connections down here. You know I'm the man down here. I run this little town. That's exactly why you should let me manage the restaurant for you. It doesn't make sense for you or Mohan to have to make trips down here every other day.

Peter sips on his coffee and looks at Steven with a pondering look on his face; he pauses for a few and looks back at Steven.

PETER. It would make sense, Steven, but you got your hands full with the sports bar. I'd been thinking about hiring a manger to run the restaurant. That way, nobody's schedule or time is conflicted. And if anything, you can stop by here and there if there are any problems.

STEVEN. Well, I thank you for being so considerate of my busy schedule, Peter, but you are right with what we got planned in the near future. Time is important to our other business ventures.

STEVEN'S DAD. You boys made an offer already on the land yet?

FELIZE. Yeah, he was happy that he got close to what he was asking. He already accepted the offer.

Peter looks at Steven's dad with a slight smile on his face and takes a bite of his breakfast sandwich.

PETER. What, you don't think we're on top of things? You should know how our we operate by now. Don't tell me you're doubting our business savvy.

Steven's dad looks at his son and Peter and turns back and looks at the land. He starts to grin a little and then looks back at all three guys.

STEVEN'S DAD. You boys doing all right so far, but you're only a few years in the game. Just make sure you maintain your lead as the game gets deep in the fourth quarter. Remember, it's not how you start out of the gate, but will you finish the race is what everybody is hatching their bets on.

Steven, Peter, and Felize nod their heads at Steven's dad, and all three men take in the strong words of wisdom that Steven's dad just told them. They all respect Steven's dad; he is a very successful construction owner. They sip on their coffee and look around the area.

STEVEN'S DAD. Well, I can get started in a few weeks if your boys are ready. Just let me know when and I will be ready. I'm proud of you, guys, and don't mind helping out. I will get started on those permits, and I will be in touch soon.

Steven's dad starts to walk away from the guys, and Steven jokes on Peter about not bringing more breakfast sandwiches.

Scene nine. Jamal stops by the office of Haseem's mother to take one of his lady friends out to a concert. Mrs. Kendricks is in the middle of a meeting with her models, discussing a photo shoot coming up. She isn't happy about Jamal dating her models. She is fully aware of the lifestyle that Jamal is living. She knows him since he was a little kid. She tells him to wait outside till the meeting is over. While waiting, he calls his boy Haseem up and tells him that his mother be on some shit. Haseem laughs about it, and he and Jamal start catching up on things going on with people they know and things they've been doing.

Jamal walks in and looks at all the beautiful models who are talking with Mrs. Kendricks; he waves and winks his eye at his lady friend, who smiles and waves back. Mrs. Kendricks notices her model smiling and looks around and sees Jamal standing there. Her face frowns up a little as Jamal waves at her.

HASEEM'S MOM. Excuse me, Jamal. I am giving an important meeting right now.

JAMAL. Ohh, I'm sorry, Mrs. Kendricks. (*He takes a seat in one of the chairs.*)

Haseem's moms looks at Jamal with an evil frown on her face and starts to walk over to him. Jamal is looking around in the back of him, wondering where Haseem's mom is walking to.

JAMAL. How have you been, Mrs. Kendricks?

HASEEM'S MOM. I'm doing fine, Jamal, but you are interrupting my meeting, and I'm gonna have to ask you to wait out in the hallway.

Jamal looks a little shocked but stands up quickly to not make Mrs. Kendricks upset.

JAMAL. No problem at all. I'm so sorry.

Haseem's moms walks Jamal to the door and starts to smile a little at Jamal. She closes the door as Jamal walks through the door. She walks back to finish up her meeting and gives Jamal's lady friend a strange stare. Jamal, out in the hallway with nothing to do, pulls out his phone and calls Haseem. Haseem is at the convenience store, getting some snacks and getting some gas also.

HASEEM. Yo, what's up?

JAMAL. Yo, man, your mother be on some shit, bro. I'm over here picking up my girl at her meeting, and your mom basically took her foot and kicked me the hell out with a mean stare.

Haseem starts laughing very hard, and he can't help to be so loud. People in the store glance at Haseem as he notices that he is a little loud.

HASEEM. Yo, you know how she is when it comes to her models, and the thought of you dating one of them probably sent her through the roof.

JAMAL. Yeah, she's very protective of her models. That probably was it. She just went beast mode on me. I thought I was good. I took a seat, trying to be quiet and stay out the way. That didn't work.

Haseem starts laughing even louder as Jamal is cracking him up by explaining the story.

HASEEM. Hey, you were better off telling her you were supposed to meet me there, and when the meeting was over, snatch Shorty up and bounce, hopefully without her seeing you. (*Haseem laughs at himself, and Jamal starts laughing too.*)

JAMAL. What's been good with you, man? What you doing, picking up dinner for you and Nadia? (*Jamal chuckles over the phone.*)

HASEEM. Something like that, whatever, man. Hey, what happened the other night on the block? I was riding through there and saw a lot of cops and detective cars out there.

JAMAL. D-Smooth's house got raided. He wasn't there though. But they found mad stuff up in there. You remember Terrell, his close friend?

HASEEM. Yeah, I remember him. What he do?

Jamal is peering through the door, trying to get a look at the gorgeous models in the room with Haseem's mom.

JAMAL. He got shot last week. He got caught up in a beef with some young cats. Haseem pays for his stuff at the counter and starts to walk out of the store.

HASEEM. That's crazy. Dudes better understand these young boys ain't playing out here.

Jamal backs up from the door in time as the models are walking out of their meeting. He looks at all the beautiful models walking out and makes some eye-popping looks. He hangs up with Haseem as his lady friend walks out, and he gives her a big hug and a bigger smile.

JAMAL. Hey, beautiful, you ready to go? I got a nice night planned for you. (*Jamal and his lady friend start walking away to leave for the night.*)

Scene ten. The crew meet up at a grown and sexy lounge that Mohan picked out for them to party on Friday night. The guys are definitely feeling the beautiful ladies, and the ladies are feeling them also. They relax in the VIP section close to where a few NFL players are partying, and an old lady friend of Haseem comes over with her girlfriends to say hi. Good music is blasting and big ballers are spending and partying the night away. Steven orders over two more buckets of champagne for the ladies to enjoy. Everyone is having fun until Haseem notices that Jamal is there with a few of his friends, and his new girlfriend is also with him.

STEVEN. Yo, Haseem, who are those girls that keep staring at you? They're looking right too. Tell them to come over in our section.

HASEEM. Oh, that's this girl I used to mess with. I don't recognize all her friends though. I got you.

Haseem motions for the ladies to come over and whispers to security to let them in. Peter and Mohan take notice of the ladies as they come have a seat in their VIP section. Peter and Mohan keep talking to each other while Steven is very happy and introducing himself. Peter looks up at Haseem talking to an old lady friend. He sips on his glass of champagne and starts back talking to Mohan.

MOHAN. Everything is in motion. Me and Haseem locked the real estate mogul deal down, and Haseem got the contract for that auto parts company. Any word yet on that seafood company up in Maine?

PETER. Not yet, but I was told not to worry about it. It's basically a done deal. I will follow up on it next week.

Both of them crack a smile and touch their champagne glasses together as a few women from out of nowhere start dancing very close to them. They look at each other and smile.

HASEEM'S OLD LADY FRIEND. So how you been, Haseem? I haven't seen or heard from you in a long time.

HASEEM. I've been on the low, trying to stack my chips, keeping myself off the radar as much as I can.

HASEEM'S OLD LADY FRIEND. You more handsome than I remember. Damn, you cute. I mean, you was cute back then, but something is different with you.

Haseem smiles as he looks around the club and notices his boy Jamal is there with a few of his friends and some light-skinned lady friend. He keeps a close eye on him as he turns back to his friend.

HASEEM. Well, they say when you reach a certain level of life, you carry a certain glow with you. Maybe that's what it is.

Both of them smile at each other, and a hot new song is mixed in. Haseem's old friend starts to dance very nasty on him. He gives very little resistance and dances back with her. Different shots of the club and everybody is partying and enjoying the music.

Scene eleven. Hours have passed and the club is about to close, but when you're VIP like the firm is, you don't have to leave right away. As things are winding down, the crew starts to make their way out. Jamal and Haseem are kicking it while everybody is heading to their cars.

Steven has decided to take a few lady friends with him. He was busy trying to convince Mohan he should roll with him to get something to eat. Across the parking lot, way in the back, sit a few undercover agents watching everything. They are amazed by the luxurious high-priced vehicles that the firm is riding in. They take a few pictures and look a little amazed by everything. Music starts to play as the firm is riding away from the club.

HASEEM. So is that your new lady friend? She got a serious fatty on her.

JAMAL. Yeah, she official, ain't she? I had to get at her. Mom dukes gonna have to understand.

They both are laughing as they walk outside the club. Steven is smiling ear to ear with three lady friends.

STEVEN. Yo, Mohan, you coming to get something to eat? I don't know if they serving fruit salad this late. (*Peter and Steven start laughing and even the girls are smiling at Steven comical jokes.*)

MOHAN. Whatever, Steven. You know I try not to eat that much meat if I don't have to.

STEVEN. Well, you gonna have to go against that rule tonight, buddy. I got a whole lot of meat for you to chomp down on. (*Steven is laughing as he gives Mohan the eye. Mohan gets his boy joke and knows what he means, so he smiles back at Steven.*)

Peter is walking to his car when one of the ladies asks if he is coming.

STEVEN. He got yoga to do in the morning! (*Steven busts out laughing again and so do everyone else.*)

PETER. Yeah, we can go get something to eat. I'm cool with that.

Peter looks at the lovely lady and escorts her to his car. The scene shifts to the back of the parking lot where two undercover agents are watching the guys leave with the girls.

UNDERCOVER DETECTIVE 1. Who the hell are these guys? I never saw them around.
UNDERCOVER DETECTIVE 2. You know Jamal, right?
UNDERCOVER DETECTIVE 1. Yeah, I see him, but he has new buddies?

Both detectives look very closely at the firm leaving and take a few photos of them to keep for their records.

UNDERCOVER DETECTIVE 2. I don't have a clue who they are, but whoever they are, you can tell they're not your typical street thugs like Jamal. And by the looks of their cars, they definitely got a lot more cash to play around with too.

The detectives look at each other again as one of them grabs his water and takes a sip; they sit back in their car seats to not be noticed as the boys are riding away, blasting their music a little.

UNDERCOVER DETECTIVE 1. I think maybe we should get a little more familiar with these guys. (*Both men look at each other again, as they watch them pull out the club parking lot.*)

Episode 3

Scene one. Monday morning meeting is the scene, and the guys are talking about investment plans and business plans for the firm. Mohan wants to get more going on Wall Street, and Peter wants to expand on the medical weed shops outside of New Jersey. Haseem thinks the guys should focus more on franchising while Steven feels that they should open up more sports bars. They never like to end Monday morning meeting undecided or unsure on business planning, so the meeting goes a little longer than expected. Peter feels they can accomplish all those things, and even more if they work hard to get it done, being more aggressive and committed is the key. As they conclude the meeting, Felize calls Peter to let him know that he got the land approval for the deal, and the sale is complete for the restaurant. Peter shares the good news with Steven to let his father know, and everybody leaves the meeting happy.

MOHAN. I don't see why we can't take a bigger percentage and invest more on Wall Street. You see the way these hi-tech technology companies are growing?

PETER. Yes, Mohan, they are growing fast. You're right, I'm going to look more into it. But I agree with Haseem and Steven, and we got to start looking more into the medical weed shops outside of New Jersey too.

Haseem is listening and looking at both Mohan and Peter, but he interrupts them with his own opinion of things.

HASEEM. I feel both of you guys, but franchising is where it's at. South Jersey is wide-open, and franchising creates a consistent residual income for us all. It's like steady money coming in every week and month for us. Plus, it gives us more leverage with the banks.

Steven is nodding his head to what Haseem is saying and gives it a deep thought as he rubs his chin, staring at the diner table. He looks at Peter with a serious face.

STEVEN. Haseem makes a strong point, and I'm on the same page with him on it. Look how good the sports bar is doing. If we open up a few more in South Jersey like Atlantic City or Seaside or something, we can make some serious cash down there with these young beachgoers. And he makes a good point with leverage with the banks. They love consistent money.

All four men look at one another and start rubbing their hair, chins, and foreheads as they are searching hard to find the next best investment. Peter looks at his friends, and they all start looking back at him, unspeaking, but they all look for Peter to make the right call for the firm. He is like the boss without the title or position appointed.

PETER. To be honest with y'all, if we really buckle down and focus real hard, we might have to shift our schedule a little more, but I think we can get all these business ventures going within the next few months. Look at how much we accomplished in only a few years. If we stay grinding and cut back a little bit more, I really believe we can do it.

All four men are in deep thought as they digest what Peter just said. It is quiet between the four of them as they all are kinda staring at the table and out the diner window.

MOHAN. Peter is right, guys. There isn't nothing that we can't do if we stick to the rules and follow our Triple D Effect.

HASEEM. Nah, that's real talk I agree too. I think with the success we had our first few years, we just trying to make sure we keep the momentum going strong, and we are a little cautious because we don't want to mess nothing up.

They all look at Haseem and agree with what he said. They take a sip on their lemon water and start back eating their breakfast. Peter's phone starts ringing, and he looks at it and answers it.

PETER. Good morning, Felize. I know when you call it's something good going on. What's up?

FELIZE. Hey, I figured you guys were having your weekly meeting. I figured I drop some good news on the table for you. The sale is complete for the restaurant.

PETER. Yeah, that definitely came at a good time. We're just finishing up our meeting with us scratching our heads on a few options, so that's great news right about now.

Peter looks at the guys and pumps his fist in the air as he looks back at his plate and eats a little bit of his food.

FELIZE. Hey, you know I don't get into your business, guys, but just continue doing what got you here. So far, it's working big-time.

PETER. Thanks, Felize. You're right on that. I will call you back later for all the details. Once again, thanks.

Peter hangs up the phone and starts to say something and then pauses; he glances back at his phone and sends a text out to somebody. He then looks back at his friends and smiles.

PETER. We got the land for the restaurant, fellas. The sale is final. Another notch under our belt. Let's keep it going while we're rolling hot right now. It's starting to feel like the chips are falling in place for us.

STEVEN. No doubt. We really haven't hit any walls yet, fellas, so let's just keep swinging.

They all look at one another and shake their head and give one another high fives to congratulate.

Scene two. Haseem rides over to his mother's photo shoot with her models. Haseem likes stopping by to see if his mother needs anything and to check up on her. Haseem tells his mother that he is so happy how things are going and how he and Nadia are ready to start looking at homes. She reminds him that everything takes time and not to hurry. While they are talking, a few of the models catch Haseem's eyes and ask him how he has been. He engages in a little side talk with them before his mom sends them back to work. Mrs. Kendricks tells Haseem that his aunt Pelynda has been asking about him and wants to talk to him. He says he will call her.

HASEEM. You keep yourself busy, I see. You really care about your models a lot, I see.

HASEEM'S MOM. You don't know how hard it is for models of plus size and African American to have any type of shot in this industry. They have to work extra harder and do a lot more to get accepted. I remember how hard it was for me to break into the industry. That's why I go all out for these girls to get their recognition.

HASEEM. Yeah, I remember when I was little how sad you used to be when you got turned down on certain jobs. It really used to make you so upset.

Haseem's mother walks with her son over to her couch, and she takes a seat as she is a little tired. Haseem stands and looks around at the models as they are enjoying their break by sipping on water and talking with one another.

HASEEM'S MOM. So what brings you by? You checking in on me?

HASEEM. Well, I was in the area, and I wanted to come see my favorite lady in the whole world and make sure you didn't need anything. I got a few hours to kill, and if you needed something done, I could do it for you.

Haseem mom smiles at her son but gives him a curious look also.

HASEEM'S MOM. Well, that is sweet of you and I appreciate that, but we're almost done here, and I already ordered lunch for us, so I'm okay. Have you and Nadia started looking for homes yet?

HASEEM. Funny you say that. We're supposed to go in a few days actually, but I don't know if I will be able to. I just got a big deal done with this auto parts store, and I got a lot of work to do.

HASEEM'S MOM. Well, I'm sure she will understand. That's great news, Haseem! That is really great news. I'm so happy for you. Things take time, and you guys just got engaged. Don't rush things. Y'all will find time to get it done.

Haseem agrees with his mother and looks her in the eye as she looks him back in the eye. Two models walk over to Haseem to say hello.

MODEL 1. Hey, Haseem, I thought that was you. How have you been?

Haseem's mother looks at the girls with a twisted look on her face and starts messing with her phone.

HASEEM. I've been good, just working on making myself a better person, mentally and physically.

MODEL 2. Well, you doing a good job at it. Your arms and chest are busting out that suit. You really been getting your lift on, I see.

Both ladies are giving Haseem that flirtatious look as they look at his diamond watch and look him up and down. Haseem's mom pauses on her phone and gives the girls a stank look on her face.

HASEEM'S MOM. All right, girls, can I have a few minutes with my boy please? Y'all can have him when I'm done, not the way y'all wanna have him, though, only conversation, that's it.

The models give Haseem a hug and smile as they listen to their boss and turn around and leave them.

HASEEM'S MOM. Your aunt Pelynda has been asking about you. She said to give her a call. She misses you.

HASEEM. Oh, she has. I'd been meaning to call her too. I got to ask her some business questions. Thanks for telling me. Well, I just wanted to make sure you were okay and didn't need anything. I gotta to go run a few errands before traffic gets crazy.

HASEEM'S MOM. Okay, sweetie. Thanks for checking on me, and come by on Sunday. I might surprise your father with a big breakfast.

They both laugh at that, and they look each other in the face, laughing very loud. Haseem starts to leave, and the scene ends.

Scene three. Steven pulls up to the office to meet up with his father. While he is there, he runs into his mother who is leaving. She gets on him about not calling or checking on her. He shrugs it off. Steven informs his dad that the deal is done and that when he is ready to start he can. He tells Steven to get the blueprints over as soon as he can. Steven's mom was ear hustling the conversation and shows a little emotion because her husband was supposed to get started on building her new salon. Steven walks out with an evil grin on his face and he tells his mother bye.

STEVEN'S MOTHER. Well, look who it is. My long lost son knows how to find his way to his dad but never to check on his mother.

STEVEN. Last time I checked, my phone receives incoming calls, and I don't recall seeing your number coming across my screen. So before you throw rocks at me, check yourself first.

Steven's mom frowns at her son as he walks by her like she's somebody on the street, and her facial expression turns to anger.

STEVEN'S MOM. So you're gonna walk right by me like I'm nobody? Steven, don't freakin' disrespect me. I don't care how much you caught up in your feelings. You will show me respect.

Steven stops and looks down at the ground, realizing his mother is absolutely right. He turns back around and walks toward her with a very sorry look on his face.

STEVEN. You are right, Mom. I apologize for that. That is wrong of me to do. I'd been overwhelmed lately, and I got things on my mind, but that is no excuse not to check on you sometimes.

Steven hugs his mom with a tight squeeze. She hugs him back, and the two of them smile at each other. Steven then pulls away and starts to walk back to his dad's office.

STEVEN. I will come by, and we can do lunch later on this week. Love you!

Steven enters his dad's office to see him on the computer, looking at things. He walks in and takes a seat. Steven's dad looks at his son and glances back to his computer.

STEVEN'S DAD. Man, you're up early this morning. You must have gone home empty-handed last night.
STEVEN. What you taught me growing up—when you know you got business to handle, push the pleasure to the side—well, I never forgot that.

Steven's dad smiles and shakes his head at his son and comes over to where he is sitting and takes a seat.

STEVEN. I just stopped by to let you know that the sale is final for Peter's restaurant and to see if you needed anything done or something.

STEVEN'S DAD. All okay. That's great. They got the sale done great. Just remind him to send me over the blueprints and all the information so we can go over it. Hey, you know, you should really think about one day starting your own construction business.

Steven looks at his dad and then thinks about that suggestion. His eyes glances away for a few seconds and then turns back to his dad.

STEVEN'S DAD. I mean, you know the business 'cause I taught you it since you were a little kid. You know what you're doing and you're a hard worker. Plus, you won't need me anymore either, but seriously, you guys can save a lot of money by doing your own building. Over years, you're talking about millions of dollars that you could be saving.

Steven leans back in his seat and really gives deep thought to what his father is telling him. He grabs his chin and looks his father in the eye.

STEVEN. I never really looked at it like that. We could save a whole lot of money by having me doing the construction. I don't know, Dad. There is a lot of work and pressure when it comes to construction. I remember seeing the stuff you had to go through, and ahh, I don't know.

Steven's dad looks at his son with a confused look on his face. He raises his eyebrows and shakes his head at Steven.

STEVEN'S DAD. So you're telling me that you're afraid of hard work even though the rewards could bring you duffel bags of money? That's not the Steven I know. I raised you better than that, and after watching you and your friends the last few years, there isn't anything you guys can't do if you put your minds to it.

Steven shakes his head and stares at his dad with a confident look on his face. His father realizes that he is reaching his son, so he leans forward in his chair.

STEVEN'S DAD. Look, I would help you get started, help you find good workers and a good manager to help you get the ball rolling. I wouldn't brush you aside like that, son. Give it some thought. Now just tell Mohan to hurry up and send me the blueprints so I can get started.

Steven and his dad stand up and shake hands and look at each other before Steven starts to make his exit. Steven stops and looks back at his dad.

STEVEN. I'm going to really think about that. Thanks for the advice, Dad.

Steven's mother was listening to her husband and Steven talk. She rushes out the hallway so Steven won't spot her, but she is too slow. Steven catches his mother and gives her a strange look and cracks a smile as he walks away.

Scene four. Peter meets up with his father to see if he can get some assistance on expanding the firm's shipping fleet. He knows he can always go to his father for advice and help. Peter's father is happy with him and encourages Peter to keep going strong and that he is really impressed with his business savvy. He also tells him to be aware of his friends because the more successful he becomes, people will become more jealous and envy will be even greater. Peter tells him he needs a little of his father's business pull to secure him and the firm's bigger contract deals for their shipping business to really take off. He tells his son not to worry as he will do whatever is necessary for his son to succeed, and he will make it happen for him.

PETER. Hey, Dad, it's good to see you home for a change. How has things been going?
PETER'S DAD. Things have been going pretty good, son. Business is expanding more, and this is a pretty good year so far. Only thing is, I can't stay to long this time around because I have

some serious contract negotiations going on back in Japan, but I will be back after that is done.

Peter's father sips on his tea and looks away for a second, looking at his surroundings a little before looking back at his son.

PETER'S DAD. How are things going with you, son? I hear and see that your investment firm is really taking off, I see.

PETER. Yeah, it's been growing and doing better than I thought out the gate. We are getting some good deals under our belt.

Peter's dad smiles at his son and sips some more of his tea. He puts the tea down on the table and folds his hands in midair.

PETER'S DAD. Just know, Peter, that the more successful you become, the more you stand out from the rest. There will be more jealously and envy. Just stay strong and ignore all that. Don't let it affect you. Keep pushing and moving forward no matter what, son.

Peter listens closely to what his father is saying. He sips on his tea and nods his head in agreement.

PETER. Father, I wanted to talk to you about improving on my shipping fleet. I know how you built your empire, and I am trying to duplicate it the best way I can. I know you have major connections here in the US, and I was wondering if you can open the door for me a little. This industry is about who you know and how many close ties you have. It's very organized as you know. It's a little hard for me to establish strong business relations with people because of my age and that they not familiar with me.

Peter's dad listens to his son, and his facial expression is saddened by what his son is telling him. He puts his balled-up fists under his chin and thinks deeply. He looks back at his son with a sympathetic look on his face.

PETER'S DAD. You know I will always do anything I could to help you, Peter. I definitely know how racially biased this industry can be, especially in the US. You are right, and I completely understand where you coming from. (*Peter's father shakes his head in disgust after listening to what his son tells him.*) Don't worry, son. I will oil up the wheels for you so you can get rolling better.

Peter shakes his head at his father in appreciation to him. Then both of them sip their tea and look around at their surroundings.

Scene five. Mohan pulls up to meet again with the real estate mogul to show him more of the work in his portfolio. He tells Mohan that he has seen enough and agrees to give him the deal. He tells him he will have his people draw up the contract in the next few days. Mohan asks him if it is for multiple years, and the mogul shakes his head and responds, "Yes, it is, but I want to see perfection."

REAL ESTATE MOGUL. Mohan, what brings you here? Is something wrong? Don't tell me you're turning my offer down.

MOHAN. No, not at all, sir. I thought about what you and your associate said about me not having a lot of experience in designing luxury homes. So I wanted to show you some of my earlier work that I did in college. I want you to see that I am capable of doing good work.

Real estate mogul looks at Mohan a little confused; he's kind of shocked that Mohan made the long trip up to show him his work.

REAL ESTATE MOGUL. Mohan, you didn't have to do this. I have seen enough of your work to know that you are capable to design our homes. You are very serious about your credibility and reputation, I see. I admire that about you.

Mohan starts to show him some of his earlier work. The real estate mogul looks at some of Mohan's work and then looks back at Mohan with a slight frown on his face.

MOHAN. Sir, I understand and really appreciate you giving me the contract to work for you, but I want you to be confident that I will do quality work to your standards, sir. My hope is that you see the hard work and dedication I give to my clients.

The real estate mogul sits up in his chair and eventually stands up and starts to walk around his office. He takes a few deep breaths and looks back at Mohan as he puts his hands in his pockets. Mohan looks a little worried and hopes that he didn't upset the mogul.

REAL ESTATE MOGUL. I believe I told you this already, Mohan. When I look at you and see your commitment to hard work and satisfying your clients every needs and wants, it reminds me of me when I got started. I believe in you and your work, Mohan, so much that I am willing to give you the whole tristate area for the next three years. I, of course, as I will put in our contract, have the ability to back out if I am not satisfied with the work.

Mohan can't believe that the mogul just gave him a three-year deal, with the whole tristate included. His facial expression is one of a person that just won the lotto. He walks over to the real estate mogul and reaches out his hand.

MOHAN. I want to, from the bottom of my heart, thank you, sir, for giving me this deal. Thank you, sir. Thank you so much.
REAL ESTATE MOGUL. I will have the contract sent over to you in a few days. Don't make me regret giving you this deal, Mohan. I want to see perfection like you promise.

The real estate mogul and Mohan finish up their long handshake and stand their smiling at each other.

Scene six. Haseem meets up with his aunt Pelynda for dinner, and they embrace each other like they haven't seen each other in years. Haseem tells his aunt that things are going good with the firm and how he thinks this may be the best year for him so far in his life. He tells his aunt about how he wants to expand in the medical weed business and wants to open up more dispensaries very soon. He asks her about what is needed to expand to other states and if it's possible if she can help him expand to the southern states in the very near future. She smiles and agrees to. She tells him that she is in the process of building better relationships in the political world, and it won't be a problem to pull a few strings to make her nephew happy.

AUNT PELYNDA. Ahh, there is my nephew. I miss you, Haseem. Why haven't you called me? You're my only nephew I have, and I need to hear from you.

Haseem and his auntie hug each other very tightly, and for a long time, they look at each other and share smiles, and they take their seat at the table, ready to enjoy dinner.

HASEEM. I am so sorry, Auntie. There is no excuse for me not staying in touch with you. I have a very small circle of family and friends, so there is no excuse.
AUNT PELYNDA. Well, I know how work can be very demanding, and I know my nephew is working very hard to turn his investment firm into a success. But a text every now and then to let me know you're okay is good enough for me.
HASEEM. Very true, very true, so how have things been with you? I can imagine all the tough decisions and people you have to deal with now in this crazy political world.

Aunt Pelynda shakes her head in disbelief as she looks down to the table; she frowns up a little as she looks back at Haseem.

AUNT PELYNDA. I wouldn't imagine all the wild behind-the-scenes stuff that goes on in politics. I will say that I have learned a lot about building bridges and not destroying them.

HASEEM. Well, that is kind of what I wanted to talk to you about, Auntie. I wanted to—

Haseem is interrupted by the waitress coming over to their table to take their order; they order drinks and Haseem's youthfulness shows by ordering some buffalo wings. Aunt Pelynda is wondering what her nephew is inquiring about as she looks back at him with a curious eye.

AUNT PELYNDA. So what do what to know, Haseem? What is it you need?

HASEEM. Well, you know how I have been building up my computer software company, and it's doing pretty good. But I wanna expand out on some of my other ventures, and one of them is the medical marijuana industry. Once again, I thank you for helping us get the ball rolling in Jersey.

AUNT PELYNDA. No problem, nephew. You know if there is anything I can do to help you, I will do it.

Haseem takes a sip of his raspberry tea that the waitress just brought over. He looks back at his auntie as she, too, takes a sip of her glass of wine.

HASEEM. I want to start expanding out of Jersey. I want to open up a few dispensaries down south like Georgia or the Carolinas. There is a very big population of stoners down there.

Haseem and his aunt start laughing at what Haseem just said as Auntie shakes her head in agreement with Haseem.

AUNT PELYNDA. You are so right about that, especially with all the colleges and universities in Georgia and Carolina. That is good business planning, Haseem.

HASEEM. I know it's very hard for a young black man to set up business moves like what I'm trying to do without some powerful connections or good influence. That is why I was hoping you can maybe give me a hand to get started down south. I'm not familiar or close with anybody important or significant down south.

Aunt Pelynda listens to her nephew and understands what he is trying to do and shakes her head while she takes a sip of her wine.

AUNT PELYNDA. So what is your time perimeter on when you want to do this?

HASEEM. I would say within the next three or four months, no more than six months from now.

AUNT PELYNDA. I am in the process of building good relationships with my political peers across the country. I know the only way to get things accomplished in this world is by building strong relationships. I know a few people I can contact to loosen up things for you down south. Don't worry, I will make it happen for you, Haseem.

Haseem smiles very hard and shakes his head. He is very happy with his aunt and her willingness to help him get things done.

HASEEM. Thank you so much, Auntie,. I couldn't do this without your help, and I appreciate it so much!

AUNT PELYNDA. I told you if I can doing anything I can to help you, I would. You're my only nephew, and I love you, Haseem. You are driven and intelligent and made smart decisions so far in life. I am very proud of you.

The waitress brings over Haseem's wings and Aunt Pelynda's salad; they both share smiles and start eating.

Scene seven. Nadia and Natalie look at a few homes with the realtor. Nadia thanks Natalie for coming with her because her friends will have her trying to buy anything, and they really don't know much about real estate. Natalie talks to her about kids and asks when she wants to start building their family. Nadia lets her know that she wants to hurry up and get this wedding done as soon as possible and that kids aren't in the near future.

NADIA. I want to thank you, Natalie, for coming with me to look at a few homes. I didn't want to take any of my girlfriends because they would be trying to get me to jump on the first thing that has a big closet.

NATALIE. Ahh, it's no problem. I understand what you mean. When it comes to buying a home, there is a lot of things to consider, and you need the right advice.

Both of them walk up to the home where they are greeted by the realtor. They shake hands and walk into the home together. The realtor is sharing some information about the first home with them as Natalie and Nadia are looking around with their eyes bulging out their heads; their mouths are wide-open as they look at the size of the kitchen.

NADIA. Wow, look at the beautiful granite marble island. It is huge enough for four people to sit at. The size of the pantry is bigger than some people's bedroom. Oh, I love the cabinets too. The kitchen leads right out to the patio and backyard also.

The realtor tells the ladies that she will let them look around the house and if they have any questions to just ask. Both ladies walk around the house downstairs. They are looking at every detail of the home. Natalie is watching Nadia face light up as she looks at the living room.

NATALIE. This is a whole lot of home. This living room is huge enough to fit fifty people in it. My house I grew up in couldn't fit ten people in it. (*Nadia chuckles to herself.*) Nadia, this is a lot for only two people. You and Haseem must be planning on having a big family.

Nadia looks at Natalie with a half smile on her face. She looks at the curtains and feels the material. She looks back at Natalie as she walks over to the fireplace.

NADIA. I don't know about big family, but I do want to have at least one kid one day down the road.

NATALIE. This is a beautiful home. I love it. This is gotta be close to million dollars. What kind of budget you and Haseem talk about?

NADIA. Budget? Haseem wants me to be happy and hasn't said anything about a budget, so I am looking at homes that I like and not really thinking about price too much.

Natalie kinda looks at Nadia with a curious look of shock on her face; her mind is wondering as she walks behind Nadia upstairs.

NATALIE. I can't get over the size of this house. This is a very beautiful mansion, not house. This is more like a mansion. (*Nadia chuckles to herself.*)

NADIA. You know, Natalie, the one thing that I respect about Haseem is that he allows me to make important decisions regarding our relationship, and he trusts me to be smart on doing that.

Natalie once again looks at Nadia with a curious look on her face. She shakes her head to what Nadia just said.

NATALIE. That is something we all want out of a man—to commit and marry us and to respect and honor our feelings and desires. But I don't know, girl. Maybe I am used to growing up different because even though my parents were financially good, they were modest and humble and taught us to be mindful on how much we spend on things.

Natalie looks at Nadia and walks with her to look at the other bedrooms upstairs. Nadia is thinking about what Natalie has said.

NADIA. I understands what you mean. I get it. But for me, I want to enjoy a taste of the good life, and I believe that I deserve to live the luxurious life and enjoy the high end of things.

Nadia looks at Natalie with a smile on her face. Natalie smiles back at her, and both of them nod their heads as they start to look at the Jacuzzi in the master bedroom. Nadia's eyes are glued on the Jacuzzi, and Natalie's eyes are wandering off, like she is a little confused by what she just heard.

Scene eight. Peter is at the office, working on a few things, when Steven walks in to talk to him about a few things. He is accompanied by a few lovely ladies. He tells Peter he has to take a business call real quick and didn't want his lady friends to hear everything. Steven tells Peter that he is about to buy this commercial property that Felize showed him to open up another sports bar. Peter tells Steven to make sure everything is right before he signs anything. Steven assures Peter that he will and says that he wants at least $350,000 budget to renovate the place and to make it really nice. Peter says okay but that it's got to be approved by Haseem or Mohan for final approval.

STEVEN. What's up, bro? I had to stop in to make a call. I don't want the girls hearing what I'm talking about.

Peter looks up at Steven and then looks through the window at the ladies Steven has with him.

PETER. Well, it's good to know you still live by the code. What's going on with you?

STEVEN. Nothing really. About to enjoy a nice afternoon out with a few friends. Hey, I met with Felize, and he showed me a few commercial properties for the new sports bar,. I saw one I really like, and I'm thinking about jumping on it.

PETER. Just make sure everything is right before you sign anything. Make sure the land is safe to build on and crunch the numbers real good before you commit.

STEVEN. Of course, of course, I will. I would like to have at least $350,000 to renovate and make it look spectacular. I want this new sport bar to be better than the first, more flat screens and VIP rooms for high-end customers. Plus, I want a bigger bar area and make a bigger outside seating area too.

Peter looks at Steven and leans back in his chair a little. He squeezes his face together as he plays with his pen in his hand. He glances back at the ladies in the other room that are getting a little loud, talking with one another. Steven notices Peter is getting annoyed with the ladies and looks at them with a mean stare.

PETER. I really don't have a problem with that because I think it's important to make it stand out more than the first one. Hell, I'm doing the same thing with my new restaurant, so I feel you. But you know that's gonna have to get approval from Haseem and Mohan when you're talking that kind of money.

STEVEN. Nah, I know, I know. We'll discuss it with them in our next meeting or something. Hey, did Mohan send my father the blueprints and information he needs to get started?

PETER. He better have. I told him to. He's always on top of things. I'm pretty sure he did. (*Steven smiles at Peter and grabs a few pieces of candy on Peter desk.*)

STEVEN. Aight. Well, let me make this call so I can get going with my afternoon session with my friends.

Steven chuckles at Peter, and Peter chuckles back at him and shakes his head while he looks back at his laptop and leans forward in his office chair. Steven turns around and walks toward his office to make his business call.

Scene nine. Mohan and Felize meet up to talk at a nightclub. They talk about what tech and pharmaceutical companies to pour some money into. Felize gives him the details on who is hot and who is on the rise and how much he thinks their firm should invest. Some gorgeous ladies are flirting with Mohan and Felize, so they send them over a bottle of champagne and tells the hostess to give them whatever they are drinking. Mohan lets Felize know that he is almost finished with the blueprints for Peter's restaurant and that he wants to get started investing in his stock recommendations ASAP. The gorgeous ladies walk over to thank the guys for the champagne and ask if they wanna hang out later on tonight. Felize and Mohan look at each other and smile and tells the ladies they know the perfect place for them to go.

FELIZE. Like I was telling Peter and I mentioned it to you before, you guys got to start doubling up on your Wall Street investing. These small tech companies and pharmaceutical companies are on the rise. I mean, they are growing fast, bro, and the time is now for you to buy some shares while the getting is good.

MOHAN. We are already buying shares in a wide range of companies, and we're getting good return for our investing. I mean, we got a lot of different things going on, Felize. We got to be careful how much we're spending too.

Felize shakes his head at Mohan and looks away. His facial expression is a little stern with no smile. He takes a sip of his drink and puts it down on the table.

FELIZE. Yeah, but you guys are investing on the sure bets the typical shit. Yeah, you're going to make money, of course, but the key to really cashing in big is by finding the hidden diamonds, the needle in the haystack. There are quite a few industries that you guys haven't tapped into. You got to open up and look at the bigger picture.

MOHAN. Oh yeah, and what's the bigger picture? What's the hidden jewels that we're missing out on?

Felize smiles at Mohan and notices a few lovely ladies dancing very sexily and looking at them with very flirty eyes. Felize, with his eyes, motions Mohan to look at the ladies. Mohan turns to see what Felize is looking at and turns back and smiles, then waves his hand to gesture to Felize to ignore them.

FELIZE. The big picture is to find the small package that will blow up with more bang than the big package that will not do as much damage. In so many words, the small companies are the ones that will bring you and the firm very huge cash-outs, especially if you let it sit for five or six years. You guys are young, still wet behind the ears, and the great thing is you're not hurting for money. It won't bother you guys to sit on it for a while.

MOHAN. Five or six years ain't long at all. I mean, it just seems like a few years ago we were eating on hot pockets, playing cards in our college dorm. I'm going to discuss with the fellas and try to convince them to do it.

FELIZE. You know me, Mohan, and how I operate. Everything that I advise you guys to do, I will do and most likely have already done it. You know I jump on any money train I see moving. I'm not trying to lose out on nothing.

Mohan shakes his head in deep thought to what Felize has schooled him on. He knows Felize is an expert on getting money and making smart business moves. He sips on his drink and looks around the club a little. He glances back at the ladies and notices that they are still making eye contact with him and Felize.

FELIZE. So are we gonna act like geeks, or are we gonna act like young men looking to have a little fun? Hell, why not? I'm gonna buy them a round of drinks, and what the heck, I will send them a bottle too. Why not?

Felize motions over to the hostess that is catering to them in the VIP section. He tells her to send over a bottle of champagne and drinks for them. He then looks back at Mohan and takes a sip of his drink.

MOHAN. I am almost done with the blueprints for Peter's restaurant. I will send it to you in the next day or so to make sure everything is right before I give it to Steven's dad.

FELIZE. No doubt. Hurry it up. You know how Peter can be. He can be a pusher sometimes.

Felize and Mohan shake their head and smile at each other as they are interrupted by the lovely ladies that walk over to their table to thank them for the bottle of champagne.

LOVELY LADY 1. Thanks, guys. That was very sweet of you.

FELIZE. Whoa, hold up with all that sweet stuff! You make it sound so soft and corny.

LOVELY LADY 2. You guys have a sexy vibe about y'all. I can smell big stacks a mile away. We been here for a while and we were getting ready to go. It seem to me like you guys ain't the type to turn in early. We're about to go get something to eat. Why don't y'all come with us so we can get to know one another better? Is there any good diners around, or do you know where we can go?

Felize looks at the ladies and then glances at Mohan. He grabs his drink and looks back at the ladies.

FELIZE. I know the perfect place where we can go, where we both can eat and unwind.

The ladies look at Felize and Mohan like they know the deal and that they're down for whatever. Felize looks at Mohan with a devilish grin on his face.

Scene ten. Felize and Mohan pull up to Mohan's crib. As they walk in, the ladies are impressed by how nice Mohan's bachelor spot is. Mohan tells them to walk around and tour his townhouse. While they are gone, Mohan texts Natalie to let her know he may be late for breakfast tomorrow with a bunch of smiley faces. Mohan puts on some music, and they are enjoying their late night with the ladies, watching them dance and entertaining one another sexually. Mohan tells Felize that this lifestyle can have its advantages sometimes with a smile. As the ladies start to triple-team Mohan and start to satisfy him, Felize jokingly smiles and says, "What about me!" The episode ends with the song of Miguel playing in the background. "How many drinks will it take you to be with me?"

FELIZE. Hey, Mohan, please tell me you do have something to eat here right. I mean, you know we got to feed them at least. Heck, I'm hungry myself.

MOHAN. I don't know why you guys think all I eat is salad and fruit. I do have a chef that comes over and cooks for me a few days a week, and it just so happened she came over and cooked yesterday, so you're in luck.

FELIZE. I didn't know they had an extra friend with them. I'm a little too saucy to bang out a doubleheader.

MOHAN. Yeah, and you're a little too young to be taking male enhancement pills. I mean, you should be able to bang out at least five minutes with them.

Felize punches Mohan in the shoulder as they walk around Mohan's bachelor crib. The ladies are kinda drunk and are loving Mohan's townhouse; they are looking around at some of his paintings and sculptures. Mohan tells them to take a tour around the house and look around. He and Felize walk into his kitchen as Mohan starts to pull out some food from the refrigerator.

MOHAN. Messing with you, I ain't gonna get out bed till midday. I'm supposed to take Natalie out for breakfast in the morning. I better let her know. Let me text her.

FELIZE. Hey, man, we didn't go looking for this. It just came our way. I was fine with going home, but as you and I know, things don't always go according to plan. (*Felize chuckles to himself.*)

MOHAN. Ahh, I forgot I got to finish some work for one of my clients tomorrow too. I got a long day ahead of me. Messing with you, Felize.

FELIZE. Listen to you, bro. I mean, what the hell, Mohan? You got to let loose sometimes, bro. You got to enjoy some of the pleasure that this lifestyle can bring you sometimes. You and freaking Peter, I swear you two would rather hang in your office on your laptop instead of having a cutie with a fat ass sitting on your lap.

Felize starts laughing so hard he bends over on the counter in the kitchen. Mohan isn't laughing. He just stares at Felize with a twisted-looking face. He walks in the living room and turns on some music. Felize follows him in the living room. He's still laughing at his joke.

MOHAN. Hey, man, I'm just sticking to the code, following the oath. I'm committed and dedicated to being a billionaire by the time I'm thirty-five. I like women, but I know they can be a distraction and get you caught up. They have brought down a lot of powerful men over the years. I ain't gonna let that happen to me.

Felize and Mohan look at each other and fix a drink at Mohan's bar. The music and the moment are making them miss out on the women entertaining themselves sexually on the couch. They turn around and notice the women are basically nude and kissing and licking each other. They lean back on the bar, and their eyes are popping out of their heads. They watch as they sip on their drink.

MOHAN. Yeah, you definitely were right, bro. This lifestyle does have some really good advantages. (*Mohan chuckles as they look at each other.*)
FELIZE. I'm gonna tell you like I was told by my pops. You know he was like a philosopher. You can lose a lot of money chasing women, but you won't lose women chasing money. They lock on very hard when you getting money.

They look and smile at each other as both of them shake their heads. Once again, they are caught off guard as the lovely ladies come over and attack Mohan sexually. They go in on him very hard, triple-teaming him very aggressively. They are not holding back their aggression on him. He is not able to fight them off as they are not taking no for an answer. Felize looks at his friend get devoured by three lovely ladies. He feels sorry for him.

FELIZE. Hey, what about me? I'd been a bad boy. I should be punished too.

The ladies feel sympathy for Felize and start to show compassion to his needs. Felize smiles and enjoys the love that he is receiving. The episode ends with the song of Miguel playing, "How many drinks will it takes you to be with me?"

Episode 4

Scene one. Haseem rides over to his parents' house to see them. He wants to tell them about his plans to open up more medical weed dispensaries. Haseem tells them he is also thinking about getting married before the year is over. His father doesn't understand the rush, and he thinks that his son needs to be make sure he really understands what it means to be a great husband. Mrs. Kendricks thinks her son is speeding things up to make Nadia happy and warns him about spoiling a woman early in the relationship.

Haseem walks in to his parents' home and surprises his parents; they weren't expecting him over. He walks over and gives his mother a big hug and pats his dad on the back as he walks by him.

HASEEM'S MOM. Well, this makes twice I'd seen my son in two weeks. Not a bad average. It's getting better, I will give you that.

HASEEM. Ahh, here you go, always overexaggerating things, and you shouldn't be the one complaining 'cause I check on you more than I do Dad.

HASEEM'S DAD. What's up, son? How's my boy making out? You know, your face has a glow to it ever since you got engaged. Somebody is happy, I see.

Haseem smiles it off and looks at his dad like, "Why you saying that?" His mother is giving him a deeper look now. She walks closer over to Haseem.

MRS. KENDRICKS. Yeah, I think you're right, baby. (*She got his nose open.*) I know my son. (*She laughs as she walks back in the kitchen.*)

HASEEM. Whatever. If I was still swinging and moving like I used to with all the ladies I had, she be pleading with me about settling down. I can't win with her. Anyway, since we're talking about my personal private love life, I wanna let you and Mom know that we're speeding up the wedding a little bit.

Mr. Kendricks looks at his son with a corner-of-the-eye stare at him; his eyebrows are raised and his facial expression looks a little confused. Mrs. Kendricks walks back in the room very slowly with a half smile on her face. Haseem walks back and forth, looking at them both.

MRS. KENDRICKS. We just had the engagement party. Wow, okay. Well, if that's what you wanna do, I, as of right now, don't really see nothing wrong with it. But I'm a little surprised and wondering what you rushing for. I mean, all women know it takes close to a year to fully prepare a beautiful wedding.

MR. KENDRICK. Son, like I told you before, marriage is not something you go in headfirst all fast. I mean, you just said it yourself. You just got all your G-Mack days out of you. Better yet, are you comfortable with yourself knowing what it really takes to be loyal? Don't be like a lot of young men who got married and were divorced in three years. I think you need the extra time to know if this is exactly what you want and, of course, if you are fully ready for it.

Haseem listens to his parents and twitches his mouth to the side. He looks away from them for a few seconds and looks back at his parents.

MRS. KENDRICKS. Listen, Haseem. Don't speed up things to make her happy. Hell, she should be ecstatic with all the nice things you have given her. All I am saying is, you have to be careful how much you give a woman early in the relationship. Some women can become spoiled and always want that treatment, then the pressure is on you to maintain it.

Mrs. Kendricks walks over to her son and pats his head and slowly waves her hand down his head. Haseem looks at her with a slight frown on his face.

MRS. KENDRICKS. One of the things that I loved about your father was that he made me feel like I was supposed to shower him with love and gifts. I never told him but the way his style was, the vibe he sent off to me, I kinda felt like I had to lock him down instead of him locking me down.

HASEEM. Okay, I didn't come over here to get a lecture on love and relationships. Enough of that. I'm an experienced grown man who knows about women, but I appreciate your concern.

Haseem looks at his parents and then walks around the room. His parents look at their son with an eye-raising facial expression.

HASEEM. Besides, what I really wanted to tell y'all is that I am going to open up more marijuana dispensaries soon. I want to expand outside of Jersey though. I want to go more south, and now I am not focusing too much on it. It's a very lucrative business and is growing fast.

MR. KENDRICKS. Hey, I don't blame you on that, son. It's about capitalizing and supplying the demand at the end of the day. I think it's brilliant thinking, and if you and your friends all agree on it, then you should go ahead and make it happen.

MRS. KENDRICKS. Your father's right on that. Smart investing is the key to success, and that is what you and your firm has done so far. It is very profitable.

Haseem cracks a smile as he looks at his parents. He rubs his stomach and starts to walk toward the kitchen.

HASEEM. I'm glad my parents see my vision, but I don't smell any food cooking I'm hungry, Mom. You ain't cook no breakfast or nothing?

Mrs. Kendricks shakes her head at her son and looks at her husband; they both just smile at Haseem as he walks in the kitchen.

Scene two. Natalie is waiting on her brother to show up for breakfast. Mohan walks in with a hangover and a little disoriented from his wild night. They order breakfast and begin to talk about things. Natalie tells Mohan about her day, with Nadia looking at homes. She kinda get a funny feeling about Nadia being a little selfish. Mohan tells her that's just her character, and at the end of the day, it's up to Haseem to decide if he can deal with it. Mohan gets a text from Haseem telling him about a surprise birthday party for Nadia. He tells Natalie she should come. He asks her if their parents got back from vacation yet and if she heard from them. He tells her about the deal he got with the real estate mogul. She is very happy for him and tells Mohan that he inspires her.

MOHAN. Hey, sis, I'm sorry for being late for breakfast. I'm surprised you haven't ordered your veggie omelet yet. So nice of you to wait for me.

NATALIE. You think I waited for you? I didn't know how long you were gonna be. I ordered my food already. And no, I didn't order a veggie omelet. I got the Western omelet instead.

Natalie smiles at her brother and motions for the waitress to come over and take Mohan's order. Mohan is looking at the menu, but he quickly closes it and looks at his sister with a half smile. The waitress walks over to their table.

MOHAN. I already know what I want. Look at you, finally eating like normal people. (*He looks up at the waitress.*) I will have the Western omelet and a side order of sausage please, and give me a short stack of pancakes too.

WAITRESS. And your drink?

MOHAN. Strawberry lemonade please. (*Mohan looks back at his sister and turns his attention to her.*) So what's up with you? You feeling all right?

NATALIE. Yeah, I'm good. I just wanted something different, that's all. I'm starting to feel skinny, and I don't like it.

Mohan shakes his head with a confused look on his face. He starts to sip on the coffee the waitress just poured for him. He puts the coffee down and wipes his face and rubs his eyes. Natalie is texting somebody and not paying Mohan attention.

NATALIE. So I went with Nadia to look at a few homes that she likes, and it was an interesting day. Haseem better keep grinding 'cause she got big taste, that's for sure.

MOHAN. Hey, well, he's getting money, and his company just got another big contract.

NATALIE. That's good for him. He works hard. I don't know. I just get a funny feeling about Nadia. It seems like she just wanna spend his money on big materialistic things. I'm not saying she doesn't love him, but it makes me wonder if it's him or the money she loves.

MOHAN. That's just the way she is. She's into high-end fashion and likes the finer things in life. She's different than you, that's all. That's just her character.

Mohan picks his coffee up and starts to take another sip. He looks around the diner and looks out the diner's window. Natalie frowns at her brother and just looks at him with a whatever look on her face. Mohan's phone goes off, so he grabs it and looks at it.

MOHAN. Besides, at the end of the day, that's up to Haseem to deal with. He got to live with that. It's his decision if he wants to deal with that. He just texted me. What a coincidence. He's throwing Nadia a surprise birthday party. You should come and hang out with us. You know how we do, sis.

The waitress brings over Natalie's food and places it right in front of her. Mohan is drooling at her food and grabs a small piece of her meat. Natalie smacks his hand away with her fork. Mohan smiles at her and tries again to steal a piece.

NATALIE. I don't think so. Not my thing. Plus, I got to catch up on some work too.

MOHAN. No doubt. I feel you. Yo, I got a big deal done with this real estate mogul. He's a billionaire, and he's feeling me. If I do my thing with him, I'm set for life, Natalie.

NATALIE. That's wonderful, Mohan. Wow, that is amazing. Look at you, doing deals with billionaire real estate moguls. I'm so proud of you for real. Wow, you really inspire me to keep grinding and working hard. You and your boys are defining the odds.

Natalie is smiling ear to ear, looking at her brother. She is cutting up her omelet and eating on some of her food.

MOHAN. You heard from Mom and Dad? Did they get back from vacation?

NATALIE. Yeah, I talked to them. They're supposed to be back in a few days, I think. You never know with them, they might stay another week. You know how they are.

MOHAN. Yes, 'bout time. Looking at you, eat is making me starve. Your food smells good.

The waitress brings over Mohan's food, and he goes in on his breakfast like he haven't eaten in a week. Natalie is shaking her head and laughing at Mohan. The way he is eating is making her laugh. She tries to take a piece of his meat. Mohan takes his fork like he was gonna stab her hand with it. He smiles at Natalie and lets her take a piece.

Scene three. Peter is meeting with the manager of his restaurants. He informs him of the Belmar expansion and his plans for the project. Peter wants him to come up with some ideas for the place and to start looking for a candidate to run it. Peter is not happy about one of his employees not cooking the food the right way. As he is walking to his car, he gets a call from Steven about the deposit for the Belmar project. Steven tells him that his father wants 30 percent down to get started. He agrees to it and will transfer the funds to him.

PETER. You already know about the Belmar project. I want you to start looking over candidates for the manger position. You already got your hands full running the other restaurants. I don't wanna put too much pressure on you.

The manager shakes his head at Peter but is a little bothered by what Peter just told him. He looks away from Peter with a hurt look on his face.

PETER. I know you can do it. That's not the issue at all. I wanna be considerate to you and your family. It wouldn't be fair to you to have that much pressure on you. You deserve some help. You're doing a great job managing the restaurants. I'm happy with the job you're doing. I don't want you to be overwhelmed.

MANAGER. I appreciate that. I really do, Peter, but you know me. If I was overwhelmed, you know I would tell you. But I respect what you're saying, and maybe I could use a little more time with the family. Kids are playing sports now, and it will be good to get to some of their games.

Peter nods his head at his manager and opens up his hands to gesture that he totally understands his family situation. He looks down at his food that he is eating, and his facial expression changes to frustration. He looks back at his manager.

PETER. This food is a little undercooked. Where is the cook at? We can't have this. That's the fastest way to start losing customers.

Peter tells the waitress to tell the cook to come here. Peter's facial expression is mad as he looks back at his manager.

PETER. This isn't your fault, but that's also one of the reasons I need you here and not having too many restaurants to manage. We got to focus and watch our workers. They have a tendency sometimes to rush and mess things up. That will destroy us if we don't monitor it more.

MANAGER. Yes, I agree. He has been getting a little sloppy lately. He's not paying attention to what he's doing.

The cook walks out of the kitchen, wiping his hands and forehead; his facial expression is confused as to what is going on. Peter and his manager are staring at the cook as he walks toward them. Peter stands up to greet his cook.

PETER. Hey, listen, I'm going to make this short, my man. This food is a little undercooked, and I can't have that anymore. If customers aren't happy with their food, they will find another restaurant to eat at. Is everything okay with you? I mean, is there something going on with you because we get rave reviews about our food here, and I owe you that? So if there is something you wanna talk about, I'm here.

THE COOK. Well, sir, I will be honest with you. I have been having some personal issues in my life concerning my family. The last few weeks have been a little rough for me, but I promise you, sir, that I will not let that happen again. I will not let it affect my work, sir. I'm very sorry, sir.

Peter takes a deep breath and shakes his head while he looks at the ground; he looks back at his cook and puts his hand on the cook's shoulder.

PETER. Hey, I'm very sorry to hear that. You should have said something to one of us. Hey, family is everything to me, and I want my workers to understand that. Family is number one. Why don't you take a few days off to get things right in your personal life? Matter of a fact, take a week off to work on your issues.

The cook starts to get a little teary-eyed, and he looks away from Peter and wipes his eye. He then looks at his manager, and the manager shakes his head and gives him a sad compassionate facial expression. He then looks back at Peter, agreeing to what his boss just told him.

THE COOK. Thank you, sir. I really do need a little time to work things out with my wife. I am so thankful and appreciate it so much, sir.

Peter hugs his cook and tells him he can have the rest of the day off. Peter looks over to his manager. Peter starts to put on his suit jacket, and his phone starts to ring.

PETER. Make sure he gets a full week off with pay, and let Antonio handle the A cook position while he is out.

Manager shakes his head and stands up to shake Peter's hand. Peter looks at his phone as he starts to leave his restaurant. He answers his phone as he is walking toward his car.

PETER. Steve, what's up, bro?
STEVEN. Hey, real quick. My old man said that he will need his 30 percent down payment to get started on the Belmar project.
PETER. Ahh, yeah, that's right. I almost forgot about that. My fault. Tell him that I will have the funds transferred to him by tomorrow morning.
STEVEN. Aight, no doubt. Hey, you going to Nadia's surprise birthday party?
PETER. Yeah, most likely I should be there before it gets too late. I got a few things to do for my mother, but I'll be there.
STEVEN. Cool, aight, I'll check you tonight.

Both of them hang up the phone, and Peter starts to drive off in his Mercedes-Benz.

Scene four. Nadia and her girlfriends are doing some shopping and talking about how things are going with the home shopping plans. Nadia says she got some more properties to look at soon but is kinda undecided on where she wants to live. They ask her if Haseem is going with her to look at the homes. They are kind of schooling Nadia about his busy schedule and why he isn't making time to accompany her. Nadia tries to explain her man's lifestyle and how he is busy pursuing big moves so they can live a glamourous life. They are enjoying a nice day out in Manhattan.

NADIA'S FRIEND KIA. Them shoes are nice. I got to buy them.
NADIA. Yeah, they look good on you too, girl. I brought me the same
    shoes a few weeks ago.
NADIA'S FRIEND SHAWNA. Damn, Nadia, can we ever get something
    that you haven't got already yet? Every time we go shopping, we
    got to try to find something that you don't already have. Heck,
    that takes up half the day.

Nadia and her girlfriends start laughing as they walk around the store, looking at more shoes. Kia is smiling as she picks up another pair of shoes and looks at Nadia for her approval. All three women start laughing at the joke. Shawna looks at Nadia as the laughing settles down.

SHAWNA. So how is the home-shopping experience coming along,
    girl?
NADIA. I mean, it's complicated, girl, It's a learning experience, you
    know. So many things you have to consider, like neighbors and
    school system, but I got some more properties to look at still.
KIA. Complicated? Yeah right. What's complicated? Do I need a
    Jacuzzi downstairs too, or is my closet space big enough, or here
    is a very hard one to decide on. How many TVs do we need in
    the house? Yeah, that's some very hard choices to decide.

Nadia smiles at her friend and shakes her head as she picks up some shoes. Shawna and Kia are still laughing over Kia's joke.

NADIA. Whatever, Kia. I'm not that clueless, girl.

SHAWNA. So how does Haseem like the whole process, or has he made time to go with you yet?

Shawna and Kia give Nadia a sharp look with a smirk on their faces. Nadia is busy trying to get the attention of the worker at the store to try on a pair of shoes. She looks back at her girlfriends with a slight frown on her face; she is thinking about her response, so she waits a few seconds.

NADIA. Haseem is a very busy man. He is out there paper chasing and landing some nice deals for his company. He is very dedicated in pursuing his dreams. I understand how busy his schedule is. Heck, his phone is always ringing off the hook. I can barely talk to him sometimes.

KIA. Yeah, well, all I'm saying is that he can't leave all this on your shoulders. He got to cut something out or something, girl.

SHAWNA. She right, girl. I mean, both of you need to be doing this together, and if I know Haseem, he makes time for his pleasure and his boys, I bet. You got to watch these men, girl. They make time to watch football and spend hours on cleaning their cars. Keep your eyes open, Nadia. Haseem is smooth.

Nadia rolls her eyes while the worker hands her the shoes she wanted to try on. She looks at her friends and looks back at her shoes.

NADIA. Well, he told me that he will be going with me soon, and I believe him. Haseem is big on his backyard and man cave. That's all he talks about. He's gonna come with me. Yeah, I'm feeling these shoes. I got the right dress to rock with them too.

Nadia looks at the shoes in the mirror. She looks at them from different angles. She then does a little dance and smiles at herself in the mirror.

NADIA. I love my man. His long hours of grinding make it good for me to buy nice shoes like this without worrying about the price.

Nadia looks at her girlfriends with a confident look on her face. Kia and Shawna look back at Nadia with a smile on their faces, and the three of them give each other hand smacks and start to laugh even louder.

Scene five. Steven and Darren are at the Rutgers football game enjoying the luxury skybox, eating and drinking and enjoying the game. Haseem and Jamal walk in, surprised that they are there, cracking jokes on Steven for eating so much food. Jamal tells Darren that he got some gas that they can blow on. Darren happily takes Jamal up on his offer. They leave out the skybox. While they are gone, Haseem and Steven talk business. Haseem tells Steven he should think about starting his own construction company, and the firm can save money by doing the work themselves instead of hiring his dad to do it. Steven likes the idea and believes he could do it because he learned everything about it from working with his father since he was eight years old. Haseem also tells him about the surprise birthday party he is having for Nadia, and he wants him to be there.

STEVEN. Yo, Rutgers always plays big when the big schools, the top twenty-five, come to town, then they look soft when they're playing schools. That ain't shit.

DARREN. That's always been them. They're like the freaking giants. They do the same exact thing. That's why I hardly ever bet on their games because you don't know what you're gonna get from them sometimes.

Darren gets up and pours him another drink. Steven is eating his steak and potatoes when the door opens up. Enter Haseem and Jamal as they stroll in laughing about an old story. They look up and notice Steven and Darren. All four men look at one another like they're surprised to see one another.

HASEEM. What y'all doing here? Steven, you're the last one I expect to see here at a Rutgers game. They always kept you pissed on how they played. Plus, it's Saturday and I know you had a wild night last night. I saw you all over social media.

STEVEN. You did? Yo, who the fuck keep posting pictures of me? I hate what I'm doing is out there for the world to see. I'm gonna stop taking pictures with people. Everybody like posting pictures on some clown shit.

All four men walk toward one another and give one another hugs and hand smacks. Jamal walks over and grabs himself a few fries and a burger at the food spread out on the table.

HASEEM. Rutgers look soft, I see. How long y'all been here?

STEVEN. We got here about twelve, so we can eat.

JAMAL. Yeah, I know you wouldn't want to miss out on the food, Steven. Damn, bro, how many different burgers and steaks do you need for two people? You're a greedy dude for real.
STEVEN. I ordered a little extra because these chicks are supposed to meet us up here. They wanna do a little tackling and hitting. You know what I'm saying.

Haseem starts laughing at Steven and shakes his head. Jamal and Darren join in laughing at Steven too. Jamal looks at Darren with an evil smile on his face.

JAMAL. Yo, Dee, I got a little gas for us to blow on, my man. Heck, it's almost halftime anyway.
DARREN. That's what I'm talking about, my dude. I haven't blown on nothing all day, bro. I'm with that, cuzzo.
JAMAL. Word, come on. Yo, Steven, when I come back, I'm going in on your steak and potatoes. Munchie time.

Jamal and Darren leave out the skybox together, smiling and joking with each other. Steven and Haseem look at them leaving, shaking their heads.

STEVEN. What's going on with you? I heard you're throwing Nadia a surprise party.

HASEEM. Yeah, that's what I was about to tell you, but I see how fast news spread around.

STEVEN. Look at you, Seem. You're really digging this one, I see. Nadia's cool, plus she's beautiful too, my dude. You got a official dime piece you snatched up.

HASEEM. Yeah, no doubt. Appreciate that. Hey, man, I was thinking the other day about things, and you know, I think you should start your own construction company one day down the road. I mean, you know all that stuff. Your old man trained you when you were little. You know the ins and outs of the business. And more importantly, think of all the money you could save the firm at the same time too. Heck, we could probably convince Mohan and Peter to kick up our yearly salary some.

Steven looks at Haseem with a very deep-thought look on his face. He is really considering hard what Haseem just said. He takes a sip of his beer and looks back at Haseem.

STEVEN. You're talking some real talk right there. It crossed my mind before, but it's a whole lot of work and politics in the construction world. Seem, you got to cut throats, mob influence, shady bidding on the real big jobs. I don't know.

HASEEM. Yeah, but the advantage you got is your father, Steven. Heck, half your family is in the business. You know they're gonna put you on, bro. They're gonna make sure you good and give you good kickback on top of it too.

Steven looks away from Haseem, raising his eyebrows and rubbing his chin with a deep-thinking look on his face. Haseem gets up and cheers on the action going on in the football game. The scene shifts to Darren and Jamal smoking in the car.

JAMAL. Yo, Dee, you still moving work down there at the shore?

DARREN. Nothing like I used to. I got a few things moving down there mainly in Wildwood and Ocean City, but on the real, I'm ready to get out the game. It's not the same no more.

JAMAL. I feel you on that. I've been thinking the same thing, bro. I made a lot of money over the years to where I mean how much you gonna stack up before them boys come kicking your door down and take your stacks while they're at it too.

Darren and Jamal look at each other in agreement with what Jamal just said. Darren takes a few more hits before passing it to Jamal.

DARREN. That's exactly how I feel too. Too many snitches out here. Plus, looking at Steven and them makes me wanna go legit. They're getting it for real, my dude. Them cats got some serious, serious stacks yo, and they can move around free, not worried about nothing. That's how I'm trying to move, bro. I wanna start cleaning up my money, buy a few Laundromats, or start a landscaping business or something.

JAMAL. No doubt. I wanna open up a real barbershop where you can come chill out and eat, get your hands and feet down, lift some weights, play some pool. You know, a real hangout spot. Charge like fifty dollars a month for membership, but you get unlimited haircuts and edge ups.

Darren looks at Jamal with a serious look on his face; he gives deep thought to what Jamal just said.

DARREN. Yo, that's a great idea, Jamal. I'm feeling that. You could really kill them with that. There ain't nothing like that in Jersey yo. That's smart, bro.

Jamal and Darren embrace the moment that they are sharing as they nod their heads in agreement with each other's ideas. Jamal passes the gas back to Darren. The scene shifts back to Steven and Haseem.

STEVEN. That quarterback is doing his thing, but his receivers are garbage. The running back is a bum too. Rutgers is a long way from competing in this conference.

HASEEM. Nah, I think they're coming up. They got a good recruiting class coming in next year. They're finally starting to snatch up a few Jersey players too.

STEVEN. Yo, I'm really gonna think hard on that construction company. Over the next ten years, we could save millions of dollars. That's a few Lamboos, Maybachs, and Ferraris we could be whipping.

Haseem and Steven laugh real loud as they shake hands real tight and shake their heads in agreement. Jamal and Darren open up the door escorted by a few lovely ladies. They are both smiling ear to ear. Haseem looks at them and smiles even harder as he looks back at Steven.

STEVEN. Hey, you sticking around for overtime, Seem?

Haseem looks at the ladies and looks back at Steven. He shakes his head and smiles. He takes a sip of his beer.

Scene six. Peter is at the office working when his manger from the firm's trucking company walks in. He informs Peter that everything is in motion for the new contract deal they got with the food company. He came by to pick up the check for the new trucks they need. He also tells Peter that since they last talked, four more companies have called about doing business with the trucking company. Peter has a shocked look on his face. He couldn't believe how fast the trucking business is growing. He tells his manager to look for some good-quality used trucks to cut spending costs and to try to get multiple years for the deals but also try to get a max deal with all the companies. Peter group texts the guys to let them know that they got to discuss business real soon. Haseem texts him back that they all can talk at the surprise party.

PETER. Hey, good morning. How has everything been going?

TRUCKING MANAGER. Things are going good, Peter. Things are really starting to take shape. I got the contract finalized with the seafood company in Maine. Here is your copy.

The trucking manager hands Peter the contract; he looks at it and reads some of it before looking back at his manager. Peter's facial expression is a bit confused. The trucking manager takes a seat and looks back at Peter.

TRUCKING MANAGER. Now before you start flipping, I know you wanted a long-term deal, but he initially only wanted to go one year so he can see how good our shipping and delivery business is, but I got him to sign for three years. I made him feel more comfortable and relaxed once I showed him our numbers the last few years. He also is willing to renegotiate after one year. And as you see, Peter, with some hard bargaining, I was able to strike a seven-digit deal. He is a tight and cheap older guy, you know.

Peter is still looking at the contract. He cracks a smile and looks at his manger. He takes a seat at his desk and puts the contract down on his desk. He and his manger are looking at each other with smiles on their faces.

PETER. I'm impressed, but I took your word. You told me not to worry about the deal, and I kinda thought about it, because we needed a company like his. His business is going to grow our trucking company exposure up there in Maine, New Hampshire, Rhode Island. This was big for us.

TRUCKING MANAGER. Well, it doesn't stop there. Since we last talked, four more companies have reached out to us and wanna use our trucks to deliver for them. Two are beverage companies, a furniture company, and another food company. We are really lighting up on the radar now. I've been in this business for over thirty years, and your trucking company has jumped out the gate faster than any other trucking company in their first three or four years.

PETER. Four more companies? You're serious?

TRUCKING MANAGER. You know me. Of course, I'm serious. I don't wanna call it luck or nothing, but that's a pretty good hot streak.

Peter shakes his head and leans back in his seat. He looks at his picture on his desk of him and his father; he smirks and nods his head. He takes a deep breath and looks back at his manager.

TRUCKING MANAGER. We're gonna need some more trucks, of course, but that's not a big issue.

PETER. True, that's a small thing. Look for some good quality used trucks. No need to get brand-new trucks right now. Maybe we can lease a few. Nah, don't do that. But do your best to cut spending costs. Do some heavy research and jump on these companies. Do your best to get max deals.

TRUCKING MANAGER. Of course, Peter. That's goes without saying, nothing less than three-year deals.

Peter looks at his trucking manger and smiles from ear to ear. The trucking manager stands up and looks back at Peter.

TRUCKING MANAGER. Oh yeah, I almost forgot. I need the check for the trucks handling the seafood company routes.

Peter looks on his desk and goes through some papers on his desk. He then stands up and looks in his file cabinet. He pulls out a folder and hands it to his manager. He then grabs his phone and sends a group text out to the fellas. He tells them that they have to discuss business real soon.

TRUCKING MANAGER. Thanks, and I will be in touch with you real soon. Hey, once again, congratulations to you and the guys. You guys are making long strides.

The trucking manger walks out of Peter's office. Peter looks at him leave and nods his head. He looks back at his phone and reads Haseem's reply. Haseem says that they can talk at Nadia's surprise party. Peter sits back down at his desk.

Scene seven. Haseem's aunt is at her office, working; she makes a call to one of her professional friends and tells them to start the ball rolling on opening up a few marijuana dispensaries in his state of North Carolina. And to make it happen, go over whoever you got to go over with to make it happen. She asks him to have their friend in Georgia to give her a call.

AUNT PELYNDA. Well, I see you're too busy to return my calls. Wow, business has you all tied up down there, I see. Congratulations on opening up your third franchise.

PROFESSIONAL FRIEND. I'm so sorry. I did call you back from my business phone. You probably didn't recognize the number, but my fault. I should have gotten back in touch with you by now, Pelynda. I can't make no excuses. I got to hire me an assistant because I hardly have any time for anything lately.

AUNT PELYNDA. Yeah, I see, but it's a great thing when you're making money and building up your brand, so I understand. Heck, I have a hard time doing things anymore. Every time I turn around, it's a meeting with this one, a meeting with that one.

Professional friend and Aunt Pelynda share laughs over the phone.

AUNT PELYNDA. Well, I've been trying to get in touch with you because I need your assistance on something.

PROFESSIONAL FRIEND. Anything, you know that. Much as you did for me and been there for me through my rough times, you know I will never forget you. What's going on?

AUNT PELYNDA. My nephew is trying to spread his wings in the entrepreneur world. He is doing pretty good so far. He got his own computer software company and he built it up pretty fast. He's trying to break in the medical marijuana industry. He's okay here in Jersey, connecting with the right people, but he looking to open up a few down in Carolina somewhere. He's not connected with anyone powerful down there who got leverage to open the doors for him.

PROFESSIONAL FRIEND. Ahh, okay, well, he picked the right industry because ever since they legalized it down here, certain people have been cashing in big-time, girl. Your nephew's right on that. The state economy is loving it, but ahh, I will get that going for you.

AUNT PELYNDA. Yes, girlfriend, I need you to make that happen for me. Do whatever you got to do and go over whoever you got to, to get that going for my nephew. He never asked me for anything, and when he came to me, I knew I had to do this for him.

PROFESSIONAL FRIEND. Yeah, when they're young and hungry and living the right way, you have to be there for them. So many young kids dealing drugs and gangbanging out here in these streets, messing up their lives, so when you have a nephew doing good and being positive, you got to have his back.

Aunt Pelynda and her professional friend chuckle in agreement over the phone.

PROFESSIONAL FRIEND. You need this right away or down the road?

AUNT PELYNDA. He said within three to four months he would be ready, so do what you got to do, and as far as money, don't worry about that. He's good with that. And, ah, our friend down in Georgia, is he still the man down there? I know a few people in the political world, but with all these investigations going on, I got to stay clear from all that.

PROFESSIONAL FRIEND. Oh yeah, he's doing big things down there. He's connected with everybody from the celebrity world to the underground world. Yeah, he's still major, girlfriend.

AUNT PELYNDA. I figured he was. He loved money too much to switch up. Do me a favor and forward me his number, girl, and thanks a lot. I really appreciate it.

PROFESSIONAL FRIEND. Anytime. Like I said, you've always been there for me. I will start getting things situated, and I will keep you informed.

Aunt Pelynda hangs up the phone and smiles as she texts Haseem not to worry about Carolina.

Scene eight. Felize is on vacation where he notices a huge commercial property lot that is up for sale. He does some research and finds out that there is no major chain stores like Walmart, Home Depot, Costco, or any other big chain stores in the area. He texts Peter that he found something that he thinks he and the firm will be interested in.

Felize is riding in a drop-top Bentley, enjoying his vacation with a lady friend on the passenger side. He has his shades on and is smoking a cigar. He looks around and notices a big-size commercial land property that is up for sale. He slows down and pulls over to get a better look. His lady friend is wondering what is wrong. She looks over at him as he opens his door to get out.

LADY FRIEND. What's wrong? What happened?
FELIZE. Nothing. I just want to check something out real quick.

Felize starts to walk over to the land to get a better view; he looks at the realtor's For Sale sign closer. He cracks a small smile on his face as he looks at his phone. He starts to make a call and look back at the For Sale sign.

REAL ESTATE AGENT. Hello?
FELIZE. I just got one question. Why did you not call me and let me know that you got something hot on your hands?
REAL ESTATE AGENT. Felize, hey, what's going on? What you talking about?
FELIZE. I'm down here in Florida on vacation, riding around enjoying myself with a friend, and I see your listing on this huge commercial property right outside Tampa. I thought I told you when you got something promising to let me know.

REAL ESTATE AGENT. Right outside Tampa? Ahh, okay, that one.

FELIZE. Yeah, that one!

REAL ESTATE AGENT. I didn't tell you about that particular listing because there is already a few mid-level developers looking at that one. They don't seem too eager to settle on a fair price though.

FELIZE. What about the area? Give me the whole rundown, will you? I mean, what's the forecast looking like? Any big chain stores or restaurants looking for land?

REAL ESTATE AGENT. Whoa, you're being very pushy. Relax, my friend. Besides, you don't have that kind of cash to place a bet on, do you? I know you and you hate rolling the dice on stuff. But yeah, there are some inquiries going on from what I was told by my sources.

FELIZE. Hey, look, I know you like me, so when you got a chance to grab a heavy bag of cash, you don't hesitate, so if you wanna get rid of the listing, I need to definitely know for sure.

The real estate agent shakes his head and looks at his drink of wine. He motions for another one. Felize is getting impatient and his facial expression is very serious as he waits for an answer.

REAL ESTATE AGENT. Yes, Felize, there is quite a few big chain stores looking for land around that area. Actually, Home Depot and Lowe's are looking aggressively. But I need to be certain that you are serious here because the owner is getting impatient and might take lower than the asking price.

FELIZE. Listen to me. Give me till tomorrow afternoon to be 100 percent certain. I got to make a few calls, but hold off for me, okay?

REAL ESTATE AGENT. Tomorrow afternoon, Felize. Tomorrow afternoon.

The real estate agent hangs up the phone, and Felize hangs up his phone. Felize starts to walk back toward his car. Felize texts Peter that he got something very interesting for him and the firm and to call him back ASAP!

LADY FRIEND. Everything okay?

FELIZE. Yeah, you know me. No matter the weather or the moment, my eyes always see green. (*Felize pulls off in his Bentley drop-top with the music blasting.*)

Scene nine. Everyone is arriving for Nadia's surprise party; it is at a very nice lounge right outside the New York City. The guys are in business mode and are greeting everyone there. They walk into a private area where they can talk about business. Steven questions Peter on what is so important that they couldn't wait till Monday meeting to talk about it. Peter starts to discuss all the good news that he has been told from the new contract proposals for the trucking company to Felize finding a gold mine property down in Florida to Mohan securing the deal with the real estate mogul. But he wants everyone to be aware that there is a bunch of expenses that come with these new business ventures, and he thinks everyone should be careful on their spending a little. All the guys are excited about the good news, and he thinks this calls for an even bigger celebration.

The guys are entering the nightclub dressed to impress. Everyone is decked out with designer suits on. They are noticed by a few people and handshakes, and pats on the back are coming from quite a few people. The ladies are definitely on notice. They make their way to the back of the club where they enter a private room. Peter looks at everyone and takes the lead role in their meeting.

STEVEN. So, Peter, what's this all about? I mean, we're here to party and celebrate Nadia's birthday. No disrespect, but couldn't this wait till our Monday meeting?

PETER. I mean, it could, but I wanted to share the good news with y'all, and since we're all together tonight to celebrate anyway, I might as well fill you guys in on things.

Mohan, Steven, and Haseem all look at Peter with a wondering look on their face. Peter walks around the room for a few seconds and then looks back at his friends.

PETER. Fellas, things are really starting to take off for us this year. Felize just told me that he found a gold mine down in Florida, and he got us a piece of property that will put a lot of zeros in our bank account real soon. Mohan just locked down a major deal with this real estate mogul, and I just scooped up a big food company in Maine that is a seven-figure deal. My boy Haseem signed a big deal with an auto parts company that is gonna pay a lot of cash for Haseem's computer skills. Things are going really good for us.

STEVEN. What do you think, we don't communicate with one another? I mean, I don't know all the details, but I didn't know about Felize in Florida or whatever.

PETER. What I wanna tell everybody is, with these new contracts and deals we just got come a lot of big expenses also. I just don't want us to be spending too much early in. The last three years has been amazing. We're doing big numbers. But I want us to mindful of what we're spending and the firm budget. We got to spend some big cash to make a boatload of cash, but when it goes down, we're gonna up everybody's yearly salary in a few.

Everybody looks very happy with the sound of those words. Everyone is smiling and nodding their heads and smacking one another's hands.

PETER. With the Belmar project and Steven's sports bar expansion and, hopefully, his construction company coming down the road, there's a lot of streams of revenue that's gonna be pouring in real soon. So let's just hold tight a little bit and curb the heavy, heavy spending a little, and I promise we will reap the benefits of our hard work later.

Haseem looks down to the ground for a few seconds. He frowns to himself and puts his hands in his pocket. Then all the guys embrace one another for a big bear hug. They are smiling and congratulating one another.

STEVEN. Yo, this calls for a real big celebration. Let's ball out tonight to symbolize this big moment. And don't worry, I will make sure we have some entertainment for us to enjoy all night long.

MOHAN. Yeah, I know I can count on you, Steven. We good as long as you and your cousin are handling the entertainment for us.

All the guys start laughing and start to make their way out of the private room.

Scene ten. Nadia and her girls are arriving at the lounge, not knowing what is going on. She thinks she is just hanging out with Haseem and the fellas to have a little fun. When she walks in, the place is dark, and out of nowhere flares and sound effects start to go off, and the lights come on and she is completely surprised by everyone screaming "Happy birthday!" The music starts to blast, and everyone is partying at the highest level. Buckets of champagne and the most expensive bottles of liquor are being ordered by the firm. Haseem lets her know how much he loves her while Jamal and Darren are busy making moves on Nadia's friends.

NADIA. I can't believe you. Yo, you really got me on this one. I didn't see this coming at all.

HASEEM. Well, it wasn't easy. I had to loop it all together in a couple of days. I know how your friends are. They can sniff something out miles away.

Nadia looks around and is really surprised. She can't believe that Haseem did all this for her. Her facial expression is in complete shock. Haseem grabs her and gives her a tight hug. He lets go and looks Nadia in her eyes.

HASEEM. I want you to know that I love you and I am happy that we're together. So far, my life is complete with you, and I look forward to us raising a family together. We got a bright future together. (*Haseem gives Nadia a slow kiss on the lips as she puts her arms around his neck.*)

96

NADIA. This is the sweetest and nicest thing you've done for me. This means so much to me, Haseem. I love you with all my heart. I have really found my Prince Charming.

Jamal and Darren walk over to Haseem and Nadia and interrupts their loving moment together.

JAMAL. Hey, are y'all gonna lock lips all night, or we gonna get lit? Come on, lovebirds, let's turn up.

Jamal pumps his fist in the air while he clutches on his expensive champagne bottle. Darren is busy dancing with his own champagne bottle in his hand also. Haseem looks at them both and starts smiling. He looks back at Nadia, and they start dancing also. The DJ switches up the music to some latest Drake songs, and everyone is partying hard.

Scene eleven. As the night is winding down, everyone is making their way out of the club when they notice a red carpet in the middle of the parking lot that leads to a brand-new purple Corvette. Everyone is surprised, and Haseem walks Nadia down the red carpet to her birthday gift. Her girlfriends are jumping up and down, yelling and screaming out in joy! Meanwhile, Peter and the guys looked very shocked by it but are smiling and happy for the lovebirds. Steven jokes with the guys about the spending squeeze that doesn't start till next week, not right now! Everybody is chuckling and laughing. The episode starts to end as a T.I. song starts to play, "You Can Have Whatever You Like."

MOHAN. Hey, Steven, you feeling aight? I don't see any ladies walking out with you.
STEVEN. Mohan, what do you take me as? I mean, you my boy. You've known me for a while now. Certain moments call for certain things. Haseem's my man, and this is a special occasion for his lady, so yes, I do know how to be classy.

Steven looks around at his boys and makes a slight smile on his face. He is awaiting some acknowledgment for his good behavior.

STEVEN. See, I got no credit when I do play the good guy. No respect, I tell you.

Everybody starts to laugh at Steven as Mohan stares at everybody's eyes to the red carpet in the parking lot. Everyone is looking at the red carpet with a confused look on their faces, then out of nowhere, Haseem pops out the crowd and calls for his fiancée Nadia's hand.

HASEEM. I know you didn't think that this birthday party was all you were gonna get, did you?

NADIA. Well, yeah, I mean, I know you spent a lot of money on the party, and I had a wonderful time tonight.

HASEEM. I'm hurt that you would think that. (*He leads her down the red carpet to a shiny purple Corvette as Nadia's friends start going crazy, jumping up and down with their hands covering their mouths.*)

HASEEM. This is your birthday gift. I hope you like it. I know it's your favorite color. Now you see why I wanted you to wear that sexy purple dress you had in your closet?

Nadia's eyes is tearing up. She is trying her best to hold back her emotions. Her girlfriends give her a hug and wipe her tears for her. Haseem stands back and watches the girls console one another. He grins and looks over to his crew that is looking amazed, shocked, and happy all at the same time. The scene shifts back over to Mohan, Peter, and Steven. Jamal and Darren are talking with a few ladies.

STEVEN. Hey, technically this spending squeeze, budget cut, it really doesn't start till next week, not right now. So he's good. He brought that way before the meeting tonight.

Peter and Mohan look at Steven and shake their heads, looking at him. They start laughing real loud as they all start walking down the red carpet toward Haseem and Nadia. The episode ends with T.I. song playing, "You Can Have Whatever You Like."

Episode 5

Scene one. Mohan is cooking breakfast, and it's been a long night for him. He hears the doorbell and is wondering who that can be since he hardly gets any company that early in the morning. He is shocked to see that his parents have paid him a visit. He opens the door and hugs them. They have just gotten back from vacation and wanted to check on him. Mohan pours them some coffee, and they sit down to talk. They ask what's been going with him and wanna know why he hasn't kept in touch. He starts to tell them about the deal he got with the real estate mogul, which will bring him and the firm a whole lot of dividends. He also tells them about the other deals the firm has recently got. His parents are happy for him and are glad things are going well for him and his friends. They tell him that he should consider investing into the medical world, and if he is serious about it, they may be willing to contribute with the initial costs to get started.

Mohan is breaking up small pieces of cheese for his omelet that he is making. He checks on his sausages that is frying on the stove. He is also looking at the morning news on TV when he hears the doorbell ring. He is baffled by who it can be. He turns his breakfast sausage in the pan and starts to walk over to the window to see who it is. He looks out the window and sees that it's his parents. He smiles as he goes to open the door.

MOHAN. What a surprise! I can't believe my eyes. I get a visit from my parents. I got to write this down in my journal.

MOHAN'S DAD. I smell some breakfast cooking. Looks like we're just in time.

MOHAN'S MOM. He and his sister don't eat like we raised them to eat. They are more "meatetarians" instead of vegetarians now that they are grown.

Mohan's parents come in the house and walk toward the kitchen to see what their son is cooking for breakfast. They take a seat at the kitchen table as Mohan checks on his food.

MOHAN'S DAD. Yeah, I can smell that pork cooking. Never mind, you can keep that, but I will take some orange juice.

MOHAN. I can make you and Mommy a cheese omelet if you want. I do have some carrots and broccoli in the fridge.

Mohan smiles at his parents as he opens up the fridge and brings out the orange juice for his dad.

MOHAN. So when did y'all get back from vacation? It would have been nice to get a text or call letting me know.

MOHAN'S DAD. We told your sister to keep you informed. I didn't want to interrupt a busy meeting or conference call. I know your business and the firm is all you care about.

MOHAN. Dad, you know what I'm trying to do with my life. I grew up watching you work sixteen hours a day sometimes to make sure your family had a good life. And Mommy you used to work doubles all the time too. What I'm saying is, I learned from you guys that hard work is the only way you can make it in this world.

Mohan's parents look at each other and look back at their son with a smile on their faces. Mohan brings over his dad a glass of orange juice and pours his mom some coffee.

MOHAN'S MOM. And yes, we are very proud of your work ethic. You and your sister have made us proud so far. How are things going with your business anyway?

MOHAN. Well, I just scored a big contract with a very prominent real estate mogul. I will be doing the whole tristate area for him. And Haseem signed a big client. Peter is expanding his restaurant business. He's gonna open up one down in Belmar, and Steven is in early stages of expanding his sports bar business.

Mohan sips on his coffee and looks very confident and proud at his parents. They are nodding their heads and looking quite impressed with what they just heard.

MOHAN. So you see, Dad, I may not of followed your road to success, but I'm driving in cruise control down my road.

MOHAN'S DAD. Well, all that sounds nice and I am happy for you, son, but I still think you should really consider going into the medical industry down the road. Look, it won't hurt to franchise a little in a multibillion-dollar industry.

MOHAN. We're already doing a little franchising already, Dad, but I will strongly look into it in the near future. I always listen to what you think is right and smart to do.

Mohan's dad smiles at Mohan as he drinks his orange juice. Mohan's mom is smiling as she checks on Mohan's food on the stove.

MOHAN'S DAD. That's what I love about you and your sister—your loyalty and confidence in your father's brilliant mind. But if you're really serious about it, I will be willing to contribute some to help you get started. I want you to know that I will always be there for you, Mohan, and I will back you if you take a turn down my road.

Mohan looks at his dad with a stern look on his face. He smiles at his dad as he shakes his hand. Mohan's mom brings her son's plate over to the kitchen table for him. As she motions for him to sit and eat his breakfast, Mohan and his parents all sit at the table.

MOHAN. So tell me about the vacation. I know it had to be beautiful over in Italy.

Mohan digs in to his breakfast and looks at both of his parents. They are looking at him eat his sausages with a disgusted look on their faces.

Scene two. Peter entertains the CEO of a major alcohol beverage company, who is looking for the right trucking company that can handle the volume of loads they have. Peter assures them that their company is definitely suited to handle their loads, and they have a professional staff of drivers who are available whenever they need them. The CEO knows Peter's father and how successful he is and trusts that Peter's track record so far in the business world is respectable. He agrees to let Peter and his firm have the contract, and the two start to enjoy the Rutgers game and share a toast together.

CEO. Peter, I don't really follow college football too much. Heck, I hardly have time to follow the professionals too much, but I will say the food and the service is first-class.

PETER. Yeah, well, you ain't missing much with Rutgers. They just can't get nothing right. It makes me upset because I went here and went to every game thinking that we were gonna get better. This is gonna be our breakout year, then reality would settle in by the third quarter of just about every game I watched.

CEO. You're only a few years removed from college, Peter, and I see you are doing pretty well for yourself. I've heard your restaurant food is great. I got to check it out soon.

PETER. Thanks, sir, I appreciate it. Yeah, I always had a vision and was inspired by my dad to work hard for myself, and to control my own destiny in life. He was very busy and wasn't around much, but he taught me so much just by his movements and the way he went about things.

The CEO takes another drink from the hostess and takes the straw and stirs the drink a little bit. Peter receives his drink from the hostess and puts it down on the table in front of him. He picks up a few potato chips and plucks them in the French onion dip.

PETER. I do a lot of reading, sir, and I read this book called *Mastermind* by Robert Greene. Very good book. In it, he wrote that you can have the most brilliant mind, teeming with knowledge and ideas, but if you choose the wrong subject or problem to attack, you can run out of energy and interest. In such a case, all your intellectual brilliance will lead to nothing.

The CEO looks at Peter like he was a student and Peter was the professor. He was really taken by what Peter just said. He fixes himself in the chair and grabs his drink and leans back in his seat. He looks away from his drink and looks back at Peter.

CEO. You know, I thought hard about what company I want to handle my distribution. I did research and had my people do research. When I ran across you, I was leery about your age and experience. But I know of your father and how he started from nothing and built from the ground up. I see that same dedication and commitment from you Peter. You strike me as the kind of guy who's gonna have his face one day on the cover of a few magazines.

PETER. Thank you. I appreciate your praise, and you couldn't be more dead on either. I will not stop for a moment until I reach my goal. Nothing will distract or disrupt me from what I'm doing.

CEO takes a sip from his drink and puts it back on the table. He leans back in his chair.

CEO. My only concern, Peter, is you guys are just getting started. Your company is young in this industry. Can I trust your fleet of trucks? Your drivers, are they dependable and reliable?

PETER. That is something I monitor every day, sir, my drivers. I keep a very sharp eye and have replaced quite a few over our first few years. I make sure they are respectful and courteous to the clerk. The person who unloads them, everyone. I also make sure that they leave and arrive on time for each stop. I will not tolerate a pattern of being late. As far as our fleet of trucks, we just purchased twenty more trucks and are in the process of looking for more, sir. CD trucking is ready to go and deliver for you.

CEO leans forward and takes a few chips and stands up and looks at the game for a few moments. He puts his chips in the dip and looks back at Peter.

CEO. You have a deal, Peter. I get a positive feeling about you, son, and I am willing to give you a chance. I believe in you and can tell you're not just talking out your ass. I will have my people draw up the contract for us.

The CEO walks closer to the window to look more at the game. Peter's face is delighted as his fist punches the air. He stands up, and he is smiling from ear to ear, knowing that this is a huge deal he just pulled off. He walks over to the CEO and shakes his hand.

PETER. I want to thank you for this opportunity. I will not let you down, sir. I promise that I will make sure your loads are handled right and product is there on time.
CEO. I truly believe that about you, Peter. I truly do, son.

The two of them look at the game and make a few sounds as they watch the football game.

Scene three. Steven goes over to his father's construction office to talk with him about starting his own construction company. Steven's father is thrilled that his son wants to go into the family business and wants to help him any way he can. Steven tells his dad that he wants no money from him and that he is grown and fully capable getting the business started. All he wants is guidance and help on picking good workers and the right type of equipment to get started with and a little help maybe on securing some big contracts from land developers. Steven's father tells him he has no problem overseeing the beginning phases, but he really wants to do more. Steven asks his dad how his mother is doing. He tells Steven how upset she was to learn that he had to postpone the construction of her beauty salon. Steven grins about it.

STEVEN'S FATHER. Stevie, my boy, stopping by to check on your pops, I see. Always good to see you, son.

STEVEN. What's up, Dad? I know you're busy, so I won't be long. I'd been doing some brainstorming, and my partners are all in on it. I want to start my own construction company, and I want to mold it the same way you built yours.

Steven's dad looks a little surprised as he listens to his son. He shakes his head and leans back in his office chair. He looks at Steven and cracks a smile.

STEVEN'S DAD. That is the best news that I heard in a long time. You know, I always wanted you to follow my lead in the construction business ever since you were little and you used to carry around your little hammer and screwdriver. You don't know how thrilled I am to hear this. I want you to know that I am willing to do whatever I can to get you going. Matter of fact, I will put my money where my mouth is. I will spot the money to get you going, son.

STEVEN. No, Dad, I want to do this on my own. I got the money and I'm backed by the firm for the rest. I appreciate your willingness to give me the money, Dad, but I wanna do this on my own.

Steven looks at his dad with a straight face, and his dad looks back at him with a straight face. Both of them are staring at each other for a few moments before Steven's dad shakes his head and looks away.

STEVEN'S DAD. Steven, you always want to do things on your own. Look, I know you're making good money, son, but you're also spending a lot of money with your lifestyle. The luxury cars, the fancy clothes, money goes quick when you're young. Let me give you a little hand, son.

STEVEN. Dad, I really thank you and appreciate you for wanting to help me, but I got it, trust me. Things are going well for us. We just signed some big contracts, and more are coming in the next few weeks. I don't need your money. What I can use, though, is help with picking the right people, good workers. You got experience with that and, of course, help with selecting the right equipment and machinery.

Steven's dad nods his head, understanding what his son is telling him; he moves around in his office chair and glances at his phone for a few seconds.

STEVEN'S DAD. Okay, I will respect that. I like your decision to open up your own company. I just feel you turning my money down because of your independent mentality, but I really do understand that you're a grown man who don't needs his daddy's money.

STEVEN. Yes, exactly, Pops. Hey, when your time is up and the clock stops ticking, I will get it anyway right.

Steven puts his right hand in the air and smiles at his dad. Steven's dad starts grinning, too, as he shakes his head at his son. He stands up from his office chair and puts his hand in his pockets. He is still looking at Steven with a smiley smirk on his face.

STEVEN'S DAD. It's funny how you got my sense of humor, but I always told you that you are the number one reason why I worked so hard all these years, why I'm always looking for bigger deals to make, so you and your mother will be good when my days are done.

STEVEN. What's up with Mom? You know, the last time I came to see you, when I was leaving, I caught her snooping on what we were talking about. I thought that was a little odd. She could have just come in.

STEVEN'S DAD. Well, your mother is still upset with me. I put off the construction of her new beauty salon. She's giving me a lot of attitude over that, and I haven't gotten too much nookie since she found that out. See what I do for you, you might have to set me up with one of your lady friends if this keeps up.

Steven and his dad laugh and shake their heads. Steven stands up and does a little stretching before he walks over to pour him some coffee.

STEVEN. Hey, your hand still works. Better choke the chicken if things don't get better.

STEVEN'S DAD. Hey, you owe me, son. I missed out on a lot of beautiful things, beautiful things over the years, mainly because I didn't want to lose out on seeing you and being there for you. It's time for a little payback.

STEVEN. So I know I can count on you, Dad, but in the early stages, if you can swing me a few big projects and help me get a few major bids, I will give deep consideration on helping you recover some pleasure you lost out on.

They both smile and give each other a hug before they start to walk out of the office together.

Scene four. Jamal surprises Natalie and her friends who were enjoying the day shopping. Natalie was shocked to see Jamal who hung with them while they tried on some outfits. Jamal couldn't help himself from flirting with one of Natalie friends. He is staring at her while she looks at how her outfit looks in the mirror. She thinks he is sexy, and she flirts back with him. They exchange numbers, and Jamal asks if he can call anytime as he doesn't want to invade on her if she is in a relationship. Natalie asks Jamal if he thinks Haseem has made the right choice with Nadia. He tells her that Haseem knows what he doing and he is well experienced with women. He tells Natalie to put in a word for him to her friend. He says he is feeling her and want to hang out with her. Natalie smiles and says maybe.

JAMAL. Excuse me, I don't know you, but watching you from behind, I would love to get to know you.

Natalie turns around and sees that it's Jamal and slaps him on his shoulder and starts to laugh. She is surprised to see him, and her facial expression is shocked.

NATALIE. Jamal, you know better. I thought you were some horny little boy messing with me. I was ready to go ham on you. Walking up on me like that, what you doing here?

JAMAL. Oh, I can't do a little shopping. I like to stay dressed to impress. You never know when you gonna run into something, so I try to stay right.

Jamal looks at Natalie's friends up and down. He is focused on one in particular as she is checking herself in the mirror.

JAMAL. What's up, Natalie? Long time no see. Where have you been hiding at lately? You and your girls should have been at Nadia's birthday party. I would have loved grinding up on her all night.

Natalie notices that Jamal is staring at her girlfriend and shakes her head at him. She is smiling at Jamal and looking at some clothes at the same time.

NATALIE. She's not your type, Jamal. You probably curse her out after a few minutes talking to her.

JAMAL. My type? What's my type? Hell, unless she slows upstairs or got some serious mental issues, I like what I see. Plus, knowing you, you don't hang with any birdbrains. She got to be educated and 'bout that life if she's your friend.

NATALIE. Jamal, you are something else, but you are right about that. I don't hang with no thot, that's for sure. Boy, I'm shopping. I ain't messing with you. Go over there and introduce yourself or something. Roll your dice and see if you crap out.

Natalie grins at Jamal with a soft smirk on her face. Jamal looks back at Natalie and then looks at her friend in the mirror. He then takes his fingers and squeezes his chin and starts to walk over to her.

JAMAL. How are you? I was over there talking to my girl Natalie, and I'm not gonna front. I couldn't take me eyes off you. My name is Jamal.

Jamal extends his hand out to greet her, and she cracks a small smile and looks back at Jamal. She gives him a very quick handshake and looks back at herself in the mirror.

MARACELLA. My name is Maracella, and it's nice to meet you.

JAMAL. Look, I'm just gonna be straight with you. That's the only way I know how to be. I run into women a lot, but there's something about you that really catches my eye. You have a mystic feeling, I sense. I can tell you not about games. You focus on your career and making moves out here and keeping it real. That's what I been waiting to find.

MARACELLA. Jamal, let me ask you something. Do you have the day off from work, or you on your lunch break or something? What makes you think that I like street guys?

Jamal gives Maracella a sexy look and sucks on his bottom lip as he watches her walk over to the chair to try on some shoes.

JAMAL. Dig, I keep it straight up raw and authentic with you. What I do is what I do, but I will tell you this. Don't judge the book by its cover because there's a lot of good information you're gonna miss out on. Listen, I know you're shopping and enjoying your day out with Natalie and your friend, but how 'bout we get to know each other over dinner somewhere, and believe me, once I break my life down to you, you will be intrigued.

Maracella gives Jamal an up-and-down look and looks at him like she's feeling his vibe. Natalie and her other friend are a few feet away, looking at them, wondering if Jamal got what it takes to pull it off.

MARACELLA. I'll give you my number, but the dinner, I'm not sure about. Got to evaluate things before that happens. But you're nice, and we'll see how it flows from here.

JAMAL. It doesn't matter when I call or text. I mean, I don't wanna cause any problems for you.

MARACELLA. Nah, I don't get down like that. I'm not what you're used to as you will find out if I take it there with you.

Jamal and Maracella exchange numbers, and Jamal gives her his best smile and handsome look. He walks away and is leaving the store when Natalie stops him.

NATALIE. Okay, I kinda doubted you a little. You got that.
JAMAL. Nah, I ain't got that yet. Hopefully soon 'cause, damn, them hips is right. But you got to put a good word in for me, a little cosigning for me, Natalie. Remember, we're family, right?

Natalie grins and shakes her head; she is looking at the perfume that she likes, and she looks back at Jamal.

NATALIE. Hey, do you think your boy Haseem made the right choice with Nadia?
JAMAL. I know Haseem knows what he's doing when it comes to women. He did his numbers back in the day and can recognize game. He ain't no sucker for love, nah.

Natalie nods her head as she ponders on what Jamal just told her. Jamal looks at Natalie's friends and glances back at Natalie.

JAMAL. Yo, I got to roll, places to go, people to see. Don't forget me, family.

Jamal walks away from Natalie, and she watches him leave for a few seconds before she looks back at the perfumes that she likes, and she sprays some on her wrist.

Scene six. Darren and some of his friends are at Steven's sports bar, enjoying the Yankees game with a few of the bar waitresses. Steven walks in, not too happy with what he sees. He greets his friends and shares a few jokes and walks back to his office and jumps on his laptop. He starts doing some research on heavy-duty construction equipment. Darren and his friends are kinda loud, and Steven just shrugs his head with a slight smile. One of the waitresses comes and checks if Steven needs anything. He says no. She tells him that his mother stopped by earlier to see him. He asks her what she wanted. "She didn't say," the waitress tells Steven. Steven just shakes his head.

DARREN. This is the year right here I'm telling you. We got the pitching, hitting. We should have gotten it last year. I mean, I wasn't too mad because Houston went through a lot with the hurricane and shit. But we were right there last year, but that only made us hungrier this year, no stopping us. I'm taking all bets this year.

DARREN'S FRIEND. Yeah, okay, we're gonna see how it play out. I might put a few yards on it because Houston got good pitching too.

Darren looks at his friend with a twisted grin on his face and stands up and puts his hand in his pocket and pulls out a big stack of money and walks over to his friend.

DARREN. I don't waste my time with yards, little homie. I put stacks down on my boys. That's how I roll. Yards? Come on now, bro. You know how I get down.

Steven walks in and sees his cousin Darren with a big grip of money and his hand and notices everybody watching the Yankees game. He walks over with a smirk on his face. Darren stands up to greet his cousin.

DARREN. What's up, cuz? I'm trying to tell these younglings in here I'm serious about my boys. They hating on us this year. We're the most hated team in all of sports, besides, maybe, the Cowboys.

STEVEN. True, true, but it's all good. They're gonna be the same ones making excuses when we're bringing it home this year. We're going to another championship parade this year, cuz.

DARREN'S FRIEND. Yo, Steven, you want some beer or a shot of something? I know you been grinding all day. Have a seat and relax, bro.

STEVEN. Not right now. I got to finish up something real quick, but I think maybe you had too many shots. This is my shit, so I can drink whatever and whenever I want. Yo, make sure he's not driving tonight, fam.

Everybody starts laughing at what Steven said, and Steven cracks a smile as he stands there and looks at his friend.

DARREN. Yo, that party for Nadia was fire. I was turned up in there. That chick that was with Nadia, she was on me too, bro. She'd been hitting me up hard on the Gram. I might go check her tonight after I ditch these dudes.

STEVEN. Yeah, I feel you. She was definitely official. She had a fatty, too. Shit, see what she's talking about if she's with a friend or something. I might ride with you.

DARREN. No doubt I'm 'bout to hit her up. See what she up to tonight.

Steven looks at his friends and notices that the basket of wings and fries are destroyed. He looks at his waitresses and see them relaxing with the guys a little too hard, but he shakes his head and kinda ignores it.

STEVEN. Y'all good. Need some more wings or something. Get them some more fries and wings. I know they're hungry with all that alcohol in them.

DARREN FRIEND. Thanks, Steven. We didn't want to take advantage of your place or nothing. Thanks a lot.

STEVEN. Don't worry about it. I ain't dumb or slow. I can tell when dude's taking advantage of me. I know y'all not like that. Enjoy. I got to finish up some work. Darren, holla at me if chick 'bout it tonight.

Steven walks in the back to his office to do some work; he sits at his desk and opens up his laptop and starts looking up some heavy-duty construction equipment. He is writing a few things down in his notepad when he overhears Darren and his friends yelling at one another about the Yankees game. He smiles and shrugs them off. One of his waitresses knocks on his door, and he tells her to come in. He is still looking at the computer.

WAITRESS. You sure you don't need anything, boss? You're not hungry or want a beer?
STEVEN. Nah, I'm good. I ate a little earlier. Don't worry about their bill tonight. I will take care of it.
WAITRESS. Okay. I forgot to tell you that your mother stopped by earlier today.

Steven stops reading on his laptop and makes a curious look on his face. He looks at his waitress with his eyebrows raised.

STEVEN. What did she want?
WAITRESS. She didn't say. She just told me to tell you that she stopped by and that she's still alive.

Steven looks back at his laptop and continues doing his reading and writing things down. He shakes his head as he looks away for a second. The waitress walks out the office.

Scene seven. Felize pulls up to the firm's office and meets with Peter. He starts to tell him about all the fun he had on vacation. He also warns Peter that the owner of that land has gotten some serious offers for it, so he needs to act quick or the firm is gonna lose out on a gold mine. Peter checks with Felize about confirmation on what he told him about a big-chain franchise looking for land in that area. Felize assures him that his source from local government tells him that a few major chain stores are looking for land around there, and the whole town is about to be developed in the very near future. Peter trusts Felize and knows that he never stirred him or the firm wrong on any business investments and agrees to put a deposit on the land while they have it inspected.

FELIZE. I see you guys been balling and having a pretty good time while I was on vacation. Some pretty nice-looking ladies in those pictures I saw online.

PETER. Yeah, well, you know it wasn't me posting anything. You know I ain't with all that showing-off stuff. But it was a good night overall. I met a few nice ladies up there, but hell, you were down in MIA where all the tropical exotic ladies at, so I know you enjoyed yourself too.

Felize takes a seat in one of the chairs in Peter's office. He looks around his office and takes a sip of his coffee. Peter is looking at his computer and leans back a little in his chair. He focuses his attention in on Felize.

FELIZE. Well, it's good to see you meeting some ladies. I was getting a little worried about you. You're all work and no play. I'm glad you're starting to have a little bit of fun.

PETER. Like I told you before, I got plenty of time to have fun and meet women. Dudes be acting like there is an expiration date on women, like in 2023, there will be no more woman on the face of the earth. I don't get that. You know how I look at it, Felize? You're hustling backward if you're chasing women. Chase the money. They come with it as a bonus.

Felize smiles at Peter as he checks his phone. He makes a concerned look on his face as he is reading his phone.

FELIZE. I hear what you're saying and I feel you, but real talk that realtor on my ass. I told him that we were gonna jump on that property within a couple of days. He just emailed me about it. You're not backing out on this, are you? I kinda gave him my word that we're in on it.

Peter looks at Felize with a concerned look on his face. He twists a little in his chair and looks back his computer screen. He looks at his fingernails and then looks back at Felize.

PETER. You know I am a man of my word, but, Felize, you got to understand, bro, we're spending a lot of money right now with new deals we just got. We got a few big expenses with these new contracts. So I need you to be certain on this because this ain't the best time to be rolling the dice.

FELIZE. Peter, I can't believe I'm hearing this. I called you in the middle of my vacation while I was getting some real nice sexual healing from this badass chick, not trying to gas you up. Nah, bro, when I call you, Peter, 90 percent of the time it got something to do with making money. Stacking serious chips is all I'm about.

PETER. Yeah, I know that, I know that. But you sure? You positive that if we scoop up this property, we gonna cash out big soon? You certain that one of these big franchises is moving in soon?

Felize shakes his head and smiles at Peter as he drinks some of his coffee. He looks down at the floor for a second, then looks back at Peter. Peter is playing with his pen on his desk and glancing back and forth at his computer.

FELIZE. My source down there whom I'd been dealing with for quite a few years now, plus the realtor whom I've known for a good while, both told me that a few big chain stores have sent their people in, looking for land in the last few months. Bro, that particular town is about to be developed, he told me—restaurants, movie theaters, grocery stores. It's a gold mine down there if you're willing to jump on it. Them guys know their shit, and they know that I don't play around. My credibility is respected, so they keep it real with me.

Peter puffs out his cheeks and looks at Felize with an understanding look on his face. He looks down at his desk and then looks back at Felize.

PETER. I know you, Felize, and I trust you. That's why we're gonna do it. I already spoke with the fellas about it, and they agree with it. Tell the realtor we're gonna put the deposit down in the next few days. And make sure you have your people inspect the land to make sure everything's right. I know you won't stir us wrong. You got our backs.

Peter stands up and walks toward Felize and gives him a hand smack. He leans on his desk and starts smiling at Felize.

PETER. So get to the good stuff, the girls. Did you think about me when you were doing your thing down there? You got something for me to hook up with while I'm down there?

FELIZE. Do I? Let's just say I got a doubleheader set up for you when we touch down there, bro.

Scene eight. Mohan goes over to his sister Natalie's business to tell her about their parents' proposal. He hugs his sister and asks if this is a good time. She tells him that she will always make time to for him. Mohan asks why she didn't come to Nadia's surprise party and tells her how the night went and how Haseem brought her a Corvette for her birthday. Natalie kinda shrugs it off and says she thinks Haseem needs to pump his brakes just a little and make sure Nadia's love is 100 percent real. Mohan tells her about how Mom and Dad came over unexpectedly and how their conscience must be eating at them because they offered to invest in him if he considers going into the medical world. Natalie smiles and tells her brother that they do believe in him, and they see his business savvy and they see how committed he is. She tries to convince him to really think about it because it's good money in this industry, and she will help him with anything he needs.

MOHAN. Stop acting like you're working hard, knowing you, looking at Macy's one-day sale or some red bottom sales.

Natalie looks up and sees that it's her brother, and her face turns to joy. She is smiling from ear to ear as she stands up and walks over to hug her brother.

NATALIE. Wow, my brother really makes time for me. Busy as you are, you make time for me.

MOHAN. Well, actually, I was on my way to a meeting not too far from here, so I figured I stop by to mess with you.

Mohan smiles at Natalie with a joking facial expression on his face. He takes a seat in one of her office chairs and drinks on some of his smoothie. Natalie shakes her head at her brother and walks back to sit down in her chair.

MOHAN. You working hard, I see. Taking care of the patients is your number one priority, I see.

NATALIE. Whatever I do, get a lunch like everyone else does, so I take advantage of it and keep up-to-date with what's on sale. You know I stay styling unlike you and your cheap no-name designer suits.

Mohan and Natalie start laughing out loud. He points to his sister and bends over laughing. He straightens back up in his chair and looks around her office.

MOHAN. So your parents stopped by and checked on me unexpectedly. I was cooking breakfast, tired as heck with only a few hours of sleep, and they wanna come by, messing with me, telling me I'm eating unhealthy. I was surprised it was them. I don't get too much company like that. Had me looking through the windows. (*Natalie is laughing at her brother telling his story as she looks at her phone for a quick second.*)

NATALIE. Yeah, you're right. That is strange for them to stop by your crib. What did they want?

MOHAN. They were on some conscience eating at me stuff to me. I mean, even Mom was in a joking mood. But Dad told me that if I go into the medical world, he would give me the money to get started, and no matter how good things are going for me, there is nothing better than being part of the medical world.

Mommy was sitting there, basically agreeing with everything he was saying.

NATALIE. Yeah, that's Mommy, sitting there, nodding her head. I don't know about all that. They're underestimating how good your engineering business is doing, and the moves y'all are making with the firm. They're old school and only see things in their tight tunnel vision.

MOHAN. I told him that I will consider it down the road. I got too much going on right now. With that new deal, I got I ain't gonna have too much time on my hand.

NATALIE. It shows me that they do believe in you. I think they were a little leery when you were in college, and they weren't sure what road you were headed down. Now they're starting to see that you're doing your thing, and your boys are doing it too. You know, success opens up people's eyes real quick.

Mohan shakes his head while he sips on his smoothie. He looks back at Natalie and twists a little in his seat.

MOHAN. What happened to you? You didn't come to Nadia's birthday party. Your ankle still hurting?

NATALIE. Nah, I feel good. Nothing keeps be down too long. You know that.

MOHAN. Yo, Haseem brought Nadia a freaking Corvette for her birthday. We were shocked by that one. It was nice though, custom rims on it.

Natalie shrugs that off as she adjusts her shoulders in the air like she can care less. She makes a frown on her face as she leans forward a little in her office chair.

NATALIE. All I'm saying is, Haseem better really think about things. He needs to slow it down a little and make sure she 100 percent authentic and not phony.

MOHAN. Why you saying it like that? Nadia's cool people.

NATALIE. I don't know, Mohan. Ever since I went with her house shopping, I get this funny feeling about her and her intentions. I might be wrong.

MOHAN. Growing up, your senses were usually sharp, but it's early yet if she on to something. Haseem will sniff it out. We had a ball in there, sis, Man, it must have been like a hundred ladies back there in VIP section. I couldn't even turn around. Every time I moved, I was bumping into asses and breasts. You missed out on that one.

Natalie looks at Mohan and just shakes her head with a fake smile on her face. She looks at her phone and starts to type a text out.

NATALIE. Yeah, I missed out. That would have been really a turn-on to be around all that asses and breasts.

Mohan laughs at his sister as he leans forward and grabs his ankle. He takes another sip of his smoothie. Natalie isn't smiling really. She is kinda serious about what she just said. She answers her text alert that she just got on her phone. She looks back up at Mohan.

NATALIE. But listen, I think you should really consider what Daddy has told you. I mean, it's a sure thing, bro, and you got me to help you out. It's kinda like easy money. Look at me.

Mohan shakes his head and looks off and thinks about what his sister is telling him. He looks back at her, and they both smile about it.

Scene nine. Haseem pulls up to his aunt's office, sipping on some coffee. He walks into her office and greets her with a big hug and kiss. He gives her a cup of coffee and a butter roll. She thanks him but rejects the butter roll, telling him she's trying to watch her weight and health. She lets him know that her connect has got the ball rolling and has already gotten back with her with good news. Legally, there won't be any issues getting it up and running, but she wants to do this as a favor for her nephew. Haseem thanks her for her kindness, but he tells her she has done so much for him since he was a little kid and that he can handle it. She tells him that he and the firm should get financing from some people her law firm represents. They're already spending a lot of money on other business ventures. Let her at least hook him up with the financing. Haseem thanks her and leaves, giving her another big hug.

HASEEM. Auntie, is this a good time? You want me to wait?
AUNT PELYNDA. Nah, you okay. I knew you were coming. I ain't that busy for my nephew.

Haseem walks in and gives his aunt a big hug and kiss on the cheek. He looks and smiles at her and takes a seat in big office chair. Aunt Pelynda walks over to the door of her office and shuts it close. She then walks back and takes a seat in one of her office chairs close to where Haseem is sitting. Haseem hands her a coffee and butter roll.

AUNT PELYNDA. Oh, thank you, nephew. You can keep the butter roll. I'm trying to watch my health. That butter ain't no good when you get my age.
HASEEM. You ain't old yet. You act like you're in your late sixties or something.
AUNT PELYNDA. Not yet, but I don't have long to go. I'd been hitting the gym and trying to get myself together. It's been working, I think. I see a few young boys checking me out.

Aunt Pelynda and Haseem start laughing. Haseem sips his coffee and puts it down on the table. Aunt Pelynda does the same thing; she takes a deep breath and looks at her nephew with a happy face.

AUNT PELYNDA. So I wanna let you know that I got the ball rolling on opening up your dispensary down in Carolina. I talked to my connection that I've known for over twenty years. She's not in the political world either so that makes it clean and leaves no traces. You know what I'm saying?

HASEEM. Yeah, I know what you're saying. With all the scandal about corruption going on, especially in Jersey, I didn't want to mess with that. I don't trust these people. Everybody's crooked in this thing. But are they a heavy mover down there and connected with higher-ups who call the shots down there, so I don't have to worry about nothing?

AUNT PELYNDA. Yes, exactly. You get it, nephew. That way, nothing can come back to me. I will tell you like this. She's good with the movers and shakers down there, and she moves fast. I just talked to her right before you came in, and she confirmed that legally there won't be nothing standing in your way.

Haseem pumps his fist in the air a little bit. He pops up and gives his auntie a little hug to thank her. She gives him a small hug without even standing up. Haseem sits back down and smiles.

HASEEM. Thank you so much, Auntie. This is the best gift you ever gave me. I put this over the trip to Vegas when I graduated college. This really opens things up for us down there. We will be able to spread our wings away from Jersey now. This is very big, very big. Thank you. I owe you on this.

AUNT PELYNDA. Haseem, you don't owe me nothing. I told you I will take care of it. Just don't tell your father with his arrogant self. I know you have it, nephew, but let me help you out with some start-up money to help get it going.

Haseem nibbles on his butter roll as he listens and thinks about what his aunt just said. He swallows his piece of butter roll and looks at his auntie.

HASEEM. You've done enough for me, Auntie. Ever since I was a little snot nose, you always gave me and did for me. I got it, plus the firm is backing this project.

AUNT PELYNDA. Haseem, you guys are young, and when you're young, you spend and go through a whole lot of money. If I can't give you the money, at least let me set you guys up with a financing company that my firm represents. They good people with very low interest rates, and that way, your firm can build up credit, and that will lead to very big loans down the road if you guys ever need it.

Haseem shakes his head at his aunt Pelynda. He is in deep thought to what she just taught him. Aunt Pelynda smiles at her nephew and sips on her coffee.

AUNT PELYNDA. I want to see you reach as high as you can. The sky is the limit and never stop climbing. Just do it the right way, not like your father. I love my brother, but he would represent anyone who would pay him. I mean, anyone. Always have class, nephew, as you go through life.

HASEEM. I understand, and that's how I strive to be. You and Mommy used to always tell me a hardhead makes a soft ass, to listen and pay close attention to what you see and hear, and my favorite was to handle your business and do what you have to because nobody owes you nothing in this world.

Haseem stands up and gives his aunt a hug. They hug each other for a few seconds. He then pulls away from his aunt and looks at her.

HASEEM. I got to run, Auntie, but keep me informed on things. I will run the business loan over with my partners, and I will get back to you. I love you, and thank you for everything. I really appreciate it.

Aunt Pelynda smiles at her nephew as he walks out of her office. She then walks back to her desk and looks over some papers at her desk.

Scene ten. Peter takes his mother to the grocery store to pick up a few things. He apologizes to his mother for not coming to check on her recently. He tells her how busy he's been but says that is no excuse. Peter's mother is understanding and knows that her son is busy with his career, and her love for her only son overrides everything. She tells him that she miss his father so much and wishes that he would start spending more time home and asks how much money and success does he needs to achieve. Peter shakes his head and feels sorry for his mother. He knows that she has spent many years alone and how loyal and patient she has been to his dad while he manages his shipping business. Peter tells his mother that he will do more for her and that she needs to get more involved with a few hobbies and get out the house more. She tells him that she has started going to the gym and doing some volunteer work. Peter is pleased to hear that.

PETER. Mom, you got to buy some meat too. You can't just live off fruit and vegetables. I mean, at least buy some chicken or something.

PETER'S MOM. For what? It's just me there. Your father and you are too busy to stop by and have dinner or spend time with me, so I don't buy too much meat like I used to.

Peter looks at his mother with a sad look on his face. He knows she is right, and his facial expression shows it. He looks away for a few seconds and then looks back at his mother. Mom is looking at the oranges to pick out some good ones.

PETER. Mom, I want you to know that I am sorry for not coming over and checking on you and spending more time with you. There is no reason why I can't come by and have dinner with you more often. I apologize for not being there. I was raised to accept my guilt and not make excuses.

PETER'S MOM. Son, I know you are young and busy trying to establish yourself in this world. I sort of understand you not coming over as much. You've been busy with the restaurant and things. I understand you. It's your father who makes me a little upset. I haven't really heard too much from him since Haseem's engagement party. He was here for a few weeks and gone again. How many years is he gonna spend chasing and building his company? He could be home more. He doesn't know how much I miss him.

Peter's facial expression is very sad as he listens to his mother hurt. He puffs out his cheeks and shakes his head.

PETER. I know, Mom. Dad has to start relaxing more and spend more time with you. You guys should be traveling more and going on some lovely vacations together. Why don't you go back home and spend time there? You have a lot of family back home that you hardly get to see.

Peter's mom looks at her son and kinda shrugs off what Peter just said. She shakes her head as she starts to put her oranges in the plastic bag.

PETER'S MOM. It's just not the same back home. It's not like it used to be. Everything is so fast-paced and money driven. The younger generation is more violent, and the people are not as hospitable and caring like they're used to be.

PETER. Yeah, but, Mom, it's the same here in the States. You shouldn't let that bother you too much. Unfortunately, it's the way of the world nowadays.

Peter and his mother start walking away from the fruit and vegetable section as they go toward the other side of the grocery store.

PETER. Hey, we got to get a few snacks to have, for when I am over there, let me load up on some cookies and sweet cakes and definitely a few gallons of ice cream too. You know, you should get a few hobbies, Mom, like joining a book club or something or do some volunteer work with the kids or at the hospital, helping out the sick people, that will take your mind off things, and you will meet new people and have a little fun.

PETER'S MOM. Yeah, you're right. I have thought about that too. I did start going to the gym and working out. I even signed up to start taking yoga classes, too, so I have realized that.

Peter smiles and shakes his head up and down. His facial expression is very happy as he looks at what cookies he wants. As he grabs three different packs of cookies and put them in the basket, he looks back at his mom.

PETER. Don't worry, Mom, it's always been me and you and we're a team. Sooner or later, our manager will come back and lead us. He loves us and cares about us. You know that.

Peter's mom smiles at her son as she looks at the cookies he puts in the basket. She looks back at him and they start walking down the aisle together. Peter puts his arm around his mother and hugs her as they are walking down the aisle.

Scene eleven. The firm meets up at their sports bar that Steven manages for a little fun and celebration. They are enjoying themselves, joking and laughing about how Haseem is deeply in love, picking on Haseem about the birthday gift. Haseem has thick skin and says it wasn't brand-new; it's certified pre-owned vehicle. Mohan says he always thought diamonds were the key to a lady's heart, but after seeing how Nadia reacted, he's not so sure. Steven tells the guys that he has decided on starting his own construction company, and his dad is going to use his leverage on getting him some good contracts to help him get started. All the guys are taking turns going over their business stories and talking about the money they made off these big deals. Peter is excited but reminds them he still wants the firm to be smart on how they are spending their money. The guys crack on Peter and tell him that he should spend some money on some better clothes. Some lovely ladies that Steven knows walk over and start hanging with the guys. Steven tells the waitress to bring over whatever the ladies want to drink. The episode is ending with the guys enjoying themselves with the ladies, watching the Yankees game. Music is playing from Drake, "I'm Way Up, I Feel Blessed!"

STEVEN. Hey, Haseem. Hey, listen, my man. I just wanna know with everything we got going on, new big contracts and more duffel bags of cash, how are you gonna be able to do it?

MOHAN. What do you mean how? He's gonna go straight home every night to his lady and stay clear of you and your wild late-night partying.

PETER. True, as long as he keep away from you, Jamal, and Darren, he should be good. But it's gonna come down to if he can keep the old Haseem locked up in his cage, and that's gonna be very hard for a young rich man to do. Hell, I even have a hard time trying to stay focused. These girls be on it, especially when you're riding in some hot shit, coming through in something foreign.

Haseem listens to his boys talk as he is smoking on his cigar, relaxing and watching the Yankees game. He smiles and checks his phone out.

STEVEN. All I'm saying is I feel the marriage thing. I really do. When the right one comes around for me, I'm gonna put her on my team, but to be honest, I don't see that happening till I get in my thirties.

MOHAN. Yeah, I feel you, Steve-O, but hey, Nadia seems like she's the one, and Haseem knows the game. She got his nose open some kind of way. She did something right for my man to go buy that Corvette with the custom rims.

Peter and Steven start laughing real loud and hitting a few tables as they are laughing. Mohan joins in with a big smile on his face but looks back at the game on TV. Haseem is taking it all in, shaking his head and smiling.

HASEEM. Hey, man, it's a certified pre-owned, and I got a good deal on it. (*Haseem laughs.*)

MOHAN. The crazy thing is I always thought diamond was a girl's best friend. You wanna steal her heart? Get her some diamonds, and you were in there. But seeing how Nadia responded and how her friends were acting, I guess car keys is the way to go now.

Everybody starts laughing real hard. Peter stands up and walks in a circle, laughing so hard. Steven almost coughs his beer up laughing. Haseem chokes on his cigar, laughing at Mohan. Mohan is keeping his same posture as he watches the game with a very big smile on his face.

STEVEN. Nah, but real talk, Seem. Nadia's bad as hell yo. She is official, my dude. She's the type of lady that makes a man be on that fabulous shit. Just throw it in the bag. Whatever you want, whatever you need, don't worry, just throw it in the bag.

All four of them continue to laugh at Haseem in good fun as four nice-looking ladies come in and are waiting on a table to be seated. Laughs kinda come to a halt as all four men take a look over at the ladies.

HASEEM. Hmm, okay, they're looking right over there.
STEVEN. I know her, the one with the tight yellow sundress. I know her. I meant to get at her, but I never got to see her again. She's with the same girls too.
PETER. I think I'm gonna like it down here. I might have to spend some time down here when the restaurant opens up.
MOHAN. But on another note, man, all of us, well, three out of four, I mean, scored some nice deals. Seven-figure deals, bro. You gotta love it.

Steven smirks at Mohan, knowing the butt of the joke is on him, but he agrees and shakes his head, along with the rest of them.

PETER. I still can't believe how fast our trucking company's taking off. That seafood company in Maine is huge, and that furniture company we just got, they're bigger than I thought they were. I can't front I didn't see us getting million-dollar deals in our first four or five years.

MOHAN. When I lay it down for this real estate mogul and he gives us the whole East Coast, I'm telling you, that's gonna really solidify us on that next level.

HASEEM. True, true, you're right, Mohan, and when I get these marijuana dispensaries going down in the dirty south, plus what we got in Jersey, we're gonna be sitting lovely for real. And like Mohan said, when I put it down for this auto parts company and he gives me the wheel for the whole country and possibly his overseas connections, man, that's gonna get me on the cover of something. I can see it now.

Haseem fakes like he's taking a picture for a magazine. He stands up and poses for the fellas. They're laughing and giving him hand smacks. They're nodding their heads in agreement with Haseem.

STEVEN. Yeah, but my next move's gonna be the one. Please believe it. Right now y'all doing it, y'all bringing in the army-style duffel bags of cash, but when I open up my next spot down in AC and my connections pull off that sports-betting license, it's game over for you, boys. Welcome to the big leagues, my friend!

Mohan, Peter, and Haseem give Steven a hand smack and a pat on the back. Their attention turns to the four ladies who are walking toward them; all four men's eyes open up wide as the ladies get closer.

LADY FRIEND 1. You look very familiar. Didn't we meet somewhere or something? I remember you. I don't forget faces.

STEVEN. Yeah, a few months back. I was trashed that night and hollered at you, but I never got back at you to see what's up with you. My cousin and I left early. But I remember you too. I was telling my boys about you when you came in.

She looks at Steven with flirty eyes, and Steven gives her the same look back. Her friends are looking at the fellas, and they're looking back at them.

STEVEN. Well, this looks like a perfect time for a replay. I can't deny an opportunity to get acquainted with someone as sexy as you are. What are you ladies drinking on? Have a seat and let's all get a little more familiar with one another.

HASEEM. You can sit right here next to me. I won't bite, but I can't help if I entice.

The ladies smile at the fellas and take a seat next to them. Steven signals for his waitress to come here as Mohan, Peter, and Haseem start conversation with her friends. Steven and the lady friend are smiling at each other.

STEVEN. So you from down this way, or you down here vacationing?

LADY FRIEND: Nah, I'm from the BX. My girls are from down here. What about you? (*Steven grins at her and takes a sip of his beer.*)

STEVEN. Me, I guess you can say I run things down here. I grew up around here not too far. (*The waitress walks over and looks at her boss Steven.*)

WAITRESS: What do you need, boss?

STEVEN. Give these ladies whatever they want to drink, and bring over a few bottles of champagne for us.

The ladies look at one another with an impressed look on their faces and place their order with the waitress.

LADY FRIEND. I see you talk it like you live it, boss, huh? This your spot?

STEVEN. Yeah, this is my place, and these are my business partners. We got our hands in a few things.

Steven gives her that look and licks his bottom lip a little bit. She looks back at him with a smile and impressed look on her face. Steven rubs her thigh very slightly not to turn her off.

STEVEN. BX, huh? You see what I'm watching? I go out there to watch my boys on the regular. We got to get up and get cozy in the box suite we got at the stadium.

LADY FRIEND. Of course, I'm with that. All you got to do is let me know when.

Steven leans back in his seat and takes a sip of his beer. He and her are smiling at each other and giving each other flirty eyes. The fellas are enjoying laughs with the ladies and having a good time. The waitress brings over the bottles of champagne with the champagne glasses. Music starts to play as the episode is ending. Drake's song is playing, "I'm Way Up. I Feel Blessed."

Episode 6

Scene one. Monday meeting is the scene, and the guys are enjoying brunch. Peter tells the guys that he thinks it's a good time for the firm to start looking for an executive manager to run the office and handle day-to-day operations of the firm so that they can handle other things. Steven blurts out, "'Bout time because he's sick of getting so many phone calls and tired of dealing with going back and forth to the office."

Haseem believes that it got to be someone who is educated in business management and business development, and everyone must agree on the hiring. Mohan, chewing on his pancakes, tells Haseem that he ran into his old high school friend Evelyn and sees that she's doing her thing out there. "What you talking about? Last I heard, she was lovestruck over some business mogul or some shit."

Mohan says he didn't get to talk too long to her, but she told him that she's running her own smoothie business and got her own talent management company. Peter blurts out, "That is exactly the type of person we need to run our firm—smart, business savvy, and driven to succeed. Try to get in touch with her, Haseem, for business purposes only." He grins while drinking his orange juice.

Steven says, "That they need a secretary too. I'm tired of typing up shit."

Scene two. Mohan pulls up to his parents' home while on a business call. He tells the person he will call them back later as he enters the front door. Mohan's parents are watching TV and relaxing. "What do we owe this occasion? Is something wrong? Are you okay because they don't get a visit to often?"

Mohan grins it off as he plays with the dog. "I stopped by because I miss my parents, and I need to come check on you guys more." Mohan's dad asks him if he's given some thought to his idea of opening up a business in the medical industry, like his sister Natalie. Mohan responds, "I didn't come over looking for a handout or asking for anything, but if I were to do business with my father it will be on my terms."

Mohan's mother loves that he stands up to his father and says, "You should do what is comfortable with you and work with what you are comfortable with."

"Exactly, Mom, and that's what I want you to understand, Dad. Let Natalie do her thing with medical treatment, and let me do what I'm good at. Believe me, Dad, there is a lot of money out there in different industries, and I am just scratching the surface on what my goals are."

Dad shakes his head and looks away, thinking about what his son tells him.

Scene three. Steven and Darren are at the mall doing some shopping and hanging out. Darren tells Steven that he's getting tired of the nightlife and wants to leave the late nights alone. "It's getting crazy out there, and every time I turn around, somebody I know is getting killed or dying." Steven listens to what Darren is saying and tells him about the drugs and dope that have these young boys doing stupid shit. "You need to think hard about changing for the better, cuz."

Darren interrupts Steven abruptly and makes a plea for Steven to think about investing in some of his business ideas. "I want to start my own business and start becoming more entrepreneur minded. There is some commercial property that is for sale, and I want to open up a tattoo shop in the shore area, maybe one day opening up a chain of tattoo shops all over the Jersey shores."

Steven admires Darren for wanting to change his life and respects his intelligence. "I'm going to give it some serious thought, but I wanna see how serious you are about it. I'll be watching your movements, cuz."

Scene four. Peter and Felize are relaxing VIP at a nightclub, talking over business. Felize reminds Peter about all the money he had made for the firm over the last few years. "You guys have made some serious dividends off my brilliant mind." Peter shakes his head and reminds Felize, "You are being paid very well for your services, but maybe it is time for a performance evaluation." Felize smiles and shakes his head while sipping his drink; he then motions for a few sexy ladies to come over to their table. Peter takes a phone call outside of the nightclub from his manager of the restaurant. He tells him that a few basketball players are there and requesting a lot of champagne, acting a little abrasive and loud. His call is interrupted by Felize and his newfound friends telling him that they wanna go have fun somewhere else. Peter looks at the ladies' bodies and agrees with what they're saying.

Scene five. Haseem pulls up to Evelyn's smoothie shop. He is decked out in a Prada linen suit with his five-karat diamond earring blinging off the sunshine. He makes sure his Rolex is looking right as he sits in his BMW 750li, unsure if he should go in. He thinks hard about it as he looks at some people walking down the street. As he makes up his mind to go into Evelyn's shop, he notices her walk out on a phone call. Evelyn talks on the phone with an attentive look on her face when she notices the shiny black Beamer. Haseem, now knowing that she noticed him, gets out of the car, playing it off like he is answering a text or something. Evelyn cracks a grin on her face as she stares Haseem up and down, then she tells the person on her phone that she will call them back. Evelyn takes a very sexy step toward Haseem and blurts out, "Where the hell you supposed to be going?"

Haseem acts like he didn't hear her and turns around real slow and responds, "I was coming to check you out, but then I thought about it and figured before I run up on you maybe I better bring you your favorite cup of apple cider tea." Evelyn sucks her teeth and grins at Haseem, "Boy, get your wack ass out of here with that wack game of yours." Haseem interrupts her, "Oh, now my shit is wack? You used to fall for everything I used to run on you back in high school."

EVELYN. As you can see, I'm not that beat airhead chick anymore! (*The two embrace each other with a big hug, and stare each other in the eye like they still had strong feelings for each other.*)

HASEEM. What's been good with you, girl?

EVELYN. I should be asking you that. I can't get a text or a call or nothing anymore. I had to hear about your engagement through friends of ours.

HASEEM. Yeah, that was corny of me. I guess I could have reached out to you more over the years. I'm hearing good things about you. Mohan told me you stacking them chips pretty high. You're owning businesses and shit!

Evelyn smiles and starts to walk down the street with a sexy slow stroll.

EVELYN. Well, I'm trying to get my little hustle on. Things kinda fell into place for me. I invested in the right time with this smoothie shop. Everybody's so health conscious nowadays.

HASEEM. You owning everything, or you got business partners?

EVELYN. You know I've never been the type to trust women too much, and after your ass, I kinda stopped trusting men too.

HASEEM. Last I heard about you, some corporate big shot had your heart in his hand, had you drunk in love. (*Haseem chuckles with a big smile on his face.*)

Evelyn doesn't find it to funny as she shrugs Haseem with a elbow. "Whatever, it wasn't like that!" The two of them enter the breakfast shop and take a seat. "You really trying to play me out. For that, you're buying me breakfast." Haseem laughs that he left his wallet home by mistake. Evelyn shakes her head in laughter.

Scene six. Peter is meeting with Steven to discuss possible expansion of his successful sports bar. The scene is relaxed at the restaurant they are dining at. There are a few sexy ladies enjoying their lunch a few tables over. While the waitress is busting out of her blouse with very huge breast. Steven can't help but compliment her on her body.

Music is playing in the background, and the atmosphere is kinda fast-paced as people are coming and going.

PETER. What's going on with your construction company plans?

Steven. It's going pretty good. I'm shopping for equipment and already got some machines and tools already. Plus, my dad got me the deal for a few projects already.

PETER. That's good. So you already got a few jobs already lined up.

STEVEN. Yeah, a strip mall and a high school expansion job. (*Steven is busy flirting with the ladies a few tables over, but brings his attention back to Peter.*) What's the deal with Felize and that land deal down in Florida?

PETER. (*Smirking at Steven.*) We're in the process of finding a construction company down there that does quality work. We got to be ready in case someone is ready to build on the land.

The waitress brings the guys lunch over with a pretty smile. She leans over to hand Steven his buffalo wings and fries. Steven smiles while staring at her breast. Steven asks the waitress her name as he picks up a wing and starts eating. The waitress smiles and responds, "Carleena, and yours?"

STEVEN. (*Handing her his business card.*) Give me a call when you get time. I might have something better for you if you're willing to travel a little.

PETER. (*Interrupts Steven.*) Yo, can we get back to business, bro?

STEVEN. My bad. You see the melons she's carrying around? But anyway, I do believe that another sports bar in Asbury will go good. They're building up the area, and people are starting to flock back there again. AC isn't a bad spot either. Things are back circulating down there too. (*Peter grins.*) I like the AC location a little better. Things are starting to come around down there, plus with the sports betting now, people are gonna be spending a lot of time down there. (*Steven shakes his head while staring at Peter. He plucks another wing in his mouth.*) We still need Mohan or Haseem to agree with us. You know Haseem's ready to get rolling with his marijuana dispensaries down south, and Mohan's bickering about his budget to expand his engineering company.

PETER. Yeah, I know, but we got to go with what the numbers tell us. It's about making the smartest investment. Fuck feelings!

Scene seven. Nadia's and Haseem's mom are doing a little jogging and working out their beautiful bodies. It's a beautiful day in the neighborhood. Kids are playing at the park and guys are getting their B-ball on at the court. They are dressed so sexy that a couple of guys flirted with them as they walked by. They didn't even flinch or nothing. They were in their workout zone.

NADIA. You know your son hasn't really bothered to go start house shopping with me yet?

MRS. KENDRICKS. Well, you know his schedule is crazy. He barely has time to call or stop by and see his parents. What irritates me is when you call him, he answers back with a freakin' text that he will call you back. Where have you been looking at? What kind of house you eyeing?

NADIA. I'm kinda thinking about going South Jersey. There is some beautiful homes down there for really good prices. Plus, it will hopefully keep his boys away.

MRS. KENDRICKS. (*Stops jogging and smirks at Nadia with a confused look on her face.*) If you think you're taking my boy down there away from his family, we're gonna have some issues. Haseem would go nuts down there in the country. He's not used to all them fields and deers!

They both chuckle out loud and stop to get a drink of water. Nadia asks Mrs. Kendricks if she ever thought about convincing Haseem's dad to move far away.

MRS. KENDRICKS. Listen, girl, you have to let a man have his joy. If you take away a man joy and happiness, it can cause him pain and hurt. Haseem loves being around his cousins and friends even though I could do without Jamal's ass! What I wanna know is when you're gonna give me my grandbaby. You and him been freaking for a good while. Please don't tell me my son shooting blanks!

Both woman start laughing while they start doing some stretching. Nadia has a loss-for-words look on her face, and Haseem mom is looking at her with a sharp stare out of the corner of her eye.

NADIA. It's coming, Mom! I'm just kinda waiting till the marriage is done with before I start squirting out babies.

MRS. KENDRICKS. Have you thought about what you're gonna be when your married life starts getting a little dull? I mean, the flame does lose its sparkle after a while. You either become a bored housewife or you find something that you like doing.

NADIA. I really haven't given that too much thought. I don't see being a housewife boring. I see it as a way of life more.

Nadia starts doing some squats and looks up in the air while Haseem's mom squirms her face and looks down at her ankle as she stretches her back and hamstrings out. The scene ends with a few ballplayers on the court hawking over the ladies stretching, making facial expressions, and grinning.

Scene eight. Natalie is in her office, working on her computer, when her secretary tells her she has a call from a Jamal.

NATALIE. Put him through. (*She has a confused look on her face.*)

JAMAL. Yo, Natte, what's up with you? I told Mohan to tell you to call me, and I called you personally a few times. What's the deal with you? I'm starting to think you're trying to avoid me.

Jamal is enjoying his day in a good mood as he rides in his Mercedes-Benz with the sunroof open. With a very big smile on his face as he rides around through the city, he waves at a few people he knows.

NATALIE. (*Natalie smiles a little but also is shaking her head, tapping her pen on her desk.*) Jamal, I've been a little busy lately, but I did get the message from Mohan. I told you that I'm not getting involved with you walking on my girlfriend's heart. You know and I know you just wanna smash and dash.

JAMAL. Whoa, whoa, whoa, hold up, Natte! Since when did you became Cupid? (*Jamal's getting a little upset on his face but is still smirking as he talks to her on his Bluetooth speaker in his car.*) How do you know that I'm not looking for something special? What do you think, I wanna keep plucking birds all my life? Hell, I'm getting older, and I wanna settle back one day, Natalie. (*He makes a big laugh and nods his head in laughter.*)

NATALIE. Yeah, okay, Jamal. I hear you talking, but I'm not beat for that bullshit. I'll tell you what I will do. I'm having lunch with her on Thursday, and I will bring you up, but I'm not sugar-coating nothing to her. If she is with it, then I will give her your number.

Jamal pulls over his car and starts to get out. He cuts off the Bluetooth and starts to walk down the street. There is a few dudes hanging out on the corner playing dice, with some hip-hop playing in the background. Jamal is wearing a throwback California Angels jersey with the matching hat, blue jeans, with a pair of matching Jordans on his feet.

JAMAL. I'm with that. Just let her know that I'm feeling her and I want to slide out with her one night, and put a few good words in for me, too, like I'm into poetry or art or some shit. (*Both of them laugh and end their call. Jamal starts to talk to a few dudes on the corner.*) It's hot as heck out here, and y'all playing for nickels and dimes, I bet. There ain't no real money in the bank. (*He walks toward them with his lip turned up and a smirk on his face.*)

Scene nine. Steven is at his sports bar, working on his laptop. He's looking up employees he's considering hiring for his construction company. He is alone in the corner of the booth, with a tray of fries and a soda on the table. In walks Carleena, the waitress he met while out to lunch with Peter the other day; she is approached by the hostess who asks her where she will like to sit. She tells her that she is here to see Steven. The hostess walks her over to Steven. Carleena is dressed very professionally and has a folder in her hand. Steven glances up and notices her. He stands up and reaches out his hand toward her. Steven is dressed somewhat casually with a black button up on with a pair of blue jeans.

STEVEN. Well, hello, I'm glad you were able to make it. It's good to see you again. Have a seat please. Would you like something to drink or anything to eat?

CARLEENA. Hmm, I will take some lemon water please.

STEVEN. I like a woman who doesn't drink alcohol early in the day. Health conscious is always a good thing. I'm planning on getting back in the gym myself. Kinda struggling with fitting it into my schedule. (*Steven grins at his anticipating of her response.*)

CARLEENA. Yeah, I can imagine it's hard for you. (*She smiles at Steven with an I-don't-believe-it look on her face.*) Thank you for the interview. I really appreciate it.

STEVEN. Ahh, no need. (*Steven waves his hand off at her comment.*) I got good senses and can read people pretty good. I had a good feeling about you.

CARLEENA. Well, thank you. I appreciate that. Finding a better job has been on my agenda, but it's kinda tough, too, because I'm trying to finish up college. I had to sit out a few years because my father died unexpectedly.

STEVEN. I'm very sorry to hear that. (*Carleena nods her head and takes a sip of her lemon water.*)

CARLEENA. Yeah, he died in a car accident a few years back. He was a little hammered coming from his friend's house. Ever since then, I haven't drank anymore. I just can't no more.

STEVEN. Understandable. I mean, I don't know what I would do if I lost my father or mother at an early age. (*Steven gives Carleena a very sad look expression on his face.*) But I like how you are still dedicated enough to battle through adversity.

CARLEENA. My father taught me growing up that you can't be weak or soft in life no matter what life brings you. You have to be hard and tough enough to battle through it. My goal is to one day become successful in the business world, so I'm saving my money and staying focused. But I want to be completely open with you, Steven. I'm not the kind of girl who sleeps around with coworkers or bosses, so I—

STEVEN. (*Steven cuts her off abruptly and starts using hand gestures.*) Listen, I'm a real dude, and I don't sugarcoat nothing. I'm not gonna front. You're sexy as hell with a banging body, but I'm professional when it comes to being a business owner. I don't fuck around with any of my workers. It's bad for business, and one thing about me is I don't play when it comes to my money. (*Steven gives Carleena a real stern look and lets her know she doesn't have to worry about that with the expression on his face.*)

STEVEN. I'm looking for a manager who has business development skills, who is creative and daring, who looks for ways to expand and grow the business, and who is willing to go the extra step if needed. If you do a good job at managing here—*Steven leans back in the chair and smirks a little with a pause*—there is no limit how far you can go working with me. (*Now with that said, Steven leans forward and looks her in the eye.*) Would you like to manage and run this sports bar?

CARLEENA. (*Carleena takes a deep breath, and her eyes looks around the sports bar. She looks back at Steven and smiles.*) Yes, I will like the opportunity to manage this place, and I thank you for the offer. I will do everything I can to make this place the number one sports bar in the state. (*The scene ends with Steven and Carleena standing up and shaking hands. Steven let's her know with a happy expression on his face.*)

STEVEN. You made a good choice, and I'm glad to have you on board.

Scene ten. Mohan is at the office, working on his computer and going over some paperwork. It's early afternoon, and he is into his work. He gets a call from one of his clients, asking questions about the proposal that Mohan sent him. He listens to the guy as he leans back in his office chair. He has a strange, confused look on his face. He notices Haseem walking in with Evelyn, and his eyebrows go up with an even more confused look on his face.

MOHAN. Yes, sir, I completely understand what you're saying, and I can assure you that the work will be completed within that time frame and no later. And that price is very considerate for all that's got to be done. So do we have a deal, Mr. Perez? (*Mohan smiles and shakes his head and starts to smile with his fist in the air.*) Great, and I can assure you when we are done, you will be happy with our work. Thank you and I will be waiting for the initial down payment, sir. Any problems, just give me a call. (*Mohan leans up in his chair and hangs up the phone. He goes back to work on his computer, muttering to himself.*)

Evelyn and Haseem are walking around the firm office as Haseem talks to her more about what Cultural Dividends firm is all about. He leads her into their meeting room which is very laid out with very nice sculptors and some nice artwork. It has very huge seventy-inch flat screen on the wall and a fancy granite marble office desk. Evelyn likes what she sees as she looks around; she is impressed with the firm's office.

HASEEM. What we're building here, Evelyn, is gonna be a conglomerate. We are making big strides in real estate and land development. Our trucking and shipping business is growing every month. My software and computer programing company is locking up big contracts. Steven is about to open another sports bar and already got some big projects lined up for his construction company. We're just scratching the surface on what we're building here. (*Haseem leans forward in the chair and hands Evelyn some papers. Evelyn reaches out and grabs the papers.*) Here are our numbers and a little more information. Take a look. (*Evelyn flips through the pages and her eyes are wide-open. Her facial expression is looking impressed.*)

EVELYN. These numbers are very impressive. You guys are really doing your thing. Everything I see here is big profits, and it's growing every month. Peter's restaurants are doing really well, I see. (*Evelyn flips through the pages and leans up in her chair. She looks at Haseem with her puckering her lip to the side while nodding her head.*) What are your long-term plans?

HASEEM. In the near future, we plan on expanding in commercial real estate and acquiring more land to develop for future franchising expansion. Expanding more on Wall Street also is key, but as far as long-term, we're trying to expand into other markets and expanding outside the country and building our brand in the global market.

Mohan walks into the conference room where Haseem and Evelyn are talking. He is decked out in his Tom Ford suit with his carrying case in hand. He tells Haseem that he just finalized the deal with Mr. Perez. Haseem grins and looks at Evelyn and invites Mohan in to greet her. Mohan ducks his head in the conference room and walks in with a shocked look on his face. Evelyn stands up and she and Mohan shakes hands.

MOHAN. It is so good to see you, Evelyn. I mean, especially in our office where I hope you consider what Haseem is telling you.

EVELYN. How you know what Haseem is telling me?

MOHAN. Let's just say that we, as a team, had discuss you, and we all think that you will be a great fit here at Cultural Dividends. We need someone like you, Evelyn, who can bring good insight and a balance to our firm and has the intelligence to make smart investments.

Evelyn shakes her head and sits back down with an amazed look on her face. She looks back at Haseem and looks back at Mohan.

EVELYN. I like what you guys are building over here. Looking at your numbers, I definitely see you guys are going hard. This can be a unique opportunity for me to be around four men who all have very high business acumen.

Mohan shakes his head in agreement with Evelyn and looks at his Rolex watch to check the time. He then tells Haseem that he has to run and will talk to him tomorrow. The scene ends with Evelyn talking to Haseem.

EVELYN. If I do decide to take the position, I will still need to check on my sister from time to time to make sure my businesses are running smooth.

HASEEM. (*Haseem, with a very slick and smooth expression on his face, stands up.*) We're already aware of that, and we understand that. We know you know how to chew gum and walk down the street at the same time.

They both laugh at Haseem's little joke, and the scene fades out with them grinning at each other.

Scene eleven. Felize is on his deck in his backyard, relaxing with his shades on. He has some cargo shorts on and a white V-neck T-shirt, with a Cuban link chain hanging around his neck. Light music is playing in the background, and his housekeeper is watering the plants. She is wearing a very tight short maid's outfit and is into her work of watering the flowers. Felize's cell phone rings, and he grabs it and answers it.

FELIZE. Tell me something good. (*He says it with a small grin on his face. He listens for a few seconds and pumps his fist in the air.*) That's what I been waiting to hear. And this is concrete in stone. There better not be any holes in your story. (*Felize sits up in his chair, and his grin gets even bigger as he listens to the other person on the phone.*)

The housekeeper walks Peter out onto the deck. Peter is dressed very casually with shorts and a polo shirt on, with shades sitting on top of his forehead. He notices Felize is grinning and looking happy. Felize hangs up the phone and looks at Peter.

PETER. What the hell are you so happy about, and why you wanted me to come over for? You could have just called me. And what the hell do you need a freaking maid to clean up after your lazy ass?

FELIZE. Bro, I don't have time to clean or cook. She comes by a few days out the week to help me out with a few things. (*Felize smiles and gives Peter a devilish look as he sips on his lemonade.*)

PETER. You act like you got a huge mansion or something. You're just lazy, bro! Anyway, what's good why you needed me over here?

FELIZE. That was my insider guy down in Florida. He keeps me plugged in on everything going on. It's official, just like I told you. Walmart, Costco, and Cheesecake Factory are all looking for land in the same area that you guys just brought your land at.

PETER. Really?

FELIZE. Yes, really Pete-e, just like I told you.

Peter walks around the deck with a shocked look on his face.

PETER. Yeah, I got to give it to you. I was a little hesitant at first only because it was a lot of money. And it came at a bad time with everything we got going on. It's not because I didn't believe you.

FELIZE. My guy said not to worry. He will be able to stir them over to your area. Bro, he also said this is easily a seven-digit deal. (*Felize walks over to Peter and looks him in the eye.*)

PETER. This is just the start, my man. I got something even bigger cooking on the stove.

Both men stare at each other with a smile on their face as Felize looks at his phone and controls his surround sound music. He puts on some Meek Mill and the episode starts to end.

Episode 7

Scene one. Natalie is driving in her Range Rover with her girlfriend, Maracella. They are talking about the party the other night that ended up in a big fight and how this is becoming the norm when it comes to hanging out.

MARACELLA. It's getting more and more dangerous out here. You can hardly go anywhere and just have a nice time. These young boys are fighting and shooting one another for the dumbest stuff. Yo, that was my girl you pushed up on. Hello, there is like five hundred women in here. Why are you idiots 'bout to kill one another over a girl who probably was flirting in the first place? You feel me? (*She gives Natalie a hand clap to acknowledge what she is saying.*)

Natalie shakes her head in agreement and pulls up to the restaurant, where she and Maracella start to get out of the white Range Rover. The restaurant's parking crew escorts them inside, and they park Natalie's truck for her. The two are dressed very classy and wearing heels and continue to talk as they are escorted to their seats.

MARACELLA. I just don't get it sometimes, girl. The good men are too busy playing the field, and the other men are just a little immature boys inside.
NATALIE. Whatever happened to that banker you were seeing?
MARACELLA. Turned out he had quite a few issues, and one of them was staying hard!

145

The two bust out laughing and cause a few people in the restaurant to take notice. The waitress comes over to their table while they are still laughing.

WAITRESS. What will you ladies like to drink? (*She also grins a little and pulls out her tab and gets ready to start taking their order.*)
NATALIE. I will take a Long Island iced tea, and you can put me an order of mozzarella sticks in please.
MARACELLA. I will have a glass of white wine with a bowl of clam chowder please.

The waitress writes it all down, and a few seconds later, she brings the ladies a basket of bread.

NATALIE. So it sounds to me like you ready to fall back and take it light.
MARACELLA. Nah, I wouldn't say that. I'm just gonna be much more careful from hereon with who I freak with.

Natalie smiles as she pauses for a few. Maracella looks at her with a wondering expression on her face.

NATALIE. Well, there is someone who's really on you. He's been on me for a minute now to get me to get you to go out with him.
MARACELLA. Who? (*She has a very surprised look on her face.*)

Natalie shrugs her shoulder as she starts to butter up a piece of bread. Maracella is very curious and waits with a sharp stare on her face.

NATALIE. Haseem's friend Jamal. He is very into you and wants to get to know you better.
MARACELLA. I knew he was on me from that time he pushed up on me when we were shopping. He is cute with a toughness about him, very masculine and edgy. His swag is sexy. He is a playboy, though, and for him, it's a body thing.
NATALIE. Sounds like you're a little interested.

The waitress brings over Maracella's clam chowder soup, and she starts to stir it with her spoon. She is looking at the soup with a slight smile on her face; she looks at Natalie with a sneaky smirk on her face.

MARACELLA. He looks like he would be adventurous, and I do like his tough-guy appeal. With me growing up with only sisters, I never got to know what it feels to be protected and safe. With Jamal, I definitely know he ain't on no sucker shit.

NATALIE. No, he definitely ain't. Jamal is charming, and from what he's swearing up and down to me, he wants to find someone to challenge his mind.

The waitress brings over the ladies' drinks, and the two of them take a sip of their drink. Natalie looks at Maracella with a little smile on her face. Maracella smiles back at her and looks around the restaurant with a debating expression on her face. Maracella nods her head as she takes another sip of her glass of wine.

MARACELLA. Go ahead and give him my number. I will peep his game if he coming at me on some BS.

The scene ends with Natalie wondering where her mozzarella sticks are at. She looks around for the waitress and grabs another piece of bread.

Scene two. Steven and Carleena are at his sports bar and are talking quietly to each other. All the other workers are looking at Carleena with a curious look on their faces. Steven calls everyone over to the bar area. The workers take their time coming over and seem a little confused to what their boss wants to say.

STEVEN. Good morning, everybody. I know it's close to lunchtime and we got to get ready to open up on time, so I won't be long because I know we all got work to do. I want to thank everyone for all the hard work that you guys have been putting in, and I appreciate all the extra work that just about everyone is doing to make this place click. My time has been getting more hectic, and my schedule is getting too much for me to balance. Obligations to other business ventures are very demanding. With that said, I have decided to hire someone who is committed, dedicated, and intelligent enough to fill in for me.

Steven looks at Carleena with a small grin on his face. Meanwhile, his workers are looking around at one another, still confused.

STEVEN. I want to introduce my assistant and our new manager here. She will be in charge of making all decisions and handling all issues for now on. You will show her respect and do what she tells you, and you will treat her with the same respect that you give me. I don't want to hear about anyone showing her a bad attitude. Let's give it up for our new manager Carleena.

Steven opens up his arms toward Carleena and starts to clap a little, followed by only a few small quiet handclaps. Carleena nods her head and walks over to where Steven is standing with a slight smile on her face.

CARLEENA. Thank you, thank you, and I want all of you to know that I'm very thankful for the opportunity that Steven has given me, and I plan to work with every single one of you on ways we can improve the workplace. My door is open to all. I welcome your comments, suggestions, complaints, and even your hard times or stressful times that you may be experiencing.

One of the workers blurts out, "That's more than we can say for Steven. He just nods his head like he is listening." Quite a few workers bust out in laughter, and even Steven is grinning slightly. Steven looks outside in the parking lot and notices that his mother has pulled up and is on her way inside. Steven's half smile quickly turns into a frown as he makes his way to the entrance to greet his mother.

STEVEN'S MOTHER. Well, I guess the only way I'm ever gonna see you or talk to you is by stopping here. Hell, if that even works. I came here last week and I'm sure they told you.

Steven gives his mother a disgusted look and tells her to shhh while escorting her to the other side of the sports bar.

STEVEN. I've been busy as heck, Mom, but what did you want?

Steven's mother angrily looks at Steven and shakes her head.

STEVEN'S MOTHER. What the hell do you mean what I want? How about a simple description of what's going with my son whose life is too busy to see if his mother is even alive.

STEVEN. I know you're alive. I'd just seen you a few weeks ago coming out of Daddy's office. Plus, I ride by your salon every other day and see your car there.

Steven's mother just stares at him and shakes her head as she looks around and notices Carleena talking to the workers. She has a frown on her face.

STEVEN'S MOTHER. Who is she? Your new piece for a few weeks? You are so much like your father when he was your age.

STEVEN. Mom, look, I don't have time for this. (*He starts to turn his attention back over to where Carleena is.*) If you must know she is my new manager and she is gonna bring some creativity to this sports bar.

STEVEN'S MOTHER. Well, I hope so. Between you and Darren and his zombie-looking friends, this place can definitely use a makeover!

Steven just looks at his mother, and she looks back at him with no smile on her face. Her face is stone-cold. Steven just laughs and shakes his head.

Scene three. Haseem and Jamal are at the Rutgers game in the firm's skybox, watching the game by themselves. There are a few other people in the skybox talking and enjoying the game. Jamal is sitting in the chair, looking at the game with a dim look on his face, like something is really bothering him. Haseem notices him looking like he lost his best friend. He gets ready to ask him what's wrong when Jamal's phone rings. Jamal looks at his phone and sees that it's Natalie, and his face lights up. He stands up and answers his phone.

JAMAL. What's up, Nat? Please tell me something that can brighten up my day. (*Natalie is at her office relaxing at her desk, smiling at what Jamal just said to her.*)

NATALIE. Well, I had lunch the other day with Maracella, and we did a little shopping and had a nice day out. I found some shoes I'd been looking for. The bad part about that is they didn't have my size.

JAMAL. Hey, explain that story on Snapchat or tweet about it. Just get to the good stuff, will you? Is she feeling the kid or what?

NATALIE. Well… (*She pauses for a few seconds. Jamal is waiting for her answer.*) She said you aight, and she wouldn't mind getting to know you a little better.

Jamal starts bragging to Haseem like he just scored a winning touchdown or something. Haseem is looking back at him like he's crazy.

JAMAL. Good-looking Natty, I owe you for this. Don't worry, I'll consider going vegan or something. Hey, listen, let me call you back. I got to rub it in Haseem's face a little, me and him at the Rutgers game.

Jamal hangs up the phone with Natalie and walks back over to his chair. Haseem is looking at him with a strange expression on his face while he takes a pull on his Montecristo cigar.

JAMAL. I knew she was feeling me. I freaking knew it. Now I know I got to step my game up. She ain't no regular chick. I got to bring my A game with her.

Haseem stays quiet while he pours him a drink. He looks at Jamal and takes another pull from his cigar.

HASEEM. Well, at least you're not looking like a sad puppy anymore. Natalie hooked you up with one of her girls, huh? Well, you're definitely right. Her friends ain't feeling that hard-core street shit. You better come correct!

JAMAL. That's exactly what got me so down today. I got to get my life together, Haseem. How can I expect to meet Mrs. Classy if I don't have a job.

HASEEM. I thought you said you live off the land. (*Haseem starts to giggle.*) You got a job. You just not on the legal books. (*He starts to giggle even more to himself.*)

Jamal looks at him like he's thinking about taking a swing on his best friend since childhood.

JAMAL. I'm serious, bro. You don't think I see how you're making moves out here, how you're running a successful company, the type of professional friends and legit connections you built. You ride around and don't have to worry about the cops, DEA on your every move, jealous ones watching everything you do.

HASEEM. Jealousy and envy are gonna follow you, legal or illegal, bro.

JAMAL. I freaking know that. (*Jamal stands up and walks over to stare at the game going on, then looks back at Haseem with a very stern face. Haseem knows his childhood friend and knows when he is being serious, so he straightens up his face and twists his lip slightly.*)

HASEEM. When you say legit, what is it you're thinking about doing? What would you want to do?

Jamal looks at Haseem and knows that he finally got his attention, and he has a relieved look on his face that his best friend is finally taking him for real.

Scene four. Peter father pulls up to his home. He is driving an all-black Maybach with factory rims on it. He walks up to the door and is greeted by his wife, who is so happy to see him. So happy that she sheds a very light tear from the corner of her left eye. They hug for a while and give each other a big kiss, then they walk inside their lovely home.

PETER'S FATHER. I know I have been gone most of the year, but I have been really doing a whole lot of thinking about you and Peter. I miss you so much! And I have decided to spend more time at home in the US, and we can start doing things that husband and wife do.

Peter's mother starts to tear even more and puts her hand on her face to hide the tears. Peter's father walks over to her and hugs her again. Peter's mother can't hold back the tears; her face is so delighted at the same time.

PETER'S MOTHER. I have been waiting for over twenty-five years for you to say those words, for you to realize how much your family miss you. Words cannot express how happy I feel right now.

PETER'S FATHER. It's time I start showing you the love you deserve. It's time you and me enjoy life and start taking some vacations, going shopping in Paris and Italy. It's time we go out for ice cream, ride our bikes in the park. I'm so sorry for not recognizing the real duties of a husband earlier.

PETER'S MOTHER. It's never too late to redeem yourself. Healing starts within your mind and shows through your actions. For you to come home today, you have showed me that. Thank you so much!

Scene five. Mohan and Peter are having a meeting with a real estate mogul who was referred to Mohan from a reliable client. Mohan and Peter are giving the mogul a presentation on how their engineering company has handled some very big projects the last few years. And they are also discussing how their construction company is reliable and has done quality work and has completed very big warehouses and huge office buildings also.

REAL ESTATE MOGUL. You know, when I first heard about you guys, I was a little unsure about doing business with you. I heard how young you and your associates are, and the first thing I thought about was immature kids. There was no way I could trust my reputation and my business brand in the hands of young kids who probably know nothing about the corporate world. But looking at your line of steady consistent work, I am very impressed with what your firm has done in less than five years.

PETER. Well, sir, our goal is to be like you, someone who has made billions and still works diligently to improve his business portfolio.

MOHAN. You see, sir, we have done our research and studied the blueprint on every industry and market out there, and we have studied how they achieved and built their empires. We hope to one day follow your footsteps and walk the same destiny.

The real estate mogul stands up out of his chair and walks around the office. He pours himself a drink and takes a sip before he speaks.

REAL ESTATE MOGUL. I have over eight projects that I plan to start in the next year just in the tristate area alone. If your firm can handle the load and complete the work in reasonable time, I might be willing to expand our deal for the whole East Coast, except for Georgia and Florida. That contract isn't available for three more years.

Mohan and Peter look at each other and then look back at the real estate mogul. They both walk around to where the mogul is standing.

MOHAN. We appreciate you giving us the opportunity to work for you, and we won't let you down, sir.

REAL ESTATE MOGUL. You guys will make a boatload of cash if you do me right, send me over the contract.

The mogul turns and starts to leave the office. Mohan and Peter wait for the glass door to shut and he is out of their sight, then they both climb on desk and throw their hands up in the air, like they just won the championship and they are the heroes of the game.

Scene six. Steven is driving in his car, a black-and-white customized 850li BMW coupe. He is sipping on a cup of coffee as he is pulling up to the jobsite of Peter's new restaurant. His dad is standing next to the office trailer on the phone. Steven gets out and is walking toward his father. Steven hands his dad a cup of coffee, and Steven starts to open his breakfast sandwich as the two enter in the trailer office. Steven's father hangs up the phone and starts to take a sip of his coffee.

STEVEN. Things are running pretty smooth over here, I see. This is coming together really fast, I see.

STEVEN'S DAD. One thing you have to always remember in the construction business, and I told you this before, you have to keep pace with your clients' needs. Every client is different, but some have that fire in their eyes like Peter, some are in no rush to get their stuff completed. You have to learn every client and buss your tail to make them happy.

Steven looks at the camera monitor and sees a few guys coming into the office trailer. His dad tells him these are Steven's new construction managers, who have over thirty years of experience each. The two men walk into the office dressed like construction workers—flannel jackets and jeans. Steven's dad introduces them to Steven, and they interrupt him and remind Steven that his dad must got memory loss. They already know Steven since he was a kid.

STEVEN. That coffee hasn't kicked in yet, huh, Dad? I remember both of these guys well. You forget how many jobsites you took me too when I was younger.

Steven's dad shakes his head and shrugs off what his son is telling him and stands up and grabs the guys attention showing them where the bagels are at.

STEVEN'S DAD. Frank and Stanley are going to oversee your projects. They know how to handle any issue that could come up and the right people in the industry to make stuff happen. They will show you the ropes on how things are done out there, what corners to cut, and who pockets you got to grease. Listen to their suggestions and do what they are instructing you to do. I relied on these guys for over thirty years, and they never hosed me down.

Steven shakes his head and listens to everything his father is telling him as he always did since he was a little kid. Steven is chewing on his sandwich and taking it all in.

STEVEN'S NEW MANAGER. Your dad told us everything going on with you, and we both are happy to help you get everything going with your construction company. We will do everything you need and show you the ropes on how things go and guide you on everything you need to know. Don't worry, we got you covered.

STEVEN'S DAD. They got all the details on your first few projects and already got the ball rolling on your new workers. So don't worry about nothing. These guys you can trust, and they will hold you down no matter what the weather is out there.

STEVEN'S NEW MANAGER STANLEY. So who will be compensating us for our services?

STEVEN. That will be me. My firm will pay you and all the workers' salary, and any issues that come up due to financing, come to me.

The two men look at Steven and then look at his dad with their eyebrows raised and an impressed expression on their faces.

STEVEN'S NEW MANAGER FRANK. I see you taught the kid right. To be independent is the first thing in business, not depending on others and taking the bull by the horn.

The scene ends as the men look at Steven and eat on their breakfast. Everybody is sipping coffee and looking at TV in the office.

Scene seven. Evelyn is at her smoothie shop, sitting at one of the tables on her laptop. When she stops and sits back in her chair and picks up her cell phone, she is drifting into deep thought for a few seconds, like her mind is in orbit. She snaps back to reality and starts to make a call on her phone. Haseem is jogging with some Jay-Z music blaring in his headphones when he receives an incoming call.

HASEEM. Well, good morning to you. I hope this is the call I've been waiting for.

EVELYN. I have considered your job offer and have given it deep thought, and I believe this will be an exciting new role for me, exactly what I always wanted. A chance to play a key role in developing an enterprise that is only a few years young and expanding on my own knowledge in the business world.

HASEEM. Yes, Evelyn, that is why we want you to manage and run our firm. We all believe in you and know you are highly educated enough to make it happen.

EVELYN. With that said, Haseem, you have to realize that it's gonna require a lot of my time, and I will have to cut back my life to make sure I succeed at being my best. I'm going to have to cut back on my own businesses and everything I got going on, so I need to be highly compensated for it.

Haseem stops jogging and starts to walk instead. His facial expression is curious and he has a slight smile on his face.

HASEEM. Highly compensated? (*He repeats with a joking voice.*) Of course you know that we will offer you a great salary to start at, plus incentives that will take care of you. What kind of salary are you looking to earn, Evelyn?

Evelyn stands up and walks over to her front window at her smoothie shop. She has a stern look on her face.

EVELYN. I'm going to need a six-digit salary of at least $100,000 to start, plus three weeks' vacation.

HASEEM. Hmm, I think that shouldn't be an issue. I think we can swing that.

Evelyn has a shocked look on her face as she listens to Haseem downplay her salary demands. She rubs her forehead in almost disbelief.

HASEEM. Let me run it by the fellas, and I will get back to you in a few days. Anything else you want or like to have?

EVELYN. No, that will be it for now, but if I start turning big profits for you guys, then I do expect a respectful bonus at the end of the year.

HASEEM. Of course, no worries on that. You do what you do and handle your handle and use that Princeton University brain to take Cultural Dividends to the next level.

The scene ends with both of them hanging up, with Haseem starting back jogging, listening to his music, and Evelyn looking through her window with a pondering look on her face.

Scene eight. Darren and his crew are hanging out at the sports bar, watching the Monday night football game. They are sort of loud as a few of the customers take notice to their behavior and language. Carleena also takes notice to it as she watches from the back office. She takes a deep breath and continues to work on her laptop. One of Darren's friends flips his tray off the table out of disgust by what happened in the game. Darren quickly gets on him about what he did and tells him to relax. Carleena has seen enough and starts to make her way to their table.

CARLEENA. Gentlemen, gentlemen, I see that you are enjoying the game, but—

Carleena is quickly interrupted by Darren as he yells at the game and looks at her with a disgusted look on his face.

DARREN. What the fuck! You're bringing us bad luck! Get the hell outta here! Go clean something!

Carleena takes a very long pause and starts an evil stare at Darren as her stare gets colder and meaner by the second.

DARREN. What are you, deaf or something? Get the hell outta here! You're bringing us bad luck. Better yet, bring us a few more pitchers of beer and some more wings.

That was the last straw for Darren and his crew. Carleena couldn't take it anymore as she motions over to security to remove them from the sports bar.

CARLEENA. Get your stuff and get the hell out of here right now!

Darren looks at her like she crazy and gets up and starts to take a step toward her. The security slowly, out of deep respect for Darren, puts one hand on his chest. Darren wipes it off like it was a fly or something.

DARREN. Who the heck you think you talking to, lady! You kicking me out? You kicking me out?
CARLEENA. You damn right. If you think you're going to be in here disrespecting me or anyone of our staff, you gotta go. You and your zombie-looking friends get the heck out right now!

Carleena once again motions for her security to remove Darren and his friends as she gives Darren a very hard stare.

DARREN. Out of respect to my little cousin, I'm not gonna disrespect his establishment, so were gonna leave, but I promise you this ain't over, sweetheart. This ain't freakin' over!

Carleena watches as security escorts them out, but her facial expression has changed to worried. She looks rattled and wondering if she did the right thing or not.

Scene nine. Aunt Pelynda and her sister-in-law are hanging with their future daughter-in-law, enjoying the day at a very posh luxurious spa, where they are getting pampered with a massage, pedicure, and good facials. They are in their robes and having a nice cocktail, relaxing. They are glancing at magazines and getting special treatment.

AUNT PELYNDA. I just love coming here. They treat you like royalty and take their time doing what you ask them to do. Other places just rush you and don't take their time treating your body the way they supposed to. They're just trying to get you out to move on to the next customer.

NADIA. I've never been here before. I had heard about it before, but I just stay close to home, plus I've been going to that one for years.

HASEEM'S MOTHER. What is going on with you, Nadia? Have you been getting wedding plans ready or your girlfriends handling everything?

NADIA. Well, they're taking care of a few minor things, but to be honest, Haseem has been so busy lately that we haven't really even got into the small details yet. He is so busy with his company and dealing with these new clients he got. We got to make some time for ourselves.

Aunt Pelynda listens and takes in what Nadia is saying while she is getting her feet rubbed. She grabs her drink and takes a sip.

AUNT PELYNDA. So what are you going to do about this because you have to make him understand that your needs and desires has to be catered to also? My nephew is very understanding and takes the time to consider other people's feelings, so you have to address it with him.

HASEEM'S MOTHER. Yeah, if she can get him to listen long enough. (*She gives her sister in-law a light wink of the eye.*) Nadia playing too laid-back, you ask me, she's not getting at Haseem about how she feels.

NADIA. No, that's not it. I have been trying to understand his heavy workload and that he and his boys are focusing on building up their investment firm.

AUNT PELYNDA. Being compassionate is respectful, I definitely get it, but being too laid-back can make him believe that you aren't worried about nothing. And he won't bother to consider your feelings. Men need to be checked sometimes.

Aunt Pelynda rubs her ankle and looks at Nadia and then look at Haseem's mother with a quick roll of her eyes. Her lips twist up as she leans back in her chair.

AUNT PELYNDA. Are you going back to school to finish up, or you plan on opening up your own business? What are you gonna do to keep yourself going? You're young, so now is the time.

NADIA. I haven't really thought about going back to college to finish up, but Mom got me thinking about my future as a wife, and to be honest, I just don't see myself as a business owner. That's not my thing, and the last thing I want to do is waste any of Haseem's money on a long-shot risk.

Haseem's mother switches her feet in the water as she is enjoying her pedicure. She looks down and tells the lady to rub more gel on her ankles and the bottom of her feet. She looks at Nadia with a slight grin and devious look on her face.

HASEEM'S MOTHER. Well, you just can't let time slip away. You got to figure out what you really have a passion for and develop a love for something.

NADIA. I got a love for shopping and working out and keeping my body right for my man. And I'm learning to cook better too.

Both Aunt Pelynda and Haseem's mother look at Nadia with a disheartened look on their faces as they both grab their drink and take another sip and start to look at their phones, as if the conversation is over and going nowhere.

Scene ten. Mohan pulls up in his Mercedes-Benz 500Sl coupe. He gets out and walks into the restaurant where the firm holds their weekly business meeting at. The guys are there, eating their pancakes and sausages. Steven is on the phone with a serious look on his face, Peter is checking his phone, and Haseem is stuffing his face with pancakes.

MOHAN. Sorry I'm a little late, fellas. Traffic was a little hectic this morning. What I missed?

PETER. Not much. We were just discussing Evelyn's salary. She did accept the job, and her demands aren't really that outrageous.

MOHAN. What she's asking for? (*Mohan stirs his coffee and picks up the menu.*) What is she looking to get paid?

HASEEM. It's $100,000, plus three weeks of vacation and a bonus at the end of the year if she turns big profits.

MOHAN. That's not too bad, considering what she brings to the table. I kinda thought she was gonna want more after looking at our numbers and upcoming business plans.

Steven hangs up the phone with a frown on his face. He looks out the window and stares out at it for a few seconds.

STEVEN. Yeah, I agree, that's not a bad asking price. Evelyn is sharp and I like her and what she can bring to the firm.

PETER. So we all agree then. We all on board with hiring Evelyn?

Everybody shakes their heads in agreement, and the waitress brings over Mohan's pancakes and turkey sausage. He starts cutting his pancakes and plucks a sausage in his mouth.

PETER. Me and Mohan locked the deal up with the real estate mogul. Turns out he got several projects he is building in the next few years around the tristate area.

MOHAN. Beautiful thing is, if we do right by him, he is willing to give us the whole East Coast, except for Georgia and Florida. Their contracts aren't up yet.

HASEEM. That's freaking nuts. You know how many people we gonna have to hire to make sure everything goes right? He is a major mogul with a lot of power. We can't mess this up.

STEVEN. We won't mess this up. You know how much money we stand to make off just these first several projects? (*Steven's eyes light up as he looks at Haseem.*) Millions on top millions, bro. I will give up whatever time it takes to make sure everything goes smooth.

All four men nod their heads in agreement and continue to eat their breakfast. The waitress asks them if they need anything. Steven says to bring him over a Western omelet with A 1 sauce.

MOHAN. Everything going all right with the restaurant construction?

STEVEN. Yeah, I was down there earlier this week. My dad and his crew are kicking ass on it. They already got the structure up. It's coming together pretty fast. Also, I start my first construction project in the next few weeks. My dad found me two good guys who are gonna guide me through the early stages.

PETER. How good is good because we're gonna need them in the near future with these upcoming building projects we just got?

STEVEN. Don't worry, I've been watching these guys since I was a kid. They are experts when it comes to land development, and construction. We are in good hands trust me!

Steven and the fellas smile and look at one another with a confident look on their faces as music starts to play in the background. As the episode is ending and the background music starts getting a little louder, Haseem says they should go to Vegas to celebrate, and the guys look at one another and they all agree.

Episode 8

Scene one. The scene starts by showing aerial shots of New York City, Times Square, Freedom Tower, Empire State Building, with smooth R & B music playing in the background. It slowly shifts to Broadway Theater slowly from a sky shot. It shows couples walking around and people enjoying their night out. The weather is beautiful out and the sky is clear. Jamal and Maracella are walking down Forty-Second Street, looking very happy. Both are smiling and walking very slowly. Jamal is wearing a very stylish cream-colored Gucci sweatshirt with the matching sweatpants to match, with all-white Gucci sneakers on. His diamond stud earring is blinking off the city lights, and his pinkie ring is very nice and flooded out with karats. Maracella is also looking very beautiful, with a tight black Prada dress on and a white blouse with black buttons. Her heels are strapped around her ankle and matching her outfit. She also is rocking a black-and-white matching Prada bag. Both of them are looking dressed to impress and are enjoying their night out.

MARACELLA. You know, Jamal, I haven't been out on a date in almost a year, and yes, there have been guys pushing up on me, but I'm very selective on who I date. And I must admit that I usually don't date your type, but I see more in you internally than what you show on the outside.

JAMAL. Yeah, I don't see you as the type riding through the hood, checking for cats on the street corner, playing dice, and drinking. You're not beat for that. Hey, I'm a little offended. What do you mean my type? (*Jamal says it with a grin on his face.*)

MARACELLA. (*Maracella smiles and looks up in the sky while Jamal is waiting for her answer.*) No disrespect, Jamal, but you know you're not a casual businessman or a lawyer or nothing. You're abrasive and edgy. You're hard-core and no-nonsense and definitely not to be messed with. But you're also charming, and I like that about you.

JAMAL. Well, I'm not going to front or sugarcoat anything. I always believe in being straight up. I played around out there in the streets for years, and I did some things when I was younger that wasn't too smart. I took risks and put myself in dangerous situations. But I realized as I got older, especially now, that the street life has a one-way street, dead or in jail.

MARACELLA. And that's what I kinda sense about you. I think you're searching for a way out but unsure exactly how you want to go about it.

JAMAL. Well, you're sort of right. I've seen too much in the game, and there isn't too many happy endings. But one thing you're wrong on, Maracella, is I know what I need to settle my life down and to bring some balance to my world.

MARACELLA. What is it that you need?

Jamal slows down walking and grabs Maracella's hand and looks her in the eye with a serious look on his face. Maracella stops and stares in Jamal eyes with a questionable look on her face.

JAMAL. I need to find someone who can tame me down and make me want to spend quiet evenings watching a movie on the couch, someone who massages my mental and has me intrigued by her personality and character, someone who wants to be with me for who I am and not what I can offer them or give them.

Maracella nods her head as she looks Jamal in the eye. She glances around the area. Jamal takes a step back and slowly lets go of her hand.

JAMAL. Come on, we better get back. The intermission is almost over, and I can't wait to see how this play ends.

MARACELLA. Yeah, you're right. It seems like time just zoomed by so fast.

JAMAL. How late can you stay out tonight? I was thinking about hanging out in the city a little bit. I'm getting hungry. We should get something to eat after the play.

MARACELLA. I'm good with that, but I ain't trying to break day our nothing. (*Jamal stops Maracella and looks at her.*)

JAMAL. You're a lady with class, not a groupie or bird chick. Don't worry, I got you.

Scene two. Peter stops by his parents' house to see his father who is back in the country. Peter is happy that his father is back home. He misses him and wishes that he could have spent more time with him growing up as a kid. As he walks up to his parents' home, he is having a conversation on the phone, and he tells his restaurant manager to make sure everything is set up nice and have champagne bottles available. Peter's father meets him at the door with a big hug and smile on his face.

PETER'S FATHER. Look at you! You are the man. I am so proud of you, son.

PETER. Father, I'm so glad you are home. I am so glad that you are here with me and Mother. There is so much to learn and talk about.

Peter and his father walk into the house with happy expressions on their faces. Peter's mother walks in and gives her son a hug and kiss. She, too, is very happy. All three head out to the patio deck in the backyard as Peter's mother pours everyone tea. They all sit and enjoy their tea with the beautiful sunny morning in the background.

PETER. So, Father, please tell me it's true what Mother has told me that you are here to stay for a while.

PETER'S FATHER. Yes, it is true, son. I realize that I have to start spending more time with my family. Me working all the time is no good. I want you to promise me that no matter how big your firm becomes, you never lose out on quality family time, son.

PETER. I can promise you that because I know what it feels like to not have your father around growing up, and I wouldn't do my kids like that.

Peter's father shakes his head as he looks at his son with a proud look on his face. He sips on his tea and looks around their beautiful backyard. Peter's mother is walking around the yard, watering her flowers.

PETER'S FATHER. You know, while I was back in Japan, I did find time to do a lot of thinking. Remember, I always taught you to make time to meditate and reflect every day, son.

Peter nods his head in agreement as he looks at his phone really quick and glances at his mother in a fast motion. His attention zooms right back to his father as he is focused on everything his father tells him.

PETER'S FATHER. I am very proud of what you and your friends have built with your investment firm. You guys have really started out the gate fast and have secured some amazing contracts. But I realized that I should be here helping you with good business advice. I know you don't want my help and I appreciate your strong individuality, but I wanna do something.

PETER. Dad, I told you before that I got this. You taught me so much already, and I watched how you handled business growing up. Believe me, you influenced me more than you realize.

PETER'S FATHER. I have an idea, son, something that I have been giving some deep thought to.

Peter's father looks at his son eye to eye with a very serious look on his face. Peter has a curious look as to what his father is about to tell him.

PETER'S FATHER. I want to help you expand your restaurant chain and open more around the United States. I think you have a great menu, and your concept and theme is very appealing. I have no doubt in my mind that Japanese people all around the country will love your delicious food.

Peter has a slight smirk of deep thought as he listens to his father. He ponders it over for a few while he sips more of his tea and looks away, looking back toward his mother. Peter's mother glances at Peter and gives him a quick fast wink and nod of her head. Peter looks back at his dad, who is awaiting his response.

PETER. Dad, I really appreciate the offer, and I do plan on one day expanding outside of New Jersey, but we got a lot going on right now with other deals and business ventures. Right now just isn't the right time. But I welcome your help, and I'm thankful for that, but give me a little more time and I will definitely take you up on that offer.

Peter's father smiles like he just closed on a multimillion-dollar deal. He is so happy that his son is willing to let him help. He shakes his head proudly and looks at his wife as she takes a seat with them and pours her some tea. The scene ends with the three of them sipping their tea and enjoying the beautiful morning sun.

Scene three. Everyone is at Peter's restaurant, sharing laughs and dressed up for a little celebration for Evelyn. The celebration is for Evelyn accepting the position and taking over as executive manager at Cultural Dividends firm. All four partners are there, along with Nadia and Carleena, and even Natalie is there with Mohan, her brother. The waiter and waitress are bringing over everyone food, and they are drinking and eating.

STEVEN. Well, Evelyn, I just want to let you know that I was the main one for months, telling these guys we need some real help around the office to hold everything together. We all are busy with our schedules, and no one is able to really build the firm up the right way. We are missing out on good opportunities, and now with you joining us, I feel confident we make some big profits.

EVELYN. Thank you so much, Steven. I really didn't see myself running a successful firm like this. I was focused on building my little empire, but when an opportunity like this comes up, you got to jump on it.

Evelyn looks at Nadia real quick and puts a fork of food in her mouth. Nadia glances back at her but looks away real quick to not show any insecurity.

MOHAN. Like I told you before, there is some things I wanna go over with you about the engineering part of our firm. I know once you get settled into your position, you're gonna find ways to build it up more. I also am glad to have you on our team.

PETER. Feel free, Evelyn, to make changes around the office as you see fit and spend on whatever you need for things to be suitable for you.

HASEEM. So, Carleena, how do you like working for Steven? Has he given you the rundown on his exclusive friends list?

Haseem grins while he eats on his chicken pasta. A few people also chuckle a little on that comment. Steven looks at Haseem with a funny look on his face.

STEVEN. She knows she has total control on the conduct of our customers, and if any of them are acting up, no matter who it is, she knows what to do.

Carleena looks around the table and looks at Steven with a proud look on her face that she was glad to hear him say that.

CARLEENA. So, Evelyn, just to let you know, if there is anything you need in reference to the sports bar or anything for that matter, anything I could do to help, please just tell me.

EVELYN. Well, thank you. That's really nice of you. That is exactly the way it is supposed to be with women in business.

HASEEM. Well, I just wanna make a toast to you, Evelyn, and on behalf of the firm, we wish you the best and much success in your first year with us. I look forward to working with you and also being supportive if you ever need anything.

Mohan, Steven, and Peter look at one another and then look at Haseem while he is talking, with a look on their faces as to not say too much in this awkward situation. Nadia has kind of a fake smile on her face as she takes a sip of champagne. She looks at Evelyn who is looking right at Haseem with a thank-you expression on her face. She smiles and nods her head to the partners around the table and glances at Nadia real fast and looks away with a devilish grin on her face. Natalie notices the both of them sharing looks at each other and whispers something to Mohan. He smiles at what she tells him.

STEVEN. Hey, what time are we meeting up for the fishing trip again?
PETER. I told everybody 2:00 PM. Is that good enough time for you? (*Peter smirks at Steven.*)
STEVEN. Yeah, that should be good enough. I know you're an early bird, Peter, and going to bed early at night is a regular for you. (*Steven laughs a little and looks around the table for others to join in on his joke.*)
EVELYN. The food here is amazing, Peter. You got great cooks here, I see. I really like their flavor and sauces.
PETER. Thank you, thank you. (*Peter gives thought about Evelyn's compliment and reflects on what his father also told him.*)
HASEEM. Yeah, it's a nice spot. My boy single-handedly picked out mostly everything too. He's just not too good on picking out the music a little, but I will help you with that. (*Haseem tries to change up the music selection on the sound system. The waitress comes over and pours everyone more champagne.*)
PETER. Haseem, make sure you keep you music selection for just back here. I don't want our customers listening to Cardi B or Migos. (*Everyone shares a laugh, and takes a sip of their refilled glasses of champagne.*)

Scene four. Jamal and Maracella are on day two of Jamal's double-header date that started last night with the Broadway play. They went home and rested up most of the day, and Jamal picks Maracella up for a nice dinner at a swanky upscale Italian restaurant. Jamal is very attracted to Maracella and wants to leave a strong impression on her. Maracella is starting to like Jamal's charming ways and thinks that he is a real sweetheart deep down. Both of them have just ordered their dinner and are gazing at each other.

MARACELLA. You know, I didn't think we'd be together most of the weekend. I know you have a busy schedule out there, doing what you do.

JAMAL. Well, this is what I call a doubleheader, and do feel proud because most women I dealt with barely get a full night out of me. But I really didn't get the chance to talk and get to know you last night. Watching that play and walking around New York, I didn't get to find out who Maracella really is.

Jamal takes a sip of his drink and gives Maracella that puppy-eye look and cracks a slight grin on his face. Maracella looks at Jamal with the same puppy-looking eyes as she takes a sip of her drink also.

MARACELLA. My story ain't complicated. It's basically typical. I mean, I've just been focused on my career more lately and going hard at that.

JAMAL. I feel you on that. Where do you see yourself in the next five years?

MARACELLA. Hopefully married and getting ready to start a family. That's why the next few years for me are critical. I have to make things happen, get my foundation straight, and maybe then a man will see that I'm worth being with.

JAMAL. Without your foundation straight, you're worth being with. You're freaking beautiful with amazing curves and one of the sexiest walks I ever seen.

Maracella blushes and looks away from Jamal and turns back to him with a beautiful smile on her face.

MARACELLA. Thank you, but I bet that's just one of your long list of lines you run on women.

Jamal grabs one of the garlic knots that the waitress just brought over and starts to dip it in the olive oil. He looks back at Maracella and gives her a questionable look on his face. Maracella also grabs a garlic knot and dips it in the olive oil.

JAMAL. I'm being real with you. I'm not gonna lie. I compliment real beauty when I see it, and believe me, I don't see to many as fine as you are. What's your makeup? I see the Indian side in you, but there something else there.

MARACELLA. My mom is American Indian, and my dad is Dominican and Cuban.

JAMAL. Damn, you're a mixed breed for real. (*Jamal chuckles while grabbing another garlic knot.*) Listen, I know that you're probably thinking that I just want to smash and dash, and yes, I do want to smash. I ain't gonna sugarcoat it. You're gorgeous and exotic, but when I look at you, Maracella, I see a shy little princess who's just really looking to be respected and treated with class. I think most men are intimidated by you or think that they can win you over by flashing money at you, but you're bigger than that. You see through that BS.

Maracella nods her head and looks at Jamal like he just hit it right on the nail. She pauses for a few seconds as she moves around in her seat a little.

MARACELLA. You're pretty much dead-on. You left out the immature mommy-boy type, but yeah, I was telling Natalie that it seems that's all I've been attracting lately.

Maracella grabs her wine and shakes her head in disgust as she rolls her eyes slightly. She then takes a small sip and looks back at Jamal. Jamal is looking back at her like he feels her pain and struggles.

JAMAL. I learned that when you search and try too hard to find love, it distances itself even further from you, almost like it runs away.

The waitress brings over their dinner to the table as they start to prepare to eat. They glance at each other as they dig into their food for the first time.

MARACELLA. I never experienced a doubleheader or whatever you wanna call it, but I feel like maybe we started out the gate right. Question is, will you be around to finish the race? (*Maracella pauses and looks Jamal dead in the eye with a sexy smirk on her face.*)
MARACELLA. Because the kind of race you got dealing with me, you might be tired after a few miles.

Jamal grins and leans toward Maracella with a more serious look on his face, he swallows his food and grabs his drink.

JAMAL. Don't worry, I'm built for the long haul. Grinding it out is what I do. Both Jamal and Maracella crack a smile on their face as they continue to eat.

Scene five. Haseem and Nadia arrive back home, and they are in a good mood as they walk into their laid-out plush townhouse. They are upstairs getting comfortable as they are smooching and are touching with each other. As Nadia is in the bathroom slipping on her lingerie, Jamal calls Haseem to find out what time is the fishing trip tomorrow. Haseem reminds him to be there by 2:00 PM sharp, and they'll leaving from AC instead of Belmar. Jamal tells Haseem a few details about his doubleheader date with Maracella. Haseem tells him that they will talk about it more tomorrow on the fishing trip. Nadia comes out the bathroom looking very sexy in her lingerie as Haseem looks at her with a lucky expression on his face.

HASEEM. You are so beautiful. I'm blessed to have you in my life.

NADIA. You're the kind of man I always wanted, driven and committed and motivated to being great!

Nadia gives Haseem a very slow kiss on his lips and gives him a sexy take-me look in his eyes. Haseem runs his hands through her long sleek hair and looks her back in the eye.

NADIA. I want you to know that I'm a little uncomfortable with Evelyn working at the firm. I know it was a quick high school fling that y'all shared, but I know she's still attracted to you, and I'm a little bothered by it.

HASEEM. I understand how you feel, baby, and for the record, it was not my ideal to hire her. Matter of a fact, I wasn't even thinking about her when we were thinking about someone for that position. Peter and Mohan thought highly of her and were the ones who really wanted her. I would have rather found someone not attached to any of us, to be honest.

NADIA. She kept looking at me at dinner with that look almost like she was saying, "I'm not over with him yet." Maybe my senses are wrong.

HASEEM. I already had a very serious talk with her during the interview, and I let her know that I'm about business and strictly business, and if I get any inkling that she's trying to rekindle anything, she won't be working there. If she can't be professional, then we don't need her at the firm.

Nadia nods her head and agrees with Haseem as she gives him a big hug and looks him in his eyes.

NADIA. I trust you, and you know I believe in you, Haseem, but I get this funny feeling about her. I think she stills has feelings for you.

HASEEM. I will not be sloppy or ratchet, Nadia. You know I don't move like that, and I will never disrespect you by sleeping with a woman that you have to see and deal with from time to time. I love you too much to let a woman have that over you. I would be rubbing pie in your face in front of everyone, and I will never play you like that.

Nadia slowly walks away and grabs her glass of wine on the table and looks at Haseem with a proud look on her face. She takes a sip and walks back over to Haseem and starts kissing him very emotionally. Haseem is into her very seductive kissing and pulls her over to their bed and pulls his head and lips away from her and looks her in the eye.

HASEEM. You are the one I love and the one I want to spend the rest of life with. No one will come between us, I promise you that.

Haseem and Nadia start back kissing and getting more sexual with each other as they start to engage in very passionate sex.

Scene six. Mohan is at his desk, looking on his computer, going over a few things. He gets a call from the driver of the Yacht.

YACHT DRIVER. Just making sure that everything is still on today for 2:00 PM. Are there any last-minute changes?
MOHAN. No, we're definitely coming. We will be there. Do me a favor and make sure the chef knows we are leaving out of AC instead of Belmar. He's a little forgetful at times.
YACHT DRIVER. No problem.

Mohan hangs up the phone and hears music playing. He gets up out his chair and notices his sister Natalie and her friends are already at his house. He has a surprise look on his face as to why they're here so early. He starts to walk to the front door to let them in. Mohan opens up the door with a funny look on his face as Natalie and her friends are dancing and singing the words to the song playing.

MOHAN. Y'all a little early, ain't you? (*No response from any of the ladies as they are enjoying themselves.*) Hey, hey, it's early in the morning. What's wrong with y'all?
NATALIE. Mohan, it's almost 11:00 AM. You should be ready by now.

MARACELLA. Yeah, it's not like you driving down. All you got to do is get in and ride.

MOHAN. Yeah, I can imagine all the gossip and man bashing I'm gonna hear. It's gonna be an exciting ride down.

Mohan looks at his sister and friends as they continue to dance with one another. He shakes his head and goes back inside his house to get his things.

Scene seven. The scene is an aerial view of Atlantic City, and music is playing in the background. Different shots of the casinos and boardwalk are being shown. It slowly shifts to a huge beautiful yacht sailing in the ocean, and everybody on board is dancing and talking, with only a few people actually fishing. All aboard are Peter, Haseem, Mohan, Steven, Natalie, and three of her friends, Carleena with three of her friends. And to Haseem's surprise, Evelyn is there with a few of her friends. Darren and Jamal have brought a few of their boys along for the trip also. Everyone is socializing and sharing laughs while the waitresses from Steven's sports bar are making sure everyone's glasses are full. Haseem and Peter are on the top deck, talking about a few things.

HASEEM. You know, it would have been nice and a little respectful if you would have told me that you invited Evelyn to come.

PETER. Haseem, she is officially part of the firm now. Why wouldn't I invite her along? Don't tell me that you feeling some type of way.

HASEEM. Nah, that's not really it. I really don't give a shit if she's here or not. I just hope Nadia don't find out.

Haseem leans over the railing of the yacht, looking at the water with a worried look on his face. Peter is smiling at Haseem and shaking his head.

PETER. Don't tell me that she's jealous, bro. She should know you're about business and not pleasure, at least 90 percent of the time. (*Peter smiles and leans over the railing, looking at Haseem.*)

HASEEM. Of course, she knows that, but you know how women are, especially when they think you're hiding stuff from them. She's gonna feel some type of way because she's thinking this is a fishing trip. She's not gonna care about any of the other women on the trip with us, but soon as she knows Evelyn was out with us, she's gonna be on some shit. I know it. Plus, she claims Evelyn was giving her a funny stare at the celebration dinner yesterday.

PETER. Hmm, I didn't know that. If I knew it would be an issue with you or Nadia, I wouldn't have told her to come. You're right though. Nadia's not gonna be too happy about her being here. This isn't gonna be long-term problem, is it? I mean, we don't need any tension or anything within the firm, Haseem. If you want me to, I will tell her to kick rocks, and we'll hire someone else.

Peter looks at Haseem with a serious look on his face, no smirk or grin, just stone-cold expression. Haseem notices that Peter is serious and appreciates his loyalty to him. He nods his head and stands away from the railing.

HASEEM. Nah, we don't have to do all that. I believe she's gonna be professional about things. Nadia will just have to understand. But I appreciate you having my back as always.

PETER. Come on now. You know I respect the rules of the game. We all vowed to them back in college, and I will always honor the rules, bro.

Peter and Haseem give each other a cool handshake and pats each other on the back and are sort of distracted by a few of the ladies on the yacht, who are walking around in sexy swimwear. Both of them smile at each other.

PETER. Hey, I ain't engaged. I can't spend all my time over here talking with you. It's time to get a little familiar with our guests. (*Haseem grins as he watches Peter walk off.*)

Scene eight. Different shots of everyone on the boat. Steven and Darren throwing shots back with their friends. Natalie and her girls are enjoying their champagne, talking and dancing, Mohan talking with Evelyn and her friends. Music is blasting, and it's a beautiful day out. Jamal and Maracella are downstairs, relaxing and playing some pool. Jamal is staring at Maracella's backside, shaking his head, while she is taking her shot on the pool table.

JAMAL. I didn't think you were gonna come out on our fishing trip. I mean, you don't strike me as a fisher or nothing.

Maracella finishes her shot on the pool table and looks at Jamal with a smirk on her face as she prepares to take another shot.

MARACELLA. Yeah, I see you guys are catching quite a few red snappers out there. I hope you let me take a few home. (*Maracella looks at Jamal with a funny look on her face, and she shakes her head like Jamal is sounding geeked out for saying that.*)
JAMAL. Okay, Miss Smart-Ass, whatever! You talking slick today, I see. I like that. Anyway, I'm not into bringing sand to the beach. That's why I didn't tell you about it.

Maracella misses her shot and is not too happy about it. Jamal gets ready to take his turn as he analyzes the table, looking for his best shot. Maracella walks around the table, giving Jamal a look like he ain't got any game-playing pool.

MARACELLA. I see you brought a few of your boys from the block with you. I hope your boys kept their guns in the car. Cops be acting funny down here in AC.

JAMAL. You got jokes today, I see! (*Jamal makes his shot on the pool table and looks at Maracella like he's ready to show his true colors of hood life.*)

JAMAL. Don't worry there in the car. We good. (*He grins as he sizes up the pool table, looking for his next shot.*) How you know I was coming anyway? I didn't mention it to you or nothing. Don't let me find out I got you chasing, and I haven't even smashed yet.

Maracella gives Jamal an evil grin as she takes a sip of her champagne. Jamal looks at Maracella to see what her comeback is gonna be now.

MARACELLA. Yeah, I was like, damn, when I saw you. Here he go 'bout to blow mine up. How am I supposed to get my pimp-stress on with him watching my every move? All the money on this boat, and I'm gonna be smothered.

Jamal's face quickly turns into a serious look, with a very curious dazed look that spells defeated. He looks at Maracella like he can't believe she said that. Maracella, sensing she got him dazed, goes in for the knock-out. She grabs her glass and gives Jamal a sexy smirk expression and walks back upstairs and starts talking to Mohan, very touchy, grabbing his arm and smiling very hard.

Scene nine. Steven and Darren are chatting with each other about some of Carleena's friends as they are looking over at them, practically drooling from the mouth. Carleena walks from behind. They never noticed her as she looks at them and shakes her head, watching them foam at the mouth. She whispers in Steven's ear, and he busts out laughing.

CARLEENA. Those are my friends from college. All you had to do was ask me their names, and I would have given you the rundown on all of them.

Darren looks over and sees it's Carleena that is talking, and quickly his facial expression turns into anger as he gives her a cold stare. Carleena notices Darren's stare and gives him one right back.

CARLEENA. Well, that ain't supposed to scare me now, is it?

DARREN. Nah, not at all, but believe me, I got something that will shut your little sassy ass up! (*Steven breaks Darren's disrespectful talk up quickly and gives him a very stern look.*)

STEVEN. Yo, what did I tell you about that? How you gonna be a businessman if you can't respect structure? She is part of our circle now, and you got to get over your feelings, cuz.

Darren looks at Steven, then looks at Carleena and walks away. He still seems upset over Carleena kicking him out of the sports bar.

CARLEENA. He'll be aight sooner or later. I know he is your cousin, but he has to let things go eventually.

Steven looks at Carleena and looks away quickly as his attention is still on Carleena's sexy friends. He takes a sip and pulls out one of cigars.

STEVEN. He's good. He just think you could have let him slide. He feels like you embarrassed him in front of his friends. But anyway, are you enjoying yourself?

CARLEENA. Yes, I am. I have never been out on a luxurious yacht like this before, and the drinks and food top it off for me. You guys do this often?

Steven lights up his cigar and takes a big pull and looks at Carleena with a you-haven't-seen-nothing-yet look on his face.

STEVEN. Only once or twice a year. It's our way of giving back a little to our close friends and family.

Carleena gives a very impressed look on her face and nods her head as she looks around the yacht. She takes a sip of her drink and looks back at Steven.

CARLEENA. This will be the best location for your next opening. AC is on its way back up. It's gonna be the premier spot in Jersey like it was years ago.

Steven nods his head in agreement as he takes another pull from his cigar. He finishes off his drink and motions for the waitress to bring him a refill.

STEVEN. We're already on it. It's already in motion. It's gonna take a little while. Some grease on a few wheels to make it start rolling faster.

Carleena shakes her head and calls her girlfriends over for Steven. He smiles like a kid just given a bowl of ice cream. He introduces himself and calls over to Darren. Darren happily makes his way over.

Scene ten. Evelyn and Natalie are talking on the side of the yacht. They are sharing laughs and enjoying themselves. Evelyn notices her sister talking to Haseem a little too friendly to her taste and gives a sharp look at them talk. Natalie, who is very observant to everything going on around her, peeps at what Evelyn is looking at and peeps at her expression also.

NATALIE. Are you ready to get started over at the firm? I know Mohan is very excited about you taking the position.
EVELYN. Yes, I am. I am very excited and looking forward to making real power moves for the firm. There is a lot of room to grow in certain industries like yours actually.

Evelyn directs her attention over at Natalie and gives her an eye-raising look. Natalie's facial expression is wondering and a bit amazed at how Evelyn is taking her position so seriously.

EVELYN. I was talking to Mohan about expanding into the medical world more in the near future. The numbers show positive gain, and it's a growing industry that will rise every year. Plus, having you around and being part of the family is a major advantage. You can help lead the way for us.

Natalie is in deep thought, thinking on what Evelyn just said to her. She looks down, contemplating what was said. She takes a sip of her champagne and nods her head, looking back at Evelyn.

NATALIE. I have been actually trying to talk Mohan into investing into a few medical care centers. You're exactly right there, huge profits in the medical industry. He is my brother, and sometimes you have to literally drill numbers and stats in his head for him to agree. But keep working on him. He is all about growing the firm to worth billions one day, so he will listen to you.

Evelyn and Natalie look around the yacht at everyone dancing to the music. They are sipping on their champagne when Carleena walks over to them and works her way into their conversation.

CARLEENA. I haven't really gotten time to talk to you, Evelyn, but I want to congratulate you on taking the position. I hope one day soon we can get together and go over ideas and business plans.

Evelyn notices that Haseem is finally by himself for a moment and is ready to go over to talk to him. She looks at Carleena and nods her head in agreement with Carleena.

EVELYN. I definitely agree with you on that. We have to get together and talk about making business moves together. Steven was right about bringing you on board. His fun time can interrupt things occasionally.

All three ladies look over at Steven and Darren dancing with Carleena's friends and laugh at him. They just shake their heads and take a sip of their drink while Evelyn starts to make her way over to where Haseem is at.

Scene eleven. Haseem is messing with his phone in a quiet area of the yacht, away from everyone so he can enjoy some quiet time for a few. Evelyn quietly approaches him from his blind side and taps him on the shoulder and dips the other direction, like she's playing peekaboo with him.

EVELYN. Taking in some quiet time, I see.
HASEEM. Yeah, a little. You know how I am. What's up with you? Are you enjoying the day out with us?
EVELYN. Yes, I am. This is really a nice way to spend your afternoon for sure.

Both of them grin at each other and look away at the ocean. They both look like they are searching for words.

HASEEM. You know, Evelyn, I just want you know how glad I am that you're with us now, but just so we're clear on things, I expect professionalism at all times from you.
EVELYN. Professionalism? Hmm, can you elaborate on what you mean? (*Evelyn takes a second pause as she puts her hand on her voluptuous waistline.*) Mr. Bossman?

Haseem plays off her smart comment with a slight grin as he looks at the ocean and then glances back at her.

HASEEM. Cut the shit, Evelyn. You know what I mean. We have to coexist on a serious business level, and I know you will do that. Trust me, I believe in that. But there will be a lot of eyes on us every time we around each other, and people will speculate and stir up things. That's all I'm saying, Evelyn.

Haseem takes a pause for a few seconds while Evelyn takes in what Haseem is saying to her. She nods her head in agreement.

EVELYN. I get what you're saying. I know your fiancée is gonna be a little uncomfortable with me, I get it.

Haseem twists his head and nods in agreement with her as they both take a sip of their drink. Haseem pulls out his cigar and lights it. Evelyn is looking around at the view of the ocean.

HASEEM. We are going to do amazing things together. We're gonna make history at this firm one day, and you're gonna lead the way for us.

EVELYN. I do truly believe that, and I am going to do everything I can to make that a reality. And I will make sure that everything I do remains respectful to you and your future wife.

Both of them smile at each other and starts to walk toward the lower level.

HASEEM. I'm 'bout to get something to eat. You good?
EVELYN. Yeah, I'm good, thanks.

Scene twelve. Aerial shots of the yacht with music playing, different shots of people socializing, dancing, eating, and drinking; everyone is having a great time. Mohan, Peter, Haseem, and Steven are dancing with different women. Evelyn and her girls are dancing close to Haseem and Peter. Evelyn gives Haseem a little twist of her hips as the two step toward each other for a quick little dance. Natalie is busy taking pictures of everybody and laughing at Mohan dancing so stiff. She records him looking clumsy on the dance floor. The scene shifts to the guys getting together for a few minutes. Peter motions over to the waitress for a refill of their glasses.

PETER. Let's have a toast, fellas, to a great year so far and an even bigger year on the way!
STEVEN. Hell yeah! In only a few years, we built a monster, and it's freaking growing crazy!
MOHAN. We're just getting started. It's only gonna get better.

STEVEN. Hey, y'all, we should go to Vegas and really celebrate this crazy year we're having. We accomplished a lot this year—big deals secured, big contracts locked down. Let's go out to Vegas and enjoy our hard work!

HASEEM. He got a point. This has been an amazing year for us. I'm down for a quick getaway!

Mohan and Peter nod their heads in agreement, and all four guys hold their champagne glasses high in the air. Music is playing in the background as the episode starts to end. Ne-Yo's song "Lets Toast It Up" is playing.

Episode 9

Scene one. Music is playing as the scene opens with Jamal and Haseem riding in Haseem's car. They are tired, and Jamal is looking out the window, nodding his head to the music. Meek Mills is playing, and both are in a relaxed mood. Haseem is looking at his phone as a text comes in from Nadia. He looks confused as he reads the text and looks at Jamal, then looks back at the road.

HASEEM. Here she goes with this bullshit. I already know what she wants to talk about, why she couldn't come with me today.

Jamal looks at Haseem with a grin on his face and shakes his head while he's still looking out the window.

JAMAL. Man, you know she's gonna be on some possessive shit now that you put the rock on her finger. Shit, that Corvette ain't helping either. I still think you went too far with that one. She knows chicks is on you hard, and as beautiful as she is, she's feeling the pressure of being with a rich man.

HASEEM. Yeah, well, she knows where my heart at and where I lay my head at every night. I ain't you where your ladies are worried and not sure where you at or, hell, if you're ever gonna call them again.

Haseem starts laughing as he looks at Jamal with a big grin on his face. He notices that Jamal ain't smiling or nothing; his face is stone-cold, and he's still staring out the window.

JAMAL. Yo, you think I got a real shot at Maracella? I mean, what do you think of her, like you read the same signs I see about her?

Haseem looks at Jamal with one eye raised. He has a confused look on his face as he looks back and forth at the road and Jamal.

HASEEM. She seems chill. I don't know much about her. I haven't really zoned in on her like that. I know that fatty-looking real soft and bubbly.

JAMAL. Yeah, that ass will definitely reel you in for sure, but let me ask you on some other shit. Is Mohan 'bout his pipe game?

Haseem looks at Jamal with a big frown on his face, like he's surprised Jamal asked a stupid question like that. He shrugs his head and pays his attention back to the road.

JAMAL. Nah, real talk, like I know he haven't banged hardly any chicks in life, and he probably choked his chicken most of his college days, but I'm saying, you know, does he pick up on flirting quick or is he stiff on his toes?

Haseem smiles as he doesn't take his eyes off the road. He looks at Jamal and starts laughing even louder.

HASEEM. Mohan and Peter is so focused on building the firm and locking down million-dollar contracts. A girl would have to strip naked and actually put their face in it before they realize they're being seduced, especially Peter. He wouldn't even take the time to call back. They're both focused on getting that paper. What you trying to get at?

JAMAL. Nothing, nothing. I just think Maracella was trying to make me a little jealous earlier. She's trying to mess with my head.

HASEEM. Hey, don't let me find out this chick got your nose wide-open, and you haven't even got to sniff, lick, finger nothing yet.

Jamal looks at Haseem like he's stupid for even saying that. He gives him a frown and looks at his phone. As he texts someone, he looks back at Haseem.

JAMAL. Come on, bro. You know how I move, but I will keep it one hundred with you. She's intriguing to me. I mean, she got that classy lady swag. She's intelligent as hell and got that getting money mentality. She's wifey material, my dude, and I got to scoop that up before somebody else does.

HASEEM. Well, if this ain't some shit, you playing with me, right?

Jamal looks at Haseem with a serious look on his face. He isn't smiling or even grinning. Haseem looks at him with a smirk on his face and shakes his head.

JAMAL. Yo, man, I ain't trying to be messing with thots all my life, bro. I mean, what you don't think I wanna find my queen one day?

Haseem notices that Jamal is for real and stops making jokes and gets serious. He starts to say something but pauses before he speaks; his eyebrows are raised as he looks at his boy and glances back at the road.

HASEEM. I see what you're saying. Trust me, bro. Just go at her the usual way you do your thing. You said she was googly-eyed when you took her to see the play on Broadway. I bet she's feeling you, but she's gonna make you work a little. You don't think she hasn't heard about how you get down out here? You got to figure she gonna try to protect her heart. Just keep doing what you do, but just understand with a chick like her, you gonna have to keep spending that bread.

Haseem looks at Jamal with a serious look on his face. Jamal looks back at him with a serious look also. He pokes out his lip and nods his head as he looks back out the window. Haseem looks back at the road and changes the music that they were listening to as the scene ends.

Scene two. Darren and Steven are walking through the casino, a little tipsy from drinking on the boat ride. They decide to stick around and sober up before they make the drive back home. They are checking out the casino floor and wondering what they should play. Carleena and her girlfriends are also hanging around the casino floor area also.

DARREN. I think I'm gonna try my luck on some blackjack. I used to run y'all pockets back in the day. I think I still got some sauce left.

STEVEN. Yeah, like you said back in the day, it's a new day now, big cuz, and that's all we used to play in college. Come on, let's see what it is. A couple of stacks can turn into a big bag of cash for us.

Darren looks at Steven with a look of happiness. He agrees with Steven as they make their way over to the blackjack table. The dealer notices them and takes their bets. Meanwhile, Carleena and her girlfriends are being hit on by a few guys at the bar.

DARREN. Come on, let's get it. I feel it in the air tonight, cuz. I haven't been down here in AC in a while either. I smell big things popping tonight.

STEVEN. Hey, my man, I'm trying to concentrate over here. Hey, sexy, can you bring me another drink please? French vanilla Ciroc please.

Steven flirts with the waitress as she smiles at him and nods her head. Carleena is paying no attention to the handsome guy at the bar who is trying to spark conversation with her. She is paying close attention to Darren and Steven.

CARLEENA'S GIRLFRIEND. I see you're in work mode. Don't worry, he hasn't started arguing with anybody yet.

CARLEENA. It's called being observant and also loyal. Think what you want about him, but Steven and his friends are going places. They are 'bout that life and they're making power moves. You're damn right, I'm gonna watch his back, and if you were smart, you watch too. You might learn a few things.

CARLEENA'S GIRLFRIEND. Hmm, somebody on one tonight, I see. Anyway, what's up with his loudmouthed boasting-ass cousin?

Carleena shrugs off her girlfriend and looks at her and rolls her eyes as she looks at the TV screen at the bar and checks her phone.

CARLEENA. He's a loose cannon, always ready to fight or argue with anybody who checks him, flashy and doesn't mind spending his paper. His temper and his street life are something he hasn't learned to control yet. He's not the type to get serious with, but he will treat you out to some nice date nights. Like I said, he's flashy!

CARLEENA'S GIRLFRIEND. You know, I noticed since you started working with Steven, you been low-key. You haven't been hanging out and your whole personality has changed. What's been going on with you? You ain't catching feelings for your boss, are you?

Carleena smiles and shakes her head as she looks at Steven and Darren celebrating over at the blackjack table. She also notices the two guys, who are trying to get her and her girlfriends' attention, are staring at Steven and Darren also.

CARLEENA. It's nothing like that at all, girl. You should know better than that. Do I come off as a chick that's trying to fuck her way to the top? I was raised and taught better than that, boo. Steven is driven. He is focused on accumulating wealth. He is motivated and inspired by his parents, and he is determined to stick to the script that he and his colleagues took an oath to.

Carleena sips on her drink and stands up out of chair and dances a little to the music playing. Her girlfriends start to join her as they all start to dance. Meanwhile, the two guys continue to watch the girls and also Darren and Steven.

Scene three. Haseem and Jamal are still riding home from AC, and they look very tired. Jamal is texting to make sure Maracella made it home. She texts him back and tells him she enjoyed hanging with him and his friends today. Haseem glances over at Jamal and grins to himself. He turns the music down a little.

HASEEM. Ahh, look at the little lovebird making sure his boo made it home safe. Yeah, she got you hooked, but hey, she might be wifey material. You never know.

JAMAL. On the real, bro, I'd been thinking more and more about what we talked about, and I hope you're on board with me.

HASEEM. What are you talking about? We talk about a whole lot of stuff.

JAMAL. You helping me go legit and help me start my own business, remember?

HASEEM. Oh yeah, no doubt, I'd been thinking about it a little. The first thing we got to do is get you on the books and make sure you're off the radar, and the only way to do that is for you to clean up your image and stop hanging out in the streets. Image and lifestyle are important for you and me if we gonna do this.

Jamal stares at Haseem with a confused look but nods his head in belief to what Haseem is saying.

JAMAL. I agree with you 100 percent and I'm ready to do that ASAP. You lead the way. You tell me what to do, and trust and believe I will follow you, bro. What's the first step?

HASEEM. First thing first. I'm gonna set you up with a job working with me, manager or assistant of something. Anyway, you start working and start earning clean money so that way when you do open up your business, no one can say nothing.

JAMAL. Working? Me working? You know I don't know about working. I never had a job before. I ain't built for cleaning toilets or being a little pea on.

Haseem shakes his head and laughs at Jamal. He looks at him like he's crazy or something. Jamal is looking back at him, wondering what is so funny.

HASEEM. Come on, man, do you really think that I would do you like that? We boys, man, we grew up together, and you always had my back out there in the streets. I would never play you like that. Basically, you be working with management and doing small technical stuff, no blood, sweat, and tears, white-collared office work, easy shit. Maybe fetching us coffee in the morning, picking up pizza for lunch, stuff like that.

JAMAL. Oh, you mean like intern work?

HASEEM. Yeah, something like that. But you won't be getting paid like an intern. Hell, they work for free most of the time.

Haseem looks at Jamal and gives him an evil grin. Jamal is smiling back at Haseem.

JAMAL. I'm with that, Hass. I'm definitely feeling that, my man. Now what kind of pay are we talking, and do you think I can get an advance on my pay? I got something I need to really do.

HASEEM. Yeah, I don't see why not. I can work that out for you.

JAMAL. Yo, I really appreciate this. I mean, I always knew you had my back, and I always knew you were a real cat. This really means a lot to me, and, Hass, I won't let you down. I promise you, bro, I got you. I know you worked hard to build your company.

Haseem and Jamal shake hands and give each other a heartwarming look. They stare each other, and happiness is on both of their faces.

Scene four. Steven is meditating over his next move at the blackjack table; his eyes are fixed on the dealer, and his cards in his hand. Carleena is standing behind him with a wondering look on her face. The dealer is looking like he is running out of patience, waiting on Steven to make his next move. Steven starts to grin with a confident look on his face.

STEVEN. Let's get it. Hit me! I got this. I ain't backing down. Scared money don't make money!

The dealer deals Steven his card and looks at him. Steven looks at the card and pumps his fist in the air. Carleena notices that her boss is happy and excited as she walks up to him. Steven looks at her and starts to nod his head.

STEVEN. I'm that dude when it comes to blackjack, I always come up no matter how bad it may look for me.

CARLEENA. I see you over here handling your business, you getting yours.

STEVEN. I can't stop now. I'm up and playing on house money. I got to keep it rolling a little bit longer.

CARLEENA. It's getting late, and me and my girls are about to head back. Plus, I don't like the vibe I'm getting from a few guys in here.

STEVEN. What few guys? Who fucking with you? Somebody said something to you?

CARLEENA. Steven, let's just go. It's been a fun day, and we enjoyed ourselves. But it's getting late and it's back to business in the morning, and the atmosphere in here is weird. I kinda feel like eyes are on us a little too much.

Steven looks at Carleena as he grabs his drink. He looks around the casino to see if he notices any strange-looking guys who might be looking in his direction. He spots Darren and sees that his cousin is having a good time at the crap table with Carleena's friends. He looks back at Carleena as he puts his drink down.

STEVEN. It is getting a little late, and I got a few meetings tomorrow. You make sense and you're right. We should go.

CARLEENA. There will be plenty of times in the future where we can splurge and enjoy ourselves down here. AC is gonna be our playground in the near future. You know what the plan is.

STEVEN. Indeed I do. There is a lot of money to make down here. Let's go get your buddy Darren and let's roll out. I'm starting to like having you around me. You make sure my vision is clear and dead-on.

Carleena smiles as she looks at her boss Steven. The two of them walk off in the direction of Darren and Carleena's friends.

Scene five. Darren and Carleena friends are sharing jokes with one another as Darren is in a happy mood after he won a little extra cash at the crap table. Meanwhile, the two men who've been watching Darren and Steven throughout the night stare even closer as Steven and Carleena make their way over toward them.

DEA AGENT 1. Seems like my little pill pusher is having a pretty good night, winning at the crap table and enjoying himself with some nice-looking ladies. This is the second time I noticed this new face hanging with him. You know anything about him?

DEA AGENT 2. Nah, I'd never seen him before with him, but then again, I don't waste my time chasing petty nickel and dime dealers either. Why you wasting your time with this kid? Jersey got so many big fish to fry, all kind of big-time criminals, and you focusing on him.

DEA AGENT 1. I never liked this loudmouthed silly asshole ever since I'd seen him knock this older man out years ago on the boardwalk down in Asbury. I'd been having a hard-on for him.

Both DEA agents look at each other with a stern look on their faces as they glance back at Darren.

DEA AGENT 2. I mean, I hear you, and I can understand those feelings you have, but I mean, with Jersey being the kind of state it is, with major kingpins and organized crime figures moving around, you would be doing yourself a little disservice worrying about this little punk. You can score a big promotion if you tackle a fat cat. But hey, do what you feel, but I think you're getting a little too personal to me.

DEA AGENT 1. Nah, see, that's where your wrong. I think this guy is affiliated with some major figures, like his bigheaded friend. I'd seen him around, driving some big-time vehicles and hanging with a few other guys who look like fresh money. I'm just trying to connect the dots here with Mr. Darren. If he's friends with these guys, then something's gotta be up.

DEA AGENT 2. Where there is smoke, there is fire most of the time.

DEA AGENT 1. Exactly my point, exactly my point. I'm gonna focus my lens a little closer on Mr. Darren.

Both agents look at each other as they smile. Darren cuts his eye toward them as he walks past them. Carleena also gives them a funny facial expression as they all make their way toward the casino exits.

CARLEENA. Steven, I'm driving your car. You'd been drinking hard all day, and you don't need to take any risks. Darren, my friends will make sure you get to wherever you decide to lay your head at.

DARREN. Hey, don't worry about where I'm gonna lay my head unless you want me to lay my head on you.

CARLEENA. Just get in the car and stop your slick talk because it doesn't work with me. You should know that by now.

DARREN. Me and Steven don't need you or your girls to drive us home. We got this and know what we're doing, boss lady. Who you think you are? You're a worker, not a freaking bodyguard.

STEVEN. She makes sense, cuz. We'd been getting trashed all day, and we're getting older and wiser. We do have to stop taking risks all the time.

Darren looks at his little cousin and has a mean smirk on his face, then he looks at Carleena and his facial expression gets angry. He waves his hand at Carleena and gets in the car. Carleena stares back at him with a serious face and tells her girlfriends to drive slow and stay close to her.

Scene six. Nadia is up, sitting in her bed, when she hears Haseem come in the house. She is looking at her phone with a mean look on her face. Haseem walks into the bedroom, looking surprised to see Nadia still up this late. He walks over to his dresser and puts his keys down.

HASEEM. Surprised you still up. You feeling aight, baby?
NADIA. Yeah, I'm feeling okay. I'm not sick physically, but I'm getting sick of your bullshit for sure!
HASEEM. What bullshit? What are you talking about?
NADIA. What I'm talking about? What I'm talking about? Oh, you really have no clue why I'm up waiting on you to come home.

Haseem looks at Nadia with a very confused look on his face. He starts to walk to his closet as he is starting to get undressed. Nadia is staring at him with an angry look on her face. She watches him as he walks around their bedroom.

HASEEM. No, I don't know why you're up this late. Can you enlighten me? I mean, you're looking at me kinda crazy. What's wrong with you?

Nadia gets up off the bed with her phone in her hand. She walks fast over to Haseem as he is near his closet, looking at her like she has two heads or something.

NADIA. Let me ask you something. Wasn't this boat trip or fishing trip, whatever the heck, was supposed to be the guys' day? "Out hanging out with my boys" day?
HASEEM. Yeah, and it was. What are you trying to say, Nadia?
NADIA. Then why the hell all I see are a bunch of skanks with their ass out sipping champagne looking real thirsty? If women were allowed to come, why didn't you invite me along?

Nadia shows Haseem her phone and the pictures from their day out on the yacht. Haseem shakes his head with a slight smirk on his face. He shakes his head and starts to take off his shoes.

HASEEM. Those are Carleena and Evelyn's friends, that's all, and for the record, I had no idea that they were coming. I damn sure didn't invite them. But Mohan and Steven figured since they kind of affiliated or associated with the firm, it was okay for them to come, no big deal.

NADIA. No big deal? You know how this looks to people who see these freaking loose chicks half dressed, hanging with you and them. It looks like a big party, a rap video. I thought I talked to you before about this Haseem.

HASEEM. Baby, you're making this more than what it is. I understand where you coming from, but it wasn't like that. I already talked to Peter about it, and he knows I was right. He didn't know they were inviting their friends either.

Nadia shakes her head as she twists her mouth up with an upset look on her face. She walks away from Haseem and then turns back around and walks toward him. Haseem starts to walk to the kitchen, and Nadia follows him.

NADIA. You just don't get it. Let me explain this a little clearer for you since you're having a hard time getting it.

HASEEM. Who sent them pictures anyway?

NADIA. Natalie posted them. Yeah, see, that's the issue. You didn't think I would see them. I'm glad she posted them. Now I see why you didn't want me to come today. You're starting to act like real suspect, and if you think this the type of stuff you gonna be doing and I'm gonna be okay with it, then you got the wrong girl 'cause I will be damn if I let you play me out like a groupie wife.

HASEEM. Look, Nadia, you're freaking out. You're making something out of nothing. First of all, I talked to you about this before. There are gonna be times that Steven, Jamal, Peter, or Mohan are gonna have women around. They aren't getting married, so you can't expect them to be innocent saints or angels. They have a right to live their lives. They're single.

Haseem grabs some juice out the refrigerator and looks at Nadia with a curious look on his face. He starts to sip his juice and walks over to the stove and grabs a plate out the cabinet to fix him some food. Nadia is furious and stares at Haseem.

HASEEM. You're gonna have to slow your roll a little. You're acting like you're trying to control me or something. I told you that you're gonna have to trust me, and how many times have I told you all I'm focused on is getting this paper and building my company and other business investments?

NADIA. No, you're gonna have to be a little more considerate to me as your fiancée and be respectful to me. You're gonna have to watch how you move and watch your code of conduct. If you really cared about me, you would have called me right away to let me know what was going on. But you didn't think about that, did you? You didn't think I would find out. I don't like sneaky people.

Nadia starts to point at Haseem as she walks toward him. Haseem is looking shocked by how angry she is.

NADIA. I'm not gonna allow you to think that this is okay. I am your fiancée, and I expect better from you, Haseem.

HASEEM. You're on one for real. Listen, baby, let's calm down and get some rest. Come on, let's go to bed.

Haseem tries to grab Nadia by the waist, and she knocks his hand down. She looks at him with an angry look on her face. She backs up from him and shakes her head as Haseem looks a little confused. She turns away from Haseem and walks out the kitchen. Haseem takes a deep breath and puts his hand on his forehead.

Scene seven. Peter is on his laptop in his office, typing something, when he cuts his eye toward his office window. He notices Felize walking toward his office and he is staring at Peter. Peter pays him no mind and continues typing on his laptop.

FELIZE. Well, it's good to see you hard at work today, Peter. I mean, with all the drinking and partying you did yesterday, I figured you would be recovering all day in bed.

PETER. I can see you're still having trouble recognizing how I move. You still haven't figured out how dedicated my drive is.

FELIZE. Yeah, I figured it out all right. I also see how I'm looked at around here and how, no matter if I think our relationship is getting stronger, at the end of the day, it's not growing like it should.

PETER. What the heck are you talking about? What are you trying to say, Felize? I mean, you know how we all feel about you, especially me.

FELIZE. You're smart, Peter, very intelligent. You should know what I'm getting at, but I will make things crystal clear for you because I know you had a long day yesterday. Why wasn't I invited to the boat trip? Everybody was there except me.

PETER. Bro, I totally forgot to tell you about it. I wasn't even onboard, and it came around so fast that I kinda forgot about it. I'd been so busy trying to structure these new deals and manage everything going on here at the firm that I forgot to tell you about it, bro. It was last minute, and I completely forgot to tell you.

Felize looks at Peter with an understanding look on his face. He walks around the office and looks out the glass window in Peter's office and notices Evelyn walking to the printer to retrieve some papers. He looks back at Peter and walks toward his desk and takes a seat.

FELIZE. You know, Peter, I do know how you can get caught up in your work. I know how focused you are on expanding and growing, but how the hell did—what's her name?—and Natalie and all these other chicks get invited and not me? I mean, I don't know, man. Sometimes I feel like all we are are business partners.

PETER. Felize, come on now. You know how all of us are thankful and grateful to have you down with us. We wouldn't be where we are right now if it wasn't for you. You played a significant role in building this firm into what it is. Don't feel like that. I simply forgot to tell you about it. Everything's been happening so fast lately.

FELIZE. I mean, I'm looking at the pictures Natalie posted and seeing all the ladies and the yacht, man, I would have loved being there, chilling with you guys. We're like family, man. I knew you guys for a while now, and I don't get close to many people. You know that.

PETER. Yeah, I know how you are, and that's one of the things I admire about you. You keep your circle tight and don't let new people enter. I promise, man, the next time I hear about us having something a function or whatever, I will definitely reach out to you about it.

FELIZE. I believe you. I know how you value our friendship, but on another note, what's going on with the restaurant down the shore? I'm hearing a few things.

PETER. Nah, nothing too serious. Building permits. Steven's father, our construction guy, has been having a few scheduling issues. Nothing too major. We're pretty much dead-on with our grand opening date. It shouldn't delay anything.

FELIZE. Did Mohan get all the details on the contract right with that real estate mogul? Last time I talked to him about it, he said he might need some help.

PETER. He told me last week everything checked out. You know how Mohan is. He will stay up for three days straight to figure things out if he have to.

Both men laugh at Peter's comment as Felize leans back in his chair with a smile on his face.

PETER. If Mohan asks me for help or needs me to help him, then I know he's really stuck and doesn't understand it. He's the kind of guy that will keep looking till he finds his answer. That's why I don't worry about him.

FELIZE. True, true, that's him, so you didn't get close to any of the ladies down there in AC. Heck, there was quite a few to choose from that's for sure.

PETER. I'd seen a few. I wouldn't mind getting to know a little better, but you know they ain't going nowhere. As long as you're accomplishing things, building on your success, they're gonna always be around, looking for some fun.

Both men nod their heads in agreement and look at each other with a smirk on their face.

Scene eight. Mohan pulls up to the gym to get his workout on when he notices his sister Natalie's car is there also. He looks a little shocked as he raises his eyebrows and walks toward the door to enter the gym. He enters and notices his sister going hard on her squats and walks toward her, trying to catch her off guard. Natalie is looking in the mirror at the gym and sees her brother approaching her. She waits till he gets close enough, and she gives him a shot to the chest. Mohan quickly defends himself and tries to block the punch.

MOHAN. I don't care how many squats you do or weights you lift. You're never gonna be fast enough to catch me off guard.

NATALIE. Believe me, I held back on you. I didn't want to strike too fast and cave that little bird chest in. I'm surprised to see you here. You must either be bored or, let me guess, you're meeting a business client here or something?

MOHAN. For your information, Miss Know-It-All, I still find time to get my lift on during the week. Most of the time, it's later in the night, but I get it in at least three days a week. It's good I ran into you because I was gonna call you later on. I got a call from Haseem, and he wasn't too happy about you posting pictures from the boat trip.

Natalie wipes her forehead and starts to grin a little as she does a little stretching in between reps. Mohan gives her that look as if he knows what his little sister is up to. Natalie smiles even more as she notices Mohan is staring at her.

NATALIE. So I posted a few pictures, what's the problem?

MOHAN. The problem is you know how we all feel about our faces blasted all over the internet. We don't need that, don't like that, and definitely not trying to broadcast our lifestyles for people to see. I think you caused Haseem some problems at home. He's not too happy with you.

NATALIE. Yeah, well, he will be aight. It's not my fault Nadia's insecure or overjealous. We were having a good time, and I was a little saucy and snapped a few pictures.

MOHAN. Listen, Natalie, I know you and you're very strategic on what you do. You up to something? You posted them pictures for a reason, I believe. I really don't care what you're up to or whatever, but you have to understand none of us want our pictures out there. We are totally against that.

NATALIE. All right, all right, I understand. I won't post any more pictures. I know how you and your friends feel about that. I know y'all like to move and float off the radar. I'm sorry, my bad.

MOHAN. You're damn right. It's your bad. You'd been warned, little sis. Don't let it happen again, or next time they will be consequences.

Mohan gives his sister a stern but playful look as he grabs a few dumbbells and brings them over to where he and Natalie are standing. Natalie looks down at the floor and glances out the window for a few seconds. She knows Mohan is serious, and he means business. She has big respect for Mohan and will not back talk him.

NATALIE. So I saw you engaging in quite a few conversations with some ladies on the boat trip. You and Maracella seemed to be getting to know each other a little better.

MOHAN. Do I look that savage? When have you ever known me to try to bang out one of your friends? I got too much respect for you, and besides, I would never subject you to that. I mean, Maracella, she's cool, but I don't look at her like that. I watched her grow up. She's almost like a little sister to me.

NATALIE. You're such a gentleman, sometimes too nice and classy, but you move around with elegance. I definitely give you that.

MOHAN. You know all I'm focused on is stacking this paper. Expanding and networking my company is all I'm focused on. You know me.

NATALIE. True, I know how you are. Nothing comes before the business or the firm. I know and I respect it.

MOHAN. Besides, it wouldn't be fair to you to have to listen to all the whining and complaining, all the crying and begging your friends would be doing if I put it on them.

Mohan starts to pump his hips in the air, smiling and laughing as he moves his hips around like he's an exotic dancer or something. Natalie starts laughing at him and hits him with her towel as she starts to walk away from him. Mohan follows her laughing.

Scene nine. Steven pulls up to his sports bar and notices his phone is ringing. He looks at it with a confused look on his face as if he's trying to figure out who is calling him. He steps out his car, looking nice, dressed to impress, and decides to answer the phone to see who it is calling him.

STEVEN. Hello, who is this?

PERSON ON THE OTHER END OF THE PHONE. Very classy way to answer the phone, Mr. Bossman.

STEVEN. Lovely voice. Unfortunately, I don't recognize it. Who is this?

PERSON ON THE OTHER END OF THE PHONE. I don't even know why I called. It's been over a month and you never reached out to me. I don't believe in chasing no man. Sorry I—

STEVEN. Hold up, hold up. I just can't catch the voice. Whoever this is, we never talked on the phone before, and I definitely don't want to disrespect and call you another name, then I'm really screwed. So I think I know who this might be. Give me a little clue.

PERSON ON THE OTHER END OF THE PHONE. (*Laughing and giggling.*) It's Bennie Blanco from the Bronx. It's me, BX.

STEVEN. Oh, okay, what's up, Bx! Tara Yellow Dress, little sunshine? What's good with you? About time you called and checked for me.

TARA. Called and checked for you? Hmm, I figured I would be the one getting checked on. I thought there was a little chemistry that night, but I guess I'm just one of the many you meet, huh, Mr. Bossman?

STEVEN. Let me be the real man and apologize for not getting at you. Shit, been a little hectic for me lately. My construction business and trying to open up another sports bar and other stuff had my schedule tied up. It definitely wasn't intentional or nothing.

TARA. I guess I'm gonna have to believe that. You seem like you're on your grind and 'bout your business, so I guess I understand. I mean you could have texted or something. Come on now.

Steven walks around in his parking lot of his sports bar and glances inside to see what's going on. He is in mack mode and starts to grin and gives a confident strut as he leans on his car.

STEVEN. Nah, that's real talk. You're right about that, but hey, look at it like this. You called because it was something about me that you're feeling. I know what I'm feeling when it comes to you. I hate that I never got at you the first time I saw you. You're so sexy and keep your body together. I can tell you work out.

TARA. Yeah, I try to keep it toned, but eating out and rice and beans are my weaknesses.

Both of them share laughs as they talk on the phone. Steven looks around the area and smiles a bit. He seems happy that she called. Tara is on her laptop at home and listening closely to what Steven is saying over the phone.

STEVEN. When can I see you? I got to redeem myself for dipping out on you like that, especially after the good conversation we had that night. You're interesting, and I wanna learn and see more. Can you make that happen?

TARA. Hmm, I guess I could, but you're gonna have to make up for lost time and everything. I don't like feeling neglected, boss man.

STEVEN. No problem. I can definitely make it up to you. How's your schedule look? I'm usually free after six o'clock. We can meet up somewhere anywhere.

TARA. Okay, we can do that. Matter of fact, the Yankees play Friday night. Since we're both big fans, let's make it happen.

STEVEN. Now you're talking my language. It's on definitely. I will talk to you before then. Bye, sunshine.

TARA. Bye, boss man!

Steven hangs up the phone and smiles to himself as he starts to walk toward the door of his sports bar. He enters the sports bar and the scene ends.

Scene ten. Jamal is talking with a group of friends outside of his recording studio that he owns in Newark. He is in his own world, counting some money, when his phone goes off. He looks at it and sees that it's Maracella. He smiles and answers his phone. Maracella is riding in her car in a good mood, near Jamal.

JAMAL. Okay now. Glad to hear from you and good to see that you're thinking about me early in the day.

MARACELLA. I wouldn't say all that, Mr. Ego, but you know I was in the area, and I decided to see what's up. You got time for a little convo, or you tied up in something, literally speaking that is?

JAMAL. What kind of question is that? Never too busy for you. Come through, I'm at my studio.

MARACELLA. I'm already looking at you, looking all suspicious, to your left.

Jamal sees her and walks over to her car. Maracella is in her Mercedes-Benz 5 series, staring at Jamal as he gets in. Jamal gets in and gives her a big hug, and she hugs him right back.

JAMAL. Man, wasn't expecting this. How you doing, sweetness?

MARACELLA. I'm good, but why you making it sound like I never came to see you? Stop that. What you doing?

JAMAL. Nothing really, just came by to pick up my bag. Haven't been over here too long, twenty to twenty-five minutes.

MARACELLA. I really enjoyed myself down in AC. It was good beating you in pool and getting under your skin, talking to Mohan. Got that on you. (*She starts laughing.*)

JAMAL. Yeah, I'm glad. That's real funny to you. Yeah, okay! Whatever, whatever, so let's cut to the chase, lovely. Look, things are doing real good right about now. No worries really. Let's get away for a few days. Can you take some time off work?

MARACELLA. Yeah, I got some time to burn. Where you wanna go?

JAMAL. Let's go to Vegas. You said you've never been, plus your girl's gonna be in concert out there too. See what I'm saying? Perfect for us.

Maracella looks at Jamal like he just said the right thing, like he found the right key to her heart. Jamal is feeling the eyes and reaches out for a kiss, and she meets him halfway. They pull away from each other, staring at each other.

MARACELLA. Come over tonight. I wanna do something for you. I'm gonna cook tonight. Stop by before nine. Some of us got to go to work tomorrow.

JAMAL. Hey, I'm up early too. I'm up and moving by twelve every day.

Jamal starts grinning, and Marcella is laughing hard at Jamal. She nudges his shoulder and is still laughing. Jamal looks at her like what he said wrong. Twelve is early for Jamal's world. He leans back in the car and looks to the right and sees some people hanging out in front of his studio. He rolls the window down.

JAMAL. Yo, yo, not in front of the studio too long. I don't want that. Take that shit inside.

MARACELLA. (*Looks at Jamal with a little princess expression. She has that look like she is surprised but also loving his flare-up. Jamal rolls up the window and looks back at Maracella with a smile on his face.*) Very interesting how you can turn up and down to romantic real quick. Very important to me. Shows leadership too.

JAMAL. Yo, I could sit here and listen to your sexy intelligent, curvaceous body all day, putting that look on me. Dangerous!

MARACELLA. Very dangerous but, sweetheart, at the same time, though, funny 'cause that's exactly what I see in you.

JAMAL. We're gonna leave in two weeks on a Friday, so put your time in soon. Looking forward to spending time with you. We're gonna have a ball yo. I'm in a very good place mentally. Future's looking good.

MARACELLA. Listen, you get three nights, that's it. You do right, then maybe a full week next time. Maybe!

Both of them start laughing very lightly. Jamal stops real fast and looks at Maracella with that "Enough!" facial expression. She notices it and nudges his shoulder again, then looks away at her phone. She glances at it and puts it down and looks back at Jamal and gives him a serious look on her face.

MARACELLA. Listen, don't be on that bull, Jamal. I'm telling you now. I don't deal with all that and wasn't raised around all that. I respect what you do and how you move and all. I don't want no crazy exes or baby mama talking slick to me. I ain't got time for that. (*Maracella mimics the song.*) I ain't got time for that!

JAMAL. Yo, you shot out, but I like it, though, funny and sexy. You know, when you're with me, you're protected and safe. I won't let nothing happen to you. Nothing's gonna happen except trips and more trips. I love weekend getaways.

MARACELLA. I hear you, playboy, but like I told you before, Jamal, I'm into cooking, movies at home, chilling, and, of course my Broadway plays. In time, we'll make it happen. I'll let u know if you're about that life, if you can be dedicated and tied down or not. Sounds real good, but I got to see it to believe all that talk.

JAMAL. You're funny. Told you I talk it like I walk it. Just be ready when I say. You understand, little homey?

Jamal gives her a nudge back on her shoulder and a sexy, smiley, serious expression. Maracella just stares at Jamal for a few seconds and starts to smile.

MARACELLA. I'm gonna see you tonight 'cause I'm about to go get a few things from the store and go see my mother for a few.

JAMAL. I'll let you know for sure. If things don't get out of control around here, I'll hit you up.

Maracella looks at Jamal like she's hot and a little confused by what he just told her. Jamal knows he ticked her off and smiles as he gets out the car. He gets out and starts walking away and looks back after a few steps and blows her a kiss and a slight head nod. Scene ten ends.

Scene eleven. It's the weekly meeting for the firm, and as usual, they are chomping down on pancakes and omelets. Haseem and Steven are in their own conversation, and Mohan and Peter are talking about a few things.

PETER. Well, first thing first 'cause we're all on pressed time. Haseem, everything going good with the new contract, right, because I haven't notice the payment hit yet?

HASEEM. Yeah, maybe because I just got it yesterday. The deal is done, and I'm hiring a few new guys for the project. Extra help is needed for this.

MOHAN. That's understood. I got to do the same because I don't have the manpower either. We could go over prospects together, Haseem.

HASEEM. Aight, I'm with that. I actually hired my first guy the other day. Jamal starts in a few weeks.

Everybody gives Haseem a look, as if they're a little shocked by his choice. They continue eating and sipping on their juice and tea. Peter looks at Steven and Mohan and then looks back at Haseem.

PETER. You hired Jamal? I'm sorry. I just didn't remember Jamal having computer science or engineer skills. I didn't know.

Peter looks around and starts laughing, and Steven and Mohan start laughing and smiling too. Haseem, seeing that he is the butt of the joke once again, just shakes his head and smiles too. He is picking around his plate like he's full.

HASEEM. Yeah, whatever. You guys sleeping on Jamal. He is gonna be a tremendous asset to our team. I see a lot of potential there, plenty of upside!

STEVEN. Yeah, whole lot of potential. I think it's a good choice if you bring him on the team. Hey, everybody deserves chances and opportunity.

MOHAN. By the way, I got on Natalie about posting them pictures from the boat trip. She's not gonna do it again, don't worry.

HASEEM. Yeah, Nadia straight tripping on that one, but she will get over it.

PETER. You ain't seen nothing yet, I'm telling you. She's gonna be popping up on you as time gets closer to your wedding. They turn into detectives and shit.

STEVEN. Best thing to do is spend the least amount of time with her as it get closer. You're going be a stressed out, dude. I'm gonna be cracking up.

The waitress comes over and fills up their drinks and brings Steven more pancakes to the table.

MOHAN. Steven, did you get all the legal stuff done for the construction company you're starting?

STEVEN. Of course. Just waiting on a few more machines and equipment to be delivered. First job coming up in a few weeks. I already got enough people to start my first few jobs.

HASEEM. How did you do down there after we left? I know you gambled some money. You can't help yourself, blackjack tables and drinks, plus ladies around. Not a good mix for you. Darren was with you too. Probably broke day out there.

STEVEN. Nah, actually Carleena and her friends got me and Darren home safe, not too early. She looked out for us. She's a good hire so far.

Steven grabs his plate of pancakes; he stuffs a mouthful and looks at Haseem with a serious look on his face. Mohan and Peter are giggling to themselves, looking at Steven. Steven notices them grinning and turns to them and shakes his head.

STEVEN. Whatever. You guys still think that I'm living wild and loose. That's where you're all wrong. I am building and growing overall. Matter of fact, I even got a more serious date tonight with Sunshine Yellow Dress from that time at my sports bar. Remember she was with a few of her friends and they came over and chilled with us?

PETER. Yeah, she had a nice ass. She was cute as hell, Steve-o. You getting up with her later?

HASEEM. Yeah, she was official. I remember that dress was fitting them hips real nice.

MOHAN. Okay, so what's the plan? She gonna be with her friends later on, or you're on some dolo stuff tonight?

STEVEN. Yeah, tonight it's solo, fellas. I got to see what she's about and let her see that other side of me. You know what I'm saying.

Peter and Haseem look at each other and raise their eyebrows, then they look back at Steven with a funny look on their faces. Mohan is stealing some of Steven's pancakes while he is not looking.

STEVEN. You know what's ill about her, why I dig her? She called me after like a month. She got at me. I probably was never gonna call her either with all the stuff I got going on. I don't want or got time for no new chicks. I'm gonna see what she's about. Might be something you never know.

HASEEM. Hey, I was thinking we should take another little quick trip to celebrate this big year we're having. We accomplished a lot this year. Let's do Vegas or Miami or something. Something real fast because Nadia. I got a feeling she ain't gonna be too happy to hear I'm bouncing again.

Haseem starts to laugh, and Peter shakes his head and starts smiling hard at Haseem. Mohan is still stealing food from Steven because he is all into his phone, not looking. Peter looks at Mohan and Steven, somewhat in agreement to what Haseem said.

PETER. Yeah, I could use a quick getaway. That sounds like a plan, Haseem. I like that.

STEVEN. Just make sure you let our stepbrother Felize know so he can't say we didn't tell him. He's so sensitive.

All of them laugh as they look at each other and sip on their drinks. Scene ends.

Scene twelve. Nadia is in the living room in her sweatpants and sports bra. She is sipping on some wine, watching TV and talking on the phone. It's late night and Haseem isn't home yet, so she is up waiting on him in a relaxed chill mode.

NADIA'S FRIEND. So why did you tell him that? I mean, if he did all that, he must really be sorry about what he did. Girl, you better calm your sensitive tail down. You're gonna mess around and lose a good one. It's a cold winter ahead. Beds get real cold at night.

Nadia busts out laughing on the phone and responds to what her girlfriend said on the phone as she sips on her wine. She notices the headlights from Haseem's car pull up. Her face turns to a frown.

NADIA. Ah, let me call you tomorrow. Haseem just pulled up, and we got some unfinished business to attend to. Girl, whatever, my situation is different than yours.

Haseem enters his home, noticing the TV is on in the living room. He is a little shocked to see Nadia still up. As he enters into the room, he starts to smile and walks over to his fiancée and gives her a hug and kiss. Nadia sits there with her glass of wine, still looking at TV, acting like she doesn't see or feel Haseem's hug or kiss.

HASEEM. How was your day, baby?

Nadia sits there for a few seconds, staring at the TV. She puts her glass down and looks at Haseem.

NADIA. It was fine. Funny how you care all of a sudden how my day was. Guilt must be sinking in.

HASEEM. No, I just wanna make sure that you're okay and listen to anything you may want to talk about. What's going on with your life is very important to me.

NADIA. Hmm, what's going on in my life is important to you? I do believe that, Haseem. I know you love and care about me. I do, but you have to understand that you're not single like Mohan, Peter, and them. I'm supposed to be by your side when you're going on different functions and events.

HASEEM. And you're absolutely right, baby, and you will be there 98 percent of the time. Once in a while, we have our little men gatherings and men fun days to unwind, talk freely, and enjoy ourselves. We're always busy handling business. So a few times a year, we make plans to do things together. It's not to disrespect you by any means.

NADIA. I get it, Haseem. My father used to do the same thing to my mother, and you know what ended up happening eventually?

Haseem puts his head down and takes a deep breath; his face has a sad frown to it. Nadia is looking at him with a sad look on her face.

HASEEM. Yes, I know. He ended up having a affair on his wife. Same thing happened to my parents, so I know what you're nervous and afraid of, I know.

NADIA. It's not so much that I don't trust you, Haseem. It's them loose thots out there; they have no respect for marriages. Only thing they see is money, and they will do whatever it takes to get some of it.

HASEEM. You're right, baby. You're right, and believe me, I see the looks and flirts from time to time, but you know where my heart is, and you know that all I ever wanted was you from day one. It took me a long time to win you over, but it was worth it.

Nadia smiles at what Haseem said as she reaches for her glass of wine. She grabs it and takes a sip and puts it back down.

HASEEM. Hey, I was thinking about you and I going to the game tomorrow night. Let's enjoy a night in the city. Walk around, maybe do a little shopping, get some good food from the spot we used to go to.

NADIA. Yeah, we haven't been to the city in a minute. You're right about that.

HASEEM. I'd been busy with this new contract and everything, but closing out the year, I want us to spend more time together and do some traveling too, especially with the holidays right around the corner.

NADIA. Okay, I would like that, and you know to show you that I am getting over our situation. I'm gonna allow you a night out with your boys as long as Jamal's nasty ass ain't around.

Haseem looks a little dazed. He is in deep thought about whether or not this is a good time to bring up the Vegas getaway. He looks at Nadia and smiles and looks back at the TV. He decides to leave it alone since everything is going so nice and sweet.

HASEEM. Ahh, come on. You know Jamal's my best friend. I can't do him like that. Why you be so hard on Jamal? He's really trying hard to find true love.

Nadia looks at Haseem and just shakes her head. She starts to laugh at what Haseem said.

NADIA. Trying to find true love, huh? If it ain't one of my girlfriends, one of your mother's models, or anything walking in his sight, he has no care or concern at all. True definition of dog is Jamal. Hey, Nadia, how you been doing? The very next question that comes out his mouth is, how are your friends doing? Knowing that's all he really wants to know anyway. He is so full of it.

Nadia and Haseem are both laughing hard. Haseem is trying not to laugh at his friend, but he knows Nadia is right.

HASEEM. He is trying. It's just gonna take more time for him to find that special one, I guess. (*Haseem is trying not to laugh.*) Hey, did you eat all my lemon cake and ice cream?
NADIA. Nah, it's in the fridge. Bring me a bowl of ice cream.

Haseem walks in the kitchen to retrieve the ice cream. He opens the fridge and cabinets and grabs what he needs. Nadia is looking at her phone and sipping on her wine when Haseem walks back in the room.

HASEEM. Why don't we go upstairs and lick on this ice cream together? Plus, I wanna try out this new whip cream and chocolate syrup.

Nadia looks at Haseem and shakes her head with a sexy smile on her face. She puts her wine down and gets up and walks over to Haseem very slowly and seductively. Haseem is smiling from ear to ear. Nadia gives him a kiss and looks at him.

NADIA. You may have to drink some energy drinks to keep up tonight, and don't forget my honey either.

Nadia turns around and walks upstairs. Haseem is looking at her with his face looking sad. He licks his lip and walks behind her. The episode ends with Meek Mill song "24/7" playing in the background.

Episode 10

Scene one. Peter is in his office, going over his paperwork. He is reading a few things to himself. His secretary buzzes him to let him know that his accountant is here for their meeting. Peter stands up from his desk and walks toward the door to meet him on his way in.

PETER. Good morning, Daniel. Good to see you.

ACCOUNTANT DANIEL. Good to see you also. Sorry I'm a little late this morning. I had an unexpected phone call from a client who needed my advice.

PETER. That's not a problem. I was kinda busy this morning also. I knew you would be coming soon.

Peter and the accountant give each other a handshake, and they take a seat to discuss a few things. Peter pours himself a cup of coffee and checks to see if Daniel, his accountant, wants a cup.

ACCOUNTANT DANIEL. Looking over things the other day and seeing the deals you and your firm have made the last few weeks, let me be the first to congratulate you guys.

PETER. Thanks. Thanks a lot. We are aggressively pursuing our goals, and we are excited about closing out the year on a good note. With that said, yes, we closed some good deals and have a few more on the table. But you know, I like staying on top of the numbers and breaking down everything. How are we looking overall?

Daniel sips on his cup of coffee and shakes his head at Peter. He pulls out his files and paperwork from his briefcase and starts to go through them. He hands over some papers to Peter and leans back in his chair.

ACCOUNTANT DANIEL. Looking over the third quarter and some of the fourth quarter so far, the only thing, if I had to highlight something, is the luxury expenses that are costing the firm a little money. For instance, the luxury skyboxes at Yankee stadium. The Knicks one has gone up the last few years, which I don't understand because they suck.

PETER. Yeah, I'm actually thinking about stopping that one, but you're right. I didn't realize how much they have gone up over the last few years.

ACCOUNTANT DANIEL. I mean, it's not to significant but it's something to keep an eye on. The other thing is start-up cost and upfront costs on these new contracts, especially Steven's construction business. The equipment and machinery is a little staggering. Haseem's new deal is gonna require him to spend a little extra also.

PETER. Yeah, I know. I talked to Steven about that, and he assured me that he wasn't gonna overspend on equipment. What about my new deal? The new trucks I brought wasn't too much, right?

ACCOUNTANT DANIEL. Nah, you did pretty good on that, Peter. Overall, the firm is bringing in millions and you guys aren't spending to crazy. I think for the age you guys are, you're doing pretty damn good! Just keep an eye on the new expansion of your restaurant and Steven's new sports bar.

PETER. You think we should delay Steven's new sports bar to later next year? (*Daniel takes a slight breath and pauses. He looks around Peter's office as he sips his coffee. Peter is looking at him, waiting for a response.*)

ACCOUNTANT DANIEL. No, I don't think you have to delay it, but to be honest, Peter, the firm is bringing in a lot of money, especially the last few years. Sometimes, when you're making a lot of money and new contracts are coming in, you start to do more spending because you have the money, and before you know it, you're in the red. I don't see that happening with you and this firm, but be mindful of things, that's all.

PETER. I understand what you're saying. I was already telling Mohan and the guys that. We're doing good and securing new deals, but just curb the extra spending because it could get out of control. I got you, Daniel.

ACCOUNTANT DANIEL. Believe me, Peter, you guys are doing amazing things here. In less than five years, this firm is making serious profits, and trust me, I will keep my magnifying glasses on your numbers. You got my word on that.

Peter and Daniel smile as they look at each other. Evelyn walks in Peter's office to say good morning. Both men look at her as she walks in.

PETER. Good morning, Evelyn. Let me introduce you to Daniel, our firm accountant. He is sharp as they come.

EVELYN. Hello, sir, pleased to meet you.

ACCOUNTANT DANIEL. Likewise. I heard that Peter has wised up and got some real help around here. I've heard good things about you and look forward to working with you.

All three of them look at one another and smile. Peter sips on his coffee and smiles at Daniel. Evelyn walks over and pours herself a cup of coffee. Scene one ends.

Scene two. Steven and Darren are walking in Manhattan. They are looking very happy as they are meeting up with Tara and her girl-friend for a double date. Steven is decked out with a nice Prada pea-coat and gray Prada sweatshirt, with black Prada jeans. Darren is wearing a stylish black leather coat with a Gucci sweater underneath and True Religion jeans. They are both in a good mood as they are on their way to meet the ladies.

DARREN. Yo, you know I don't be messing around with these blind-date chicks. I hate meeting a person for the first time, and we're both wondering if this is what I want. For me, most of the time, it's like hell no! Have you seen her friend, cuz? She better be official!

STEVEN. Man, I told you I'd only seen a picture of her, and she looks right, I'm telling you. Long hair with a phatty, the way you like them.

DARREN. Yeah, that's the way I definitely like them, thick hips, and if they pushing a nice whip, I'm all in.

Both of them share a laugh as they continue to walk down the street. Darren stops and grabs a hot dog on the street corner. Steven looks at Darren and shakes his head as he looks at his watch. Darren notices Steven's facial expression and starts to put mustard on his hot dog.

DARREN. What, man, I got the munchies. You can't turn down a New York hot dog. Even down the shore dogs can't mess with New York dogs. Look at you. This chick got you all on time and shit. This is your second time out here too. She got your little nose open, huh?

STEVEN. Whatever, man. We're already twenty minutes late already. You ain't gonna never change fam. You never gonna be on some grown man classiness, are you?

Darren bites down on his hot dog and looks at Steven. Steven looks at his phone as he receives a text from Tara.

DARREN. Yeah, one day I will change. When? I don't know. Maybe this one will spark my interest.

STEVEN. Come on, man, they're waiting on us. I knew I should have left your ass. That's what I get for trying to plug you in on something nice.

Both Darren and Steven continue walking down the street as Darren is still munching on his hot dog. Steven is looking at some ladies as they walk ahead of him and Darren.

DARREN. How far is this place, cuz? Seems like we'd been walking for a mile already. Heck, we should have driven the car a little closer. This place don't have VIP parking?

STEVEN. Will you stop complaining? It's right down the street. You getting lazy and old acting.

DARREN. Old acting? Man, you act like it's the summertime or something. It's cold out here. I'm telling you, if she looking like a thot, you gonna be on your own, bro. I'm out. Heck, I'll catch the train back.

Steven and Darren walk into the restaurant and both are looking around. Steven notices Tara and her friend sitting at a table near the entrance. She and her friend walk over to them. Darren's eyes rise up as he notices Tara and her friend. His facial expression is shocked as he looks at Tara's friend up and down. Steven looks at his cousin and smiles.

STEVEN. Pick your lip up, my man. I told you she was official.

TARA. Hey, boss man, 'bout time. We were just about to order. Hello! You must be Darren. How are you?

DARREN. So we finally meet. You're Tara, the one who got my little cuz running back and forth to the city.

TARA. Well, I'm going to be coming to Jersey eventually. I'll like you to meet my friend Myeisha.

MYEISHA. How are you? You got a little mustard on your chin, by the way.

DARREN. Yeah, I grabbed a dog on the long hike here to the restaurant. I'm Darren, and you look sexy as all hell. Looking forward to getting to know you.

Myeisha smiles at Darren and looks at Tara and looks back at Darren. The ladies lead Steven and Darren back to their table. Darren is staring at Myeisha's booty, and he makes a facial gesture of amazement. He taps Steven on the shoulder, and Steven looks back at him and laughs. End of scene two.

Scene three. Haseem and Nadia are enjoying their night as they are eating dinner in a very romantic setting at a fancy high-end Italian restaurant. Both are dressed formally, very nice. Haseem is wearing a nice suit, and Nadia has a nice dress on with her diamond necklace on.

HASEEM. I'm really feeling this food. I've never been here before, but I must say that I picked a pretty good place. Maybe I'm just starving too.

NADIA. Nah, the food is good, the garlic knots are delicious, and the pasta noodles are light, not too heavy when you swallow. I guess you did aight even though Google really directed you to it, but I will give you credit.

HASEEM. Ahh, Google put me on, huh? Hey, I read up on the reviews and checked out the menu and ratings. That was, at least, time-consuming.

Nadia smiles at Haseem and nods her head as she sips on her wine and glances around the restaurant. Haseem looks at his phone and sees a group text page sent out from Peter. It's the flight confirmation for their trip to Las Vegas and all the details on where they will be staying. Haseem looks back at Nadia and starts back eating his dinner.

HASEEM. So are you enjoying your Corvette? You hardly been driving it.

NADIA. Oh yeah, I meant to tell you about that. That car's too fast for me. That's why I don't drive it too much. I was thinking you let me drive your car more and you drive the Corvette.

HASEEM. That car is too small for me. It's tight and my knees are jammed up. But we can switch sometimes. I just can't drive it too long because, for one, it's purple and that's more of a lady's color.

NADIA. Yeah, that's true. You won't look too masculine driving a purple Vet around. Have you talked to your mother? She told me you'd been MIA.

HASEEM. I texted her a few times, but I haven't stopped by to see her in a while. I know her schedule is crazy and mine has been too lately with this new deal I got.

NADIA. How is that coming along? You said you gotta hire some help, right?

HASEEM. Yeah, I actually started the hiring process. I even hired a really good candidate with tons of experience, whom I think is gonna be a huge asset to the company.

NADIA. That's great. That's exactly what you've been needing, someone to take a little pressure of you and free up some of your time, then maybe we can have more quality time together. How is his credentials? What school did he graduate from?

HASEEM. He, huh…he, huh, well, he didn't graduate college, but his track record is impressive.

NADIA. Okay, no college experience at least. How old is he? What other companies he worked at? What's his name?

HASEEM. You know him pretty well. I hired Jamal.

Nadia almost chokes on her pasta. She reaches for her wine and takes a sip to avoid choking. She waves her hand as if she's having a heat flash or something, Haseem leans back in his seat and gives her a look like, what's wrong with her? His facial expression is smiling with his eyebrows raised like he doesn't know why Nadia is acting like that.

HASEEM. You finished? I mean, I don't understand what's so funny. Jamal is very intelligent and has a little business savvy with him. You sleeping on him?

NADIA. Sleeping on him? I'm knocked out snoring and drooling on him. Haseem, Jamal has no clue on how to even work computers besides maybe send an email. He damn sure doesn't know anything about being a computer technician. I don't get this one, but I know you're not dumb and you love and worked hard to build your company.

HASEEM. Well, the thing is, Jamal is really, really serious about starting his own business. He's been talking to me about it for a while now. He wants to be legit and follow in my footsteps. He's tired of the street game and wants to become an entrepreneur. He needs me to put him on the books so he won't look suspicious when he starts his business.

NADIA. Oh, I get it. I understand that. That's real of you to do. My only suggestion is make sure his job ain't answering the phones. Imagine him trying to talk professional. "Yo, yo, I'm saying my dude. What's good with you?"

Both Haseem and Nadia start busting out laughing. They are laughing so loud a few people in the restaurant are looking at them. They realize how loud they are and look around the restaurant a little embarrassed. They sip on their drinks and quiet down but are still chuckling.

HASEEM. You ain't lying. I'm definitely keeping him from answering the phones.

NADIA. Yeah, maybe you need to take him shopping too and not at the mall either. Tims and Air Jordans don't look right when prospective clients are coming to the office.

HASEEM. Yeah, I was already thinking ahead of you. Trust me on that. Ah, listen, on another note, me and the guys are taking a business trip out to Vegas next week. Peter and Felize wanna met with a high-level player out there in the real estate game. Peter is considering opening up his restaurant out there. We will only be out there for a few days.

NADIA. Hmm, few days, huh? Business trip, huh? You sure this just isn't a getaway trip for the fellas?

HASEEM. Well, it's kinda like a two-for-one thing, double whammy, kill two birds with one stone, all mixed in one.

NADIA. You so stupid. All mixed in one whatever.

Nadia smiles and shakes her head as she sips on her wine. She looks at Haseem and glances at the waiter to signal for another drink.

NADIA. Just make sure you bring me something back, and if your lady colleagues do accompany y'all, please have the respect to let me know, Haseem.

HASEEM. You got my word on that, but they're not coming on this trip. It's just us the firm going. I really am loving this moment and look forward to later on tonight, but before we reach our climax later on, let's make sure we both saucy, you feel me?

Nadia and Haseem smile and give each other a toast, and the scene ends.

Scene four. Mohan and Evelyn are back at the office, going over business and investment opportunities for the new year that is approaching fast. Mohan is listening to Evelyn's ideas about what the firm needs to do next year.

EVELYN. So looking at things so far, I definitely see areas that the firm can expand in. There are industries and certain territories that are untapped. For instance, Peter's restaurant chain should expand into New York. As we know, the Japanese population is growing rapidly in all five boroughs, especially Manhattan.

MOHAN. Yeah, I mentioned that to Peter before, but everything is about timing and budgeting with him. But that's something we got to go over with him. One thing about him is if the numbers make sense, he will roll with it.

EVELYN. I'm also not to sold on the Atlantic City expansion for Steven's sports bar even though the numbers show that people are slowly flocking back there. It's not as overwhelming as you might think. And with more and more people gambling online, the percentages are more negative than positive.

MOHAN. So what do you suggest?

EVELYN. Honestly, I think it comes down to location. If we can't get the boardwalk or joint venture in with a casino, it may not attract a good following. Maybe we should closely monitor that and get Felize involved on his connections down there to see if we can land a prime location.

Mohan looks over the numbers and paperwork and starts to rub his chin as he looks down to the ground and then looks back at Evelyn, nodding his head. Evelyn is looking back at Mohan and waiting for his response.

MOHAN. Steven won't be happy if we delay that expansion. He kinda thinks we drag our feet on his business ideals, but you're right, and I'll discuss it with him. What else you looked into?

EVELYN. Well, this is something that may not be on the agenda for next year, but down in southern counties of South Jersey, land is going real cheap, and there is a need for strip malls for franchises and small businesses that need space. South Jersey is starting to develop as more and more people are migrating south to avoid the high cost of living up North Jersey.

MOHAN. I don't know. It depends on what counties, like Salem County is dead money. But Burlington County is starting to really grow. Ocean County is growing also. Look more into it and check with Felize about it. He knows exactly what areas we can dump some money into.

EVELYN. I was thinking about it and looked into it recently, and there is a need for more day cares for children. Parents are working longer hours and kids are being neglected more and more. I think if we open a few day cares that are open a little later for parents that work later, it would really appeal to the masses.

MOHAN. Yeah, but the state is anal and strict on child laws and guidelines concerning children. I don't know about that. Maybe something along the lines of entertainment centers for kids to be able to go after school and have fun will be the way to go.

EVELYN. That's exactly the market I was aiming at. There isn't enough youth centers for children to go to enjoy themselves. If we focus on more of the urban areas, then it could be a huge success.

Mohan and Evelyn look at each other and nod their heads in agreement as Mohan checks his phone real quick.

MOHAN. What's the situation with the furniture company that needs shipping to their other locations across the country? Did you look into that?

EVELYN. Oh yeah, that's an intriguing thing. They actually are growing faster than they predicted. They are growing big online and just secured a deal with a few major hotels. I already scheduled a meeting with them. I already told Peter about it also. He was thrilled about that.

MOHAN. Oh yeah, by the way, we're not going to be here next week for a few days. We got some business out in Vegas to attend to. Peter and Felize might be locking down a big opportunity for the firm. So we will get together when I get back. Also, have the numbers and research ready for the Florida project that Peter and Felize got going on.

EVELYN. Will do. I will keep you posted on things while you guys are away also.

Evelyn stands up and leaves out the conference room. Mohan looks over the paperwork that she left for him to review. He looks at his laptop and starts clicking away on it. End of scene.

Scene five. Natalie and Maracella are having a treatment day, getting their nails, feet, hair done. They are at the spa, enjoying themselves and catching up on things. They are drinking some wine and relaxing in the sauna.

NATALIE. This exactly is what I needed, girl, a day of being pampered. We haven't done this in a while, and we got to do this more often.

MARACELLA. You're the one always caught up with work, girl. I keep telling you to hire more help so you can free up more of your time.

NATALIE. Yeah, I'm thinking about that more and more. I feel like I don't have any time for myself to do anything. I ain't gonna never find a man or have the time to even date or nothing.

Both ladies sip on the wine and grin about what Natalie just said.

NATALIE. I know what I forgot to tell you. Oh, how did I forget to tell you this? So check this out, girl. Mohan comes into the gym, right? And I'm going in on my workout. You know I'm doing my thing trying to get right. Mohan walks over to me and tells me off, girl. He's going in on me about posting a few pictures from the fishing trip.

MARACELLA. What! Get the heck outta here. He was going in on you?

NATALIE. Yes! Don't be posting no more pictures of us while were out. We don't do that social networking stuff. You know better and it better not happen again.

Both ladies start laughing and are hitting each other and rolling to the side, almost dropping their wine glasses. They are cracking up so hard about Mohan's strict demands.

MARACELLA. I can't believe he was going ham on you like that for posting a few pictures. Who cares? I mean, I get how they are so private and don't like their faces out there like that, but damn, take it down a notch.

NATALIE. You know what it boils down to? Haseem must have gotten at Mohan about it because his fiancée, Queen Nadia, was feeling some type of way because she wasn't there. Chick, get over yourself. Are you that insecure? I mean, Haseem ain't even that type of dude. He's focused on his paper not banging chicks. Know your man better!

MARACELLA. That's exactly what it seems to me. If she's gonna be on it like that where Haseem can't be around other woman, then she ain't gonna make it too long with him 'cause I can tell you right now, Haseem doesn't move like that, and he's gonna get tired eventually of her hounding him about being with him when he's chilling with his friends. She got a lot to learn!

NATALIE. There's something about her. She comes across as a little controlling to me, and she's so spoiled by the way Haseem treats her.

MARACELLA. So your boy Jamal wants to take a little trip with me. He wants to get away for a few days to Miami. I done been to

South Beach quite a few times, so I told him let's go to Cali or Vegas or something.

NATALIE. Yeah, Miami is getting a little played out for us. Vegas is always right because there is so much to do out there. So you got Jamal's nose open, I see. He's on you, chick. He's that dude though his swag is official.

MARACELLA. He's starting to grow on me too. I stopped by to see him a few times, and he really treats me like a lady. He got a touch of class and a little romance with him.

NATALIE. Ohhh, you know I'm thinking, girl. Maybe Vegas will be good because they're all supposed to be going out to Vegas in a few days for a business trip. I might have to slide out there too.

Both woman smile at each other as they stand up and sip their drink together. They are fixing their hair and fixing their robes. They start to slowly make their way to the door to leave the sauna.

MARACELLA. I'm reading your mind, girl. I'm reading your mind. You're so slick with yours.

NATALIE. Yeah, I think I'm gonna have to go do a little shopping and make some arrangements at work because you know, girl, what happens in Vegas stays in Vegas.

Natalie gives Maracella that look, and Maracella gives her that look back. They both smile at each other as they walk out the sauna together. End of scene five.

Scene six. Peter and Felize are riding together as they pull up to the construction site for Peter's restaurant in Belmar. They are riding in Felize's Porsche truck and have sort of a serious facial expression. Steven's father is sitting down, looking things over from afar. He is instructing his workers from his chair.

PETER. I see where Steven gets it from. I guess they both have a hard time getting going in the morning.

FELIZE. Yeah, that and they love giving orders, sitting on their asses!

Both men are laughing as they are walking up toward Steven's father. He doesn't notice them at first, but after a few seconds, he looks their direction and spots them walking toward him. His face is a little surprised, but he stands up to greet Peter and Felize.

STEVEN'S DAD. Well, what a pleasant surprise to see you young punks early in the morning. What, and no Starbucks coffee in your hands? What the heck you young bucks want?

PETER. Well, good morning to you, old man. I see you're really working up a sweat.

FELIZE. Yeah, let me guess. You're probably still buzzed off a case a beer from last night, having a hard time getting going, I see. You remind us of a close dear friend of ours.

STEVEN'S DAD. Yeah, yeah, you little geek squaders. What's going on with you, boys? Checking up on the old man? We're getting things done.

All three men embrace one another with hugs and smiles as Steven's dad walks them into his office on-site. Peter and Felize take a seat and Steven's dad stops to talk to his secretary for a second. Steven's dad walks in the office and pours himself some coffee.

STEVEN'S DAD. I would offer you guys some coffee, but I know you guys like that fancy stuff. I drink the cheap stuff. What can I do for you, guys, looking all fancy with your name-brand suits?

PETER. Nah, we just stopped by to get some advice on some things. By the way, your team is really working fast, and it's good to see things are rolling along kinda fast.

STEVEN'S DAD. Well, Peter, you're like family, and you told me you wanna be up and running by next summer, so as you know, my wife got me sleeping on the couch 'cause I had to delay her stuff. You guys should give me an extra bonus for stress or something.

FELIZE. Nah, you know we appreciate that, but we're going out to Vegas in a few days to meet with connections I know out there. We're trying to acquire some land out there to expand Peter's restaurant chain and maybe even Steven's sports bar chain if everything goes right.

STEVEN'S DAD. That's what I'm talking about. You guys and my son are hungry and always looking to grow your business. That's why I like helping you guys as much as I can. So what do you boys need me to do? I think I already know.

Peter and Felize look at each other and grin and then look back at Steven's dad. Steven's dad is sipping on his coffee and puts it back down on his desk. He glances back and forth at Peter and Felize with a slight grin on his face.

PETER. Well, we know you are connected with major people out there in Cali and Vegas, and we're kinda hoping that maybe you can pull a few strings or grease a few wheels so we can get some traction going out there.

FELIZE. I know some players out there, but they're a little inexperienced and not all the way in with the big fish out there, and from knowing your line of work and respect you have, maybe you can help us out.

STEVEN'S DAD. Hmm, I don't know, fellas. Vegas is a close-knit family out there, and they don't like dealing too much with people from the East Coast. They got burned a few times back in the day, so they're real funny who they let in out there.

PETER. What do you think about our plan? Do you think it's smart? Or are we jumping around a little too fast? Should we wait some years before we make a big move like this?

STEVEN'S DAD. Well, I kinda think you should stay working the East Coast heavy. There is a lot of green to be made down south and in Florida, and that's the market you guys are starting to tap in. But I also don't believe in limiting yourself either. No need to put muzzles on your future.

FELIZE. That's what I've been trying to tell this hardhead right here. The sky is the limit, so let's keep climbing.

Steven's dad leans back in his chair and looks up in the ceiling with a deep thought facial expression on his face. He twists his mouth and looks back at the guys. Peter and Felize are both looking like puppies waiting to be rubbed with love and affection.

PETER. If you can pull this off for us, sir, you know I will compensate you very well.

STEVEN'S DAD. I don't expect nothing from you guys. You know that. I get enjoyment out of seeing you boys knock down doors and building new relationships. I think I might be able to get someone who will take a swing for me on this. He got credibility and power out there. When are you guys leaving for out there?

FELIZE. In a few days.

STEVEN'S DAD. Okay, let me see what I can do. I can't promise anything, but I got some old friends who might be able to connect the dots for me. We go back a lot of years.

PETER. Ahh, thank you so much, sir. Thank you so much!

STEVEN'S DAD. Peter, cut the sir shit stuff out. You're making me feel like an old man. Regardless of what you guys think, I'm still pulling in some looks from the girls.

Peter and Felize look at each other and laugh, then they look at Steven's dad, and all three of them start laughing together.

End of scene.

Scene seven. Jamal is in the kitchen, warming up some food in his microwave. Haseem is over talking with his best friend. They are discussing things needed for Jamal to do with his new business he wants to get started. Both of them are relaxing and enjoying each other's company.

JAMAL. So the way I vision my whole gentleman club is for it to be more than just a barbershop. I want it to be a place where guys can come and hang out and enjoy themselves, where you can get a massage, play pool and video games, work out on the treadmill, or just sit back and watch TV with a drink waiting on your haircut.

HASEEM. Yeah, well, there isn't nothing around here like that. I mean, it can be the start of something different that people will take to really quick, something that you can expand on to different locations. A barbershop is supposed to be like a sanctuary for men to get away.

JAMAL. Word. That's what's I'm talking about 'cause real talk, men need somewhere where they can come chill and relax, get away for a few hours from wifey or the kids, a place where they can escape too.

HASEEM. True that. You figured out how you would charge people yet?

JAMAL. I figured the best way is to charge like a membership, where you pay a certain amount to get unlimited haircuts or edge ups. You can come play pool and lounge, but the extra stuff like cigars and food will be extra. Unless you're part of the VIP club, then you get all the full-scale benefits, and believe me, it will be worth to have the VIP card, if you feel me.

Jamal looks at Haseem with a little smirk on his face as he eats on some of his food and drinks. Haseem looks back at Jamal and nods his head in agreement with what he just said. Haseem looks at his phone and responds to a text. Jamal gets a text at the same time and responds to his text.

JAMAL. So what's good with Nadia? She was on your ass a little hard about the boat trip. You better get used to that because it ain't gonna stop, bro.

HASEEM. Yeah, I mean, she understands that Peter invited Evelyn. I told her it was just supposed to be a guys' day out fishing. She knows that, but at the same time, I think she's a little threatened by Evelyn working there.

JAMAL. Shit, it's more than just Evelyn working there. You're gonna have to deal with that stuff every time you're out late with the fellas or just working late at work or something. That's why I think on some real talk, you should have taken your time on this marriage thing, homey.

HASEEM. I mean, I talked and talked to her about the life and the dedication it takes, the commitment it takes to get to the top or accomplishing your goals you set out. I don't know if she fully understands it, but she's gonna have to because, like I told her, I'm not gonna stop until I get there and that I'm not letting anything distract me or disrupt me from getting it.

JAMAL. I feel you, but the thing I don't get sometimes with women, not Nadia specifically, is women pray and hope they meet a man that is 'bout his business and committed to achieving success, then when they meet them, they can't deal with what comes with the territory. Haseem, your lifestyle is real, bro. I mean, you're living it, and 'bout that life, from your clothes to your whip to your business smarts, I don't think Nadia can handle it, real talk.

Haseem looks at Jamal with a curious look on his face. He looks away for a few seconds and then looks away at the ceiling like he's in deep thought. Jamal is still munching down on his food and responds to another text that he receives.

HASEEM. What you got going on? You're all smiles every time your phone goes off. Somebody's excited. Maracella must be on her way over or something.

JAMAL. You're on point with it. She is on way over to chill with me. She's on it, my dude. It took a minute, but I pierced her heart.

HASEEM. Yeah, I guess you did, telling her about trips to Miami and Vegas and shit, Broadway plays and all that. You went in on her for real. But I see why though. She's bad as hell, and she got a good head on her shoulders too. Talking about me, you gonna be cuffed up real soon, big homey.

JAMAL. Yeah, but the big difference with me and you is how I'm moving and how you moved. It's gonna take years before she get a ring, trust me, but if she sticks around and her code of conduct is right, then hey, she might be wifey.

HASEEM. Yeah, okay, playboy, I hear you talking, I hear you talking. Anyway, make sure you get me your social security card and a well-put-together résumé, detailing work history and references, so we can complete the hiring process. Until I get that, I won't be able to give you your needed advancement money, which I still kinda feel funny about.

JAMAL. Haseem, go ahead with that. I keep telling you that I need that to get the ball rolling with everything. Do you realize how much money is needed to get equipment, supplies, furniture, and everything needed to just get started? I really wanna lay it out real professional and fancy. It's gotta have a look to make men feel at home and make them wanna chill out. You know what I'm saying?

Haseem looks at Jamal with a understanding facial expression. He nods his head in agreement as he grabs one of Jamal's buffalo wings. Jamal notices he got company as his doorbell camera alerts him that Maracella is there; he wipes his face and stands up to make sure he is looking right before he answers the door. Haseem notices that his boy is excited about Maracella coming to see him. He smiles to himself as he finishes up his buffalo wing. Jamal walks over to open the door for her as Haseem stands up and gets ready to leave.

MARACELLA. Hey, it's kinda late and having the light on will make me feel a little bit safer in this neighborhood.

JAMAL. Stop being so nervous about coming to see me. I told you that you're good around here. This is a well-protected area for the most part.

MARACELLA. Hello, Haseem, how are you?

HASEEM. I'm doing good. Just over here listening and checking on my boy. Good to see you. Glad to see y'all putting in quality time together. I still don't quite understand what you see in him, but hey, opposites do attract.

JAMAL. Whatever, man. Get your punk ass outta here. Yo, I will make sure I give you that before you bounce to Vegas. I got you.

Haseem looks at Jamal with a slight smirk on his face as he looks at Maracella when she walks in the living room. He looks back at Jamal with his eyebrows raised. He gives his boy a hug and walks out the door. Jamal watches him walk to his car for a few seconds. Then he turns around and notices Maracella is waiting on him with a very sexy outfit on and a very sexy facial expression on her face. End of scene even.

Scene eight. Carleena is talking with one of the workers. She is also closely monitoring Darren and his friends as it seems that they are in the middle of a debate or disagreement. Steven walks in and notices Darren and his friends having a disagreement. He acts like he doesn't even notice it as he makes his way back to his office. He nods his head at Carleena and looks around his establishment, making his way to his office. Steven enters his office and takes a seat and flips open his laptop. He looks at some paper on his desk and looks up to see Carleena walk in.

CARLEENA. Hey, you aight? You don't look like you're in a good mood.
STEVEN. Yeah, I'm aight. Just gotta get a few things done before I leave. I told you about me going to Vegas to handle some business. I'm going to need you to keep a sharp eye on things while I'm away.
CARLEENA. That's not a problem. I have been training Rosina to be more of a crew leader when you or I are not available. She is smart and picking up on things pretty well so far.
STEVEN. Do you have the time to go over things or your training?
CARLEENA. Well, yeah, I mean, it's not much. I just wanted to go over my observations and ideas for growing the business. I always got time, but I know you're busy and got a lot to deal with. It can wait till you get back from Vegas.

Steven looks at Carleena with a serious look and looks back at his laptop. He types a few things and glances back at his documents on his desk. He looks up at the cameras and looks at Darren and his friends and then looks back at Carleena.

STEVEN. I hired you to make this place better, and no matter how busy I am, I will always find time to listen to you. Never worry about that. What's going on? What do you think we can do better around here?

CARLEENA. First thing I noticed is we need to expand on drink specials and sweeten up our after-work hours to appeal to a larger crowd. I mean, 70 percent of your customer base are men. I want to add a karaoke night also. Women like to sing with their girlfriends and dance and perform.

STEVEN. Hmm, yeah, we could use more ladies hanging around. That's always a good thing.

CARLEENA. We also need to look into renovating and building more seating area outside for when the weather gets hotter. I can't believe you never thought about expanding outside seating.

STEVEN. I mean, I considered it, but I kinda think it's gonna bring unwanted drunks and people that just wanna sit around and cause problems. We will have to have a security guard out there because the young boys be on some dumb stuff.

CARLEENA. I agree with that. Ahh, what about your cousin? I mean, listen, I don't want you to think I'm messing with him or nothing, but he be running up a serious tab with his friends. I just wanna make you aware of it, that's all. I just want you to be aware.

STEVEN. Yeah, I will talk to him about that. Trust me, I'd been watching his loose spending. Sometimes people go too far because they think they're entitled to.

CARLEENA. Should I start getting things rolling on the AC project or wait for your okay?

STEVEN. Wait up on that. That's not all the way green-lighted yet. That's actually something that's gonna be talked about on our business trip. Hey, listen, I wanna thank you for handling and being observant down there that night in the casino, making sure me and knucklehead didn't get behind the wheel that night.

CARLEENA. Steven, no need, but I appreciate it dearly. You put me in a good place to succeed and gave me a nice opportunity working with you. I appreciate what you'd done for me, and I will always watch your back.

Steven looks at Carleena with a slight grin on his face as he glances up at the cameras to observe what's going on in his sports bar. He notices Darren and his friends leaving. His phone goes off, and he grabs it and sees his mother is calling him. He flips it back on his desk and shakes his head.

CARLEENA. Oh yeah, your mother called earlier. I told her you weren't in till later. She said to call her before you leave outta town.
STEVEN. Yeah, I might. Has my father been here lately?
CARLEENA. No, I haven't seen him.
STEVEN. Go ahead and advertise and make the changes you wanna do. I trust you will do things right. Whatever you need for spending, just let me know and I will sign off on it.
CARLEENA. Thanks. I will make sure things are done right and look right. I promise you won't be disappointed, boss.

Carleena stands up and leaves out the office. Steven goes back to work on his laptop as the scene ends.

Scene nine. Mohan is packing his luggage and getting ready for his trip to Vegas. The TV is on, and he is also glancing at it as he packs. He suddenly remembers something and looks for his phone. While he is looking for it in his room, it starts to ring. He finds it and looks at it and sees that it's Natalie, his little sister; his facial expression is a little puzzled as he answers the phone.

MOHAN. Good morning, sis. What are you up to this morning?
NATALIE. Nothing much, just running around, doing a little shopping, about to stop and get some breakfast. What you doing? You wanna meet up for breakfast?
MOHAN. Hmm, I could use some pancakes, that's for sure. My stomach's bubbling this morning, but I can't. I'm running a little late.

NATALIE. Too busy for me all of a sudden? You always make time for me. I'm offended, bro.

MOHAN. Well, you will be all right, I'm sure. Besides, I would meet with you, but I got to get to the airport.

NATALIE. Airport? Where you going?

MOHAN. I told you that we got an important business meeting out in Vegas. I'm running a little late, but yeah, I will be back in a few days.

Natalie gives an evil smile as she listens to her brother on the phone. She waits a few seconds before she responds.

NATALIE. Ahh, yeah, you did mention that, but I didn't think it was this soon. Oh, okay, well, be safe and try to have a little fun out there in Sin City, something you hardly do.

MOHAN. Yeah, I'm gonna sit in my hotel room every night and twiddle my fingers and drink tea and watch TV.

NATALIE. Yup, that sounds about right! (*Natalie laughs.*)

Mohan starts to cut off his TV, and grabbing his luggage and heading to the door, he checks the stove in the kitchen and makes sure he puts his food in the refrigerator. Natalie pulls up in her white Range Rover to get her some breakfast.

NATALIE. Well, I will see you when you get back. Good luck, and I hope you and your partners do your thing out there. You coming back Monday, right?

MOHAN. Yes, Ms. Nosy. I will talk to you when I get back, sis. Gotta go.

NATALIE. Or maybe I will holla at you tomorrow or something to make sure you're good.

Natalie smiles as she hangs up the phone. Mohan hangs up the phone and starts to load up his luggage bag into his car. End of scene nine.

Scene ten. Felize and Peter are at the airport already. Felize is talking to a lovely lady that works at the airport, and Peter is reading a magazine. His phone rings, and he looks at it to see that is Evelyn; he answers it and stands up to talk to her.

PETER. Evelyn, is everything all right?

EVELYN. Peter, you know you forgot some of your files and folders that you wanted to take with you, right?

PETER. Nah, I got everything. I thought I grabbed up everything that I had left on my desk that I wanted to take with me.

EVELYN. Yeah, you did get the folders on your desk, but you forgot the ones that you had in the conference room. Remember we were talking yesterday in the conference room and you said that you wanted to bring the blueprints and contracts from Mohan's engineering company to show while you were out there?

PETER. Ohhh, shoot, that's right. I knew I should have stopped by the office on my way. I knew it was something else I needed before we left to the airport. Freaking Felize was taking forever, and I completely forgot about it.

EVELYN. What do you want me to do? Should I scan everything and send it to you in emails?

Peter pauses before he answers. He looks at Felize running his smooth talk on the pretty lady he's talking to. He rubs his forehead, and his facial expression is upset and puzzled.

PETER. I hate that kind of information being scanned and possibly being intercepted by hackers. Damn it! I can't believe I forgot that stuff. Freaking Felize! I hate to do this, but yeah, just scan everything and email it to me, Evelyn.

EVELYN. Are you sure that's what you want me to do?

Peter pauses again and looks around the airport and notices Haseem and Steven walking up. He shakes his head and looks frustrated and angry because of the mistake he made.

PETER. Yeah, go ahead and send it me.

EVELYN. All right, I will. Enjoy yourself and good luck to you guys.

PETER. Thanks! See you when I get back.

End of scene ten.

Scene eleven. Haseem and Steven walk up behind Felize. He doesn't even notice them because he is so focused on talking to the lady that he isn't aware of Steven and Haseem making fun of him. Steven is giving the lady his charming look and making fun of Felize's shoes. He points to them and the girl starts to grin at Steven. Steven then models for the pretty girl and shows off his diamond watch and tries to impress the girl. Felize is wondering what the girl is grinning about and turns around and notices Haseem and Steven.

FELIZE. Yo, man, can I do my thing here please?
STEVEN. Do your thing? The lady looks like you're boring her. I mean, we watched you for the last five minutes, and it don't seem like you're getting anywhere, bro.
HASEEM. Yeah, man, I mean, she didn't start to smile until she saw me and Steven. She knows good looks when she sees it.
FELIZE. Whatever! You guys are some haters for real, hating on me, man. I was right there. I run my game a little slower than you young bucks. Anyway, let me do me please. Go check in or something. Find your own ladies to talk to.

Felize turns his attention back to the lovely lady and continues to talk to her; he hands her his business card. Haseem and Steven walk over to Peter as he looks a little upset still from leaving the folders back at the office.

HASEEM. Yo, what's wrong with you?
PETER. Nothing really. I'm good. I just forgot some paperwork that I needed to bring with me to Vegas.

STEVEN. Just have Evelyn send it to you. She will take care of it.

PETER. Yeah, she is. I just talked to her.

HASEEM. Where the heck is Mohan?

STEVEN. Knowing him, he's probably somewhere stuffing his face with his laptop open, going over last-minute presentation stuff.

PETER. Yeah, he should have been here by now. Normally he's the first one ready to go.

The announcement comes over the intercom that the flight to Vegas is now boarding. Steven, Peter, and Haseem look at one another. Jogging up to the terminal is Mohan with his facial expression, looking tired and winded. Felize walks over to the guys with a confident look on his face. All four men head over to start boarding the plane. End of scene eleven.

Scene twelve. All four men are sitting in first class right across from one another; they are cracking jokes on one another.

FELIZE. Yo, fellas, this can be the start of a major expansion for the firm. We get this done and we're on our way up for real!

HASEEM. Let's get it. Let's make history, baby!

STEVEN. No doubt this will definitely put us on the map if we score this.

MOHAN. Oh yeah, no question. This will be major, major if we nail this.

PETER. There is no if or maybe. We got this! Matter of fact, let's have a toast before we take off.

Peter pulls out a bottle of vodka from his bag. Everybody looks a little surprised at what Peter is doing. He shares a shot glass with all the fellas, and they share a toast. The stewardess comes over and gives the guys a look. She knows the guys are wrong for what they're doing.

She gives them a warning but smiles as she warns them about what they are doing. Peter folds up a $100 bill and hands it to her. She gives an even bigger smile and she walks away. The plane is ready for takeoff, and everybody is smiling and excited. Music starts to play as the plane is taking off. The episode ends! End of episode ten.

Episode 11

Scene one. Aerial shots of Las Vegas is being shown with music being played in the background. Different casinos are being shown with people gambling and drinking. Peter, Steven, Haseem, and Felize are trying their luck gambling with different ladies and hanging around them. They are enjoying their first night out in Vegas and are hanging out at different nightclubs, drinking champagne and enjoying the ladies who are all over them like they are famous celebrities.

STEVEN. Oh, man, we should have been out here years ago. This is the place to be, fellas. I mean, look around at all these beautiful Cali women we're meeting. The atmosphere here, Jersey or New York just don't give you the same feeling!

HASEEM. True! Indeed, I couldn't agree with you more. The nightlife here is electric and off the chain. I mean, I could stay out here for two weeks straight and wouldn't get tired of it. Hey, in the future down the road, a few years maybe, I might have to buy a getaway spot out here, somewhere I can get away for a few days!

FELIZE. Now you're talking my language, Hass. We chip in together and get like a mansion out here, and it can be somewhere we come and recoup and relax ourselves. You feeling me?

MOHAN. I must say my first night out here, nothing compares to it. I mean, South Beach is live and beautiful, but it doesn't have nothing on Vegas. I'm all in headfirst. This is where it's at, and everywhere you freaking look, you see nothing but thick thighs and tight dresses.

Peter shakes his head with a big smile on his face. He looks at the guys one by one and just smiles. He puts his glass of champagne down

241

and turns his facial expression into a more serious look. All the guys start to glance at Peter as he sits up in his seat and puts his glass down on the table. It's like they know what's about to come.

PETER. Believe me, I'm definitely feeling this too. I agree. We should have been out here a few years ago for real. But you guys know we got business to attend to tomorrow, and this is a business trip, so I think we should get ready to take it down.

STEVEN. Correction, business trip for you and Felize. You guys are the ones with the big meeting. Me, Mohan, and Haseem got some downtime. And I definitely plan on getting something nice to lie down with me on my downtime. Hey, I got to enjoy this, Peter. You understand, right?

PETER. Yeah, I get it. Trust me, I get it, but I wanna meet with you guys before me and Felize go to our meeting, so don't get too caught up out here.

MOHAN. Definitely, Peter. We agreed to an eleven breakfast meeting. I will be there. No worries, bro.

HASEEM. Yeah, no doubt, man. Don't get it twisted. We know what we're out here for, but the night is still early, so I got to enjoy the entertainment a little.

FELIZE. Yeah, Peter, our meeting ain't till two o'clock, bro. Relax a little and enjoy the scenery like I do. Matter of fact, I think I'm gonna get my two steps on, a little bumping and grinding before my night is over.

Felize finishes up his drink and puts his glass of champagne down on the table. The guys look at Felize with a grin on their faces. Felize gives a few ladies a sexy look, and his eyebrows are raised up to suggest he wants to know if they wanna dance. The ladies smile and give Felize the turned-on look back at him as they meet him over at the dance floor.

STEVEN. You know, having Felize around is a plus. His Latin swag does well with the ladies, that's for sure. I don't know if it's the ton of gel in his hair or his slick dance moves. Whatever it is, he does his numbers with the chicks. He's that dude.

PETER. Yeah, that's the man when it comes to the chicks. He just better be the man tomorrow at the meeting. That's what matters to me. Well, look, I'm about to take it down, playboys. Just remember we enjoyed ourselves all day out here. Tomorrow is game time.

MOHAN. Yeah, it was smart of you to give us a full day of chilling and relaxation. You be on top of things when it comes to planning things out. I will give you that.

Peter looks at Mohan and nods his head as he finishes up his drink. He gives Haseem and Steven a hug and pat on the back to say goodbye. Then he gives one to Mohan before he walks away from the table where they were at. He walks over to Felize and gives him a hug and pat on the back also. End of scene one.

Scene two. Steven is lying in the bed with a very attractive, exotic-looking lady that he met from last night. The sun is shining brightly in the room. Steven and Felize are sharing a penthouse suite, and in the other side of the large suite, Felize is also knocked out with the two ladies he was dancing with at the club. The alarm goes off, and Steven grabs the pillow and puts it over his face. He bangs on the pillow out of frustration and then hits the alarm to shut it off.

STEVEN. Freaking bullshit. Damn it, this some real BS.

STEVEN'S LADY FRIEND. Ahh, is it that time already? Damn, the sun is so bright. Why didn't you close the shades?

STEVEN. Why didn't you close it? You put me out for the count, so you should have closed it. I don't even remember going to sleep. All I remember is you jumping up and down on me and those big-ass melons of yours slapping me in my face.

STEVEN'S LADY FRIEND. Shut the heck up. You were on some drunk shit, that's all. Barely got ten minutes outta of your bitch ass. Is that how you Jersey boys get down 'cause I won't give anyone else from Jersey a look or nothing.

STEVEN. You talking slick, huh? Okay, keep on talking and I'm gonna stuff that mouth for you this morning. And I guarantee you won't be able to talk then with your mouth full.

Steven's lady friend hits him with the pillow a couple of times. Steven protects his head and grabs a pillow and hits her with a pillow. They are both laughing loudly as Felize stumbles in the room on his way to the kitchen to get something to drink. They don't even notice Felize in the kitchen as Steven climbs back on top of her and begins kissing and squirming on her. Felize just shakes his head as he drinks some orange juice. He then walks back in his part of the suite. He sits on the edge of the bed, looking at his lady friends lying in the bed.

FELIZE. Where the heck is the remote at? Hey, one y'all lying on the remote?

FELIZE'S LADY FRIEND. (*Moaning out.*) You had it, I don't know. What time is it?

FELIZE. Unfortunately, time for me to get ready for my meeting. Believe me, I'd rather lie back down and continue getting the royal treatment.

Felize's lady friend shakes her friend to wake her up. She turns around in the bed to see who is shaking her. She looks at her friend and then shuts her eyes again. The sounds of moaning is coming from the other room. Felize looks at the ladies and the ladies look at each other. They then give Felize a look with a smirk on their face. Felize jumps on top of one of the ladies, and the other lady jumps on top of him. End of scene.

Scene three. Peter is drinking on some coffee at the table, going over some papers for his meeting later on. His phone goes off and he looks at it. It's a text from Evelyn. Mohan walks in the room, already dressed on the phone with a friend. He walks over to the balcony and goes outside to have a little privacy. Haseem is lying down, looking at the TV. He stands up and stretches and starts to walk toward Peter.

HASEEM. Yo, why you didn't wake me up?

PETER. You look like you just went to sleep, mouth drooling, snoring all loud. I was about to wake you up, bro. You looked messed up, so I figured to let you get all the sleep you could get.

HASEEM. Felize and Steven is shot out. Yo, they locked the doors and tried to force me to stay with them and their chicks from the club. Believe me, it was tempting. Steven bagged this nice Costa Rican hottie, bro.

PETER. For a chubby fat kid with no kind of game, chicks be falling for him.

HASEEM. What's crazy. Is he was cursing the chick out for eating on his wings at the club? Yo, you should have seen him. He was going in on her.

PETER. That be the funniest shit yo. He be spazzing on chicks and he be dead serious too. It's like that shit turns them on or something. They get horny by it and wanna jump on him.

Peter and Haseem start cracking up, laughing. Mohan, still on the phone, looks back into the suite to see what they're laughing at. He then turns around on the balcony and lights up a cigar. Haseem heads to the kitchen to get something to drink when the doorbell rings. Peter gives Haseem a look with a smirk on his face. Haseem's eyebrows are squeezed together with a curious look on his face as he looks at Peter, wondering who's at the door. Peter walks over to open the door.

HASEEM. I know them cats ain't dressed and ready before me.

PETER. Evelyn! When you asked what casino I was staying in, I figured it was to send over the paperwork we needed.

EVELYN. Like you said, this is confidential personal information related to the firm, and it shouldn't be sent over through fax or email. Account information and all stuff could be hacked like that.

Evelyn walks in and looks around Peter's penthouse suite and nods her head as she is impressed. Peter says hello to Evelyn's girlfriend. Evelyn notices Haseem and gives him a stunned charming look with a slight grin. Haseem gives her a slight grin as he drinks on his orange juice.

EVELYN. Good morning, Haseem. How are you?

HASEEM. Tired as hell, but I'm good. Hey, you could have brought us some coffee, a bagel, doughnut, something.

EVELYN. You are so ungrateful. I see you haven't changed that yet over the years. I flew all the way out here to make sure y'all meeting go right, and all you worried about is your stomach.

HASEEM. You know I'm just messing with you. We're about to go fuel up on some breakfast in a few. Who's your friend, Ms. Disrespectful? (*Haseem walks over to greet her friend Peter is looking over the files that Evelyn handed him.*)

EVELYN. Tanasha, this is Haseem, a good friend of mine as you already know the story.

HASEEM. Nice to meet you. I can just imagine what you heard about me. I'm sure Evelyn broke everything down to you and then some.

TANASHA. She has explained how nice a gentleman you are and how caring you were to her back in the day. It's good to finally meet you.

PETER. Evelyn, I really, really owe you. I want to thank you so much for stopping everything and flying out here so last second. I really needed these files.

EVELYN. It's no problem, Peter. I know how important this meeting is to the firm and how this is a very big opportunity out here in Vegas. This deal can have a tremendous impact on our future growth.

PETER. Haseem, I'm so glad you convinced her to manage our firm. She is really in our corner for real.

Mohan walks in off the balcony with his cigar in his hand. He's still on the phone as he reaches for his laptop to take out on the balcony with him. He glances at Evelyn, and his facial expression is shocked and amazed to see her. He walks over to give her a hug and whispers thank you to her with his hand over his cellphone.

PETER. Hey, listen, I hate to see you come all the way out here just to hand over some folders. Hang out with us till we fly back. Tell Lynn to forward important calls to you, that's all. That's the least I can do.

HASEEM. Yeah, I mean, it doesn't make sense for you to fly right back. Do some shopping, partying, and drinking like what we're gonna be doing.

EVELYN. Well, that does make sense, I guess. Tanasha, you got to get back right away?

TANASHA. Girl, even if I did have to, I wouldn't care. I ain't never been to Vegas and ain't nothing that important back home that can't wait. I wanna visit the MGM and do some swimming and shopping.

Evelyn laughs at her friend, and Peter and Haseem join in on the laughs too.

HASEEM. Well, I better get dressed. It's almost about that time.

PETER. Yo, Hass, we're just going to our breakfast meeting, so no need to pour on cologne and get all Don Juan DeMarco on us.

Haseem laughs as he leaves the room. He gives Evelyn a hug to thank her again. Evelyn smiles as she watches him leave out the room. Tanasha looks at her friend watch Haseem and smiles. Peter walks out to show Mohan something in the folder Evelyn brought to him. End of scene.

Scene four. Jamal and Maracella are at the airport bar, having a drink. Natalie is being talked to by a guy at the bar a few seats down. Natalie seems to be a little bored of the guy's conversation but is not being disrespectful.

MARACELLA. Did you tell Haseem we're bringing Natalie?

JAMAL. Nah, I didn't tell him, but I know him. He's not gonna really care about it. Hass and Steven are the more laid-back of the firm. They're more understanding and relatable. You feel me?

They're not gonna get upset so quick. But don't get it twisted. If they think you're gonna mess up their business or money, they will go ham on you real quick.

MARACELLA. I've never been to Vegas. There is so much I wanna see and do. The MGM is the first place I wanna hit up.

JAMAL. Yeah, well, I wanna hit up a couple of whorehouses and see what's the deal. I heard a lot of crazy stories about them. You know you're more than welcome to come. I know you're a little freak on the low. Besides, I don't believe in being greedy. I was raised to share and give to the needy.

Jamal starts laughing to himself as he sips on his drink. Maracella slaps him on the shoulder and smiles as she gives him a funny look and shakes her head. They both are laughing and sipping on their drinks as they glance over to Natalie. Natalie is in conversation with her bar friend.

NATALIE. So you travel to LA often to just get your chill on, huh? Hmm, you sure it ain't to check in on your girl or wife even?

BAR FRIEND. Wife? Nah, I'm way too young for that. That ain't happening no time soon.

NATALIE. No time soon, huh? Yeah, you're like most men I meet, not trying to leave the playgrounds until they get bored and tired.

BAR FRIEND. I'm not going there with you, but most women I date or hang out with don't know what they really want. They're still searching to find Prince Charming and waste their best years thinking he's gonna come sweep them up off their feet and spoil her with lavish gifts and luxury trips.

NATALIE. You're dead-on with that one. I mean, I don't need anything financially from a man, but a woman deserves to know and feel secure and safe. Certain requirements are important to us, but some ladies go a little too far, demanding huge child support payments and alimony. I understand why most men play the field and not settle.

BAR FRIEND. Exactly, exactly, but I can tell you're educated and not on some gold-digging mess. That is very alluring because I hardly meet that nowadays. Listen, I don't wanna take up all your time. I noticed your friends keep eyeing us, and dude looks like he's 'bout that life. I don't need any problems.

Natalie looks at Jamal and Maracella and then back at her bar friend. She smiles as she rubs her hair. Bar friend gives her a smile and charming look back at her. Jamal is in story mode as he is making Maracella crack up to his jokes and storytelling.

JAMAL. So I peep the whole thing out. Peter, Mohan, none of them knew what was going down. They really were dumbfounded and didn't have a clue. I give it to Hass a little. He figured it out like a few days later.

MARACELLA. Stop playing. They didn't peep it. They didn't notice it?

JAMAL. You know what's funny? Real talk, I remember when I used to go up to their dorms when they were in college, and this was when they were eating Hot Pockets and noodles for dinner. They never acted out of character. They were committed and focused from day one. I'd seen their hunger and vision back then.

MARACELLA. I know Peter and Mohan had to be a little uncomfortable around you. I mean, how you were moving back then.

JAMAL. On the real, they always accepted me and never were funny style toward me. They took me in like family. That's the thing about them. They might be a little geeked out, but they know the code. Loyalty and trust is part of their obligation. I respected their vision and dedication from the start. Years later, seeing how far they come, it motivates and gives me that drive.

Maracella nods her head as she looks Jamal in the eye and is thinking deep to what he just told her. She looks away at Natalie as she is looking at her phone and finishing up her conversation with her bar friend. Natalie walks to the ladies' room, and Jamal orders more drinks for them.

MARACELLA. I see the level of respect you have for Haseem, and I admire that. Guys are so fake and phony nowadays with their self-centered attitude. You're a real dude, and I guess that's why I'm taking this trip with you.

JAMAL. Code of conduct is everything. If you can't respect realness, how you expect anyone to show you respect? I mean, I always got their backs because they're good dudes with big hearts. Watch the love and money they spend out in Vegas with us. You don't be a grimy cat to dudes with good hearts like that, you feel me?

MARACELLA. Nah, no doubt, I definitely feel that. You gotta respect it.

NATALIE. Damn, I didn't think he was ever gonna leave. I kept trying to tell him that I'm chilling with my people, but he kept freaking talking. He was cool, though, but he wasn't beat for Jamal. He thought you were about to get at him.

JAMAL. For real?

NATALIE. Yeah, he was nervous on how you were looking at him. That was definitely a turn off for real.

Maracella and Natalie start laughing, and Jamal is grinning also. He gives the ladies the drinks the bartender brings over to them. They all give a small toast to one another and continue to smile about Natalie's scary bar friend. End of scene four.

Scene five. The guys are chomping away on their breakfast while Peter and Mohan are talking among themselves. Felize is busy texting someone, and Steven and Haseem are discussing their meeting later on. Steven gets a text from Darren about why he can't come out there and hang out since Jamal and Natalie are on their way out there.

STEVEN. Freaking Darren yo. He mad because I told him this is a business trip and he can't come on this one. Now he's all in his feelings because Jamal and them are on their way out here. Thanks a lot on that one, bro. He's not gonna let me leave this one down.

HASEEM. Nah, Steven, you can't get at me on that one. Maracella's got Jamal open on her, and he's on some playboy stuff. He's coming out here on his own thing. I didn't invite him, yo real talk.

Matter of fact, he was supposed to take her down to Miami. She convinced him to go to Vegas because she's never been here. That's what happened.

STEVEN. I hear you, no doubt. I just get tired sometimes of our friends and family feeling like they have to be everywhere we are at. I mean, I get it. I know they love and care about us, but yo, like, fellas, this is business we're doing here.

HASEEM. Nah, I feel you. I know what you're saying. I totally understand what you're saying. There are times when we can't be mixing business with pleasure.

PETER. Business with pleasure! Steven, you're the last one to be talking about mixing them together, especially after last night. But I do hear you had some official exoticness with you last night, so I don't agree with it, but I understand!

Everybody at the table starts laughing and grinning at what Peter just said. The waitress comes over and fills everybody's cups up. Steven is grinning as he contemplates telling Peter about his cousin Darren's hunger to come to Vegas.

STEVEN. Yeah, well, you know, I mean, hey, the chubby kid can still pull them in. She was feeling your boy, and I mean, can you really blame her?

MOHAN. Whatever, man, anyway.

FELIZE. I still think he slipped her some Molly. She had to be on something. What, you took some pills from Darren to help you bang something nice out here?

Everyone laughs at what Felize said.

STEVEN. Whatever, Rico suave. Anyway, speaking of Darren, Peter, he wants to know if it's all right for him to come out here and hang with us. He's on some lonely shit, I think. He just texted me.

PETER. Darren, what the heck! We just got out here! Man, we are truly missed, I see. Your cousin loves you. He can't be away from you too long. He got to keep an eye on you for real.

STEVEN. Yeah, he's always been like that. It's the Vegas thing that's got everybody on it.

PETER. Yeah, I don't care. He's family. But talk to him, bro, and make him understand this is a business trip and not an orgy festival. You and Haseem meeting at four, right?

STEVEN. Yeah, four.

MOHAN. That was good your aunt hooked that up, Haseem. The more opportunities, the better for us.

FELIZE. Yeah, it's a massive market out here for that. Sin City smoke and drink your night away.

Everybody chuckles at what Felize just said. Steven grabs some toast that Haseem's not eating. Mohan flips open his laptop to look up something. Peter is pouring some more orange juice, and Haseem gets a phone call from his Aunt Pelynda. He stands up to take the call. He plucks a sausage in his mouth first.

HASEEM. Wow, we spoke her up. Let me take this call.

MOHAN. Felize, you gonna be able to come with me to my meeting later on, right?

FELIZE. Yeah, me and Peter should be done in a couple of hours tops.

STEVEN. Hopefully we can go three for three today, but I'll settle with two for three.

PETER. The first meeting's gonna be the toughest to swing. These old-timers out here are very traditional and very leery about young entrepreneurs, especially from the New York area.

FELIZE. Nah, that's true, but this guy we're meeting today is the nephew of a big, big dog out here. He a shot caller and been one for years. Heck, he was making moves when the Rat Pack was doing it out here.

STEVEN. So we're clear, Peter? If this guy is feeling our presentation and offer, can we confirm a deposit if he wants one?

Peter takes a small deep breath as he munches down on his food, then looks at Mohan to see how he feels about it, then he looks back at Steven and nods his head. Felize and Steven are looking at Peter for an answer.

PETER. Yeah, we can guarantee a deposit if needed, but as you already know, swing for something light down 10 percent, no more than 20 percent, and make sure he can have the contract done before we leave. This is Vegas, and everybody got some game and slickness with them.

HASEEM. Yo, fellas, we in there? My aunt just told me that her connect's gonna let us in on a piece of the action. We'll just gotta run our charm and show our professional swag and we're good.

PETER. Cool, that's big, really, really big, bro! Yes, that's what I'm talking about.

MOHAN. You the man, Hass! You scored and got us on the board first. Big moves, bro. Way to come through for the team.

STEVEN. Hey, I owe you tonight, my man. This is big for us. We're planting our flag out here in Vegas. Tonight, I got you, but hey, listen, just remember sometimes my gifts can be a little overwhelming for a guy, especially one that's about to get married.

FELIZE. Hey, as long as he remembers the motto and stick to the code, he'll be all right.

All five men look at one another with big, big smiles on their faces. What happens in Vegas stays in Vegas. They all stand up and give one another hugs and clap hands; they are in a very good mood after the good news Haseem just shared. End of scene five.

Scene six. Evelyn and her friend are doing some walking down the infamous Vegas strip. They are taking in the all the action as this is their first time in Las Vegas. Both women are dressed comfortably and are smiling and enjoying themselves. They notice a few cute guys while they are walking, and quite a few guys notice them also.

EVELYN'S FRIEND. Wow, there is so much to do out here. I can't believe that I finally made it out here. Vegas Sin City!

EVELYN. Yes, girl, I guess you can say it. We're doing things early in life. I'm glad that I took this position working with this firm.

EVELYN'S FRIEND. We got to check out old Vegas too, girl. I heard so much about all the history and legendary things there. Hopefully we can go see the Hoover Dam.

EVELYN. You act like we're gonna be out here for a week. We don't have that much time out here, so I think we should just stick with the shopping. This won't be our last time out here, trust me, especially if Peter and Haseem can get these new contracts.

EVELYN'S FRIEND. Speaking of Haseem, girl, I didn't know how fine and charming he is in person. Pictures from back when he was in high school definitely don't show it. I mean, he just seems cool and laid-back, and you can tell he hits the gym quite often.

EVELYN. Well, when you're signing million-dollar deals, you're gonna be full of charm and laid-back. That money makes you relaxed and calm.

EVELYN'S FRIEND. My point exactly, Evelyn. How are you able to do it, girl? I know how you felt about him in high school. I don't know if I can see him looking all good, walking around dressed up, smelling all good. I would be on his fine ass.

Evelyn laughs to herself as she and her friend walk down the strip. She looks at her friend and then glances around, looking at the casinos and stores. Her friend is looking her back straight in her eye, waiting for a response from her.

EVELYN. I mean, at the end of the day, girl, Haseem is that dude that touched my heart, but we were younger, and since then I realized that we just weren't meant to be. I mean, don't get it twisted. When I see him, I do have inner thoughts about him, but there was too much time in between us.

EVELYN'S FRIEND. Too much in between, y'all. What, girl, people rekindle after twenty years of not seeing each other. So what you saying, all I know is life is short and you only live once. If you don't follow your heart, then you're never gonna feel right, I'm telling you.

EVELYN. Tanasha, I feel what you feel, but it's not that deep as you think. I was in high school and, I have matured so much since then. Haseem did some stuff that really hurt me, and I just don't think he ever cared about me like I cared about him.

Tanasha and Evelyn walk into Caesars Palace and stop and talk for a moment. Tanasha is giving Evelyn a sad but understanding look. She understands where her friend is coming from but thinks she should let him know how she really feels. Evelyn is looking around the casino and at the people dressed up in their Roman costume.

TANASHA. Girl, I've seen the way you were looking at him when he went to get dressed. When he came back in the room after getting dressed, you still like him. Evelyn, I know you and see it in your eyes.

EVELYN. Whatever, Tanasha. You just don't understand. You don't get it. Even if I do still like him, he is engaged for one thing.

TANASHA. Engaged, not married. Meaning, there is still time to take him from that selfish-ass chick.

EVELYN. When he came to see me that day to offer me the job, there was a part of me that wanted him to open up to me about how he misses me, how he still cares and thinks about me. But he didn't and hasn't, so regardless of how I might feel, I got to guard my heart and, most importantly, stay professional.

Evelyn looks at her friend Tanasha, and her facial expression is sad but also confident in what she is saying. She looks around the casino and looks at her phone. Tanasha shakes her head and raises her eyebrows as she understands the position her friend is taking. She also starts to look around the casino and looks at people walking around.

EVELYN. I mean, this position at the firm means a whole lot to me, girl. I walked into a six-figure deal with them. They believe in me. They trust in me to grow their firm and help grow their various businesses. If I do right by them, ain't no telling how much I can make in five years and the different opportunities that might come my way. To me, that's more important than anything. My career is first and foremost.

TANASHA. I understand. I know your drive and passion to be successful. I get what you're saying.

EVELYN. Haseem is one man, girl, one man. At the end of the day, I believe in destiny, and if it's meant for us to be together, I'll know and he will know. But I got to stay professional and classy. I don't want to let Peter down or Mohan. It will look like I took the position because of a ulterior motive.

TANASHA. You're such a freaking lady. Such a freaking lady, I tell you. Me, I wouldn't care about all that. I would be getting some of that fine muscular ass, forget all that.

Evelyn starts laughing at Tanasha and shakes her head; they start walking again, and Tanasha is doing all kind of hand and facial expressions as they walk through the casino.

EVELYN. Come on, girl. With your crazy tale, let's do some shopping and check out Vegas Shoe game.

TANASHA. I'm with you on that, girlfriend. Now you're talking my language. Let's get to it!

Scene seven. Peter and Felize are in the lobby, waiting for their meeting. Peter is looking a little nervous, pacing back and forth. Felize is comfortable and relaxed, looking at his emails on his phone. The secretary walks into the lobby and tells them Terrance will be with them shortly. She asks them if they would like something to drink. They both say no.

FELIZE. Peter, will you take a seat and relax, man? You look like a man with no confidence, walking back and forth. Chill out, will you?

PETER. For the third time, I am relaxed, Felize. I'm just going over things in my mind, that's all.

FELIZE. Okay, if you say so. I'm just saying you look nervous and Terrance will peep that, so just be calm like you always are.

PETER. You sure this guy, this Terrance guy, knows the right people to get us the deal, Felize?

FELIZE. You see, now I feel disrespected. Of course he does, Peter. Terrance is well-connected and his bloodline is well respected. I keep telling you he is a shot caller out here. This dude's family go back to the old Vegas and the gangsters who built this out here. Bro, if he likes you and feeling you, you're in there with no question. You got to trust me on this, Peter. Have I steered you wrong yet?

Peter looks at Felize and stares at him for a few seconds, and he finally relaxes and takes a seat. Terrance walks into the lobby and greets his boy Felize. Felize and Peter both stand up to greet him back.

TERRANCE. Yo, my man, good to see you. What's been going on with you, Felize?

FELIZE. Hey, man, you know what I'm about all day every day. This is my boy, my good friend Peter, I was telling you about.

TERRANCE. Yes, I have heard some good things about you, Peter. It's a pleasure to meet you.

PETER. Likewise. I'm glad to meet with you also. Thanks for making time for us.

TERRANCE. Come on, let's go to my office. You guys want anything to eat, drink? There is steak and ribs in the conference room. We just ordered lunch, so help yourself.

FELIZE. We're good, we actually just had brunch, but thanks though.

Terrance leads Peter and Felize to his office. Felize and Peter can't help but notice the beautiful woman working there at Terrance's company. Terrance tells his secretary to hold his calls for at least thirty minutes as they walk into his office. Peter and Felize look at how big and spacious his office is, equipped with a bar and bathroom also. They look around Terrance's office in amazement and then look at each other.

TERRANCE. So how's your trip been so far? Enjoying the Vegas nights yet?

FELIZE. Yeah, man, we had good first night here. Vegas welcomed us with open arms literally.

TERRANCE. Yeah, I bet it did, Peter. I don't know how you swing with this guy. I mean, he will keep you up all night drinking and partying and then have you up in two hours, riding to a meeting three hours away.

PETER. Yeah, tell me about it. He doesn't need sleep. He just keeps rolling and rolling, but you got to love his ambition, that's for sure.

TERRANCE. How long you guys out here for?

PETER. Just a few days. We're heading back on Monday.

TERRANCE. Oh, okay. If my uncle ain't too busy, he would love to meet with you guys, but if not, I'm sure this won't be the last time you guys will be out here.

PETER. Nah, definitely we will be back, that's for sure. I just hope I can come back feeling proud that we're making a little money out here to substitute the money we're spending out here.

FELIZE. Yeah, 'cause one thing about this guy, he is the definition to cheap. He's about that tight-budget cheap life.

TERRANCE. Hey, you don't succeed out here if you're spending it as fast as you making it. Trust me, I've seen quite a few guys come here with their shoulders spread out to leave with their heads down back and shoulders hunched over. This place will suck you dry before you know it. With that said, you guys are ready for this life out here. It's nothing like you'd never seen, I'm telling you.

PETER. Well, that's why we don't want a full plate. We just want a small nibble right now, not a full bite of the action. Enough to see if we like the taste and wanna swallow, or is it too much to swallow and maybe we better spit it back out.

TERRANCE. I like that. A wise man never jumps in headfirst unless he's sure he can swim and handle the current.

FELIZE. Terrance, speaking of jumping in headfirst, what the hell with all these beautiful woman working here? Man, I'm surprised you ain't got kids all over the place.

TERRANCE. This dude, man! Yo, you never gonna change, Felize. I got you. I got you. Don't worry, bro. So, Peter, getting to the point here, cutting corners, what exactly do you and your firm try to accomplish out here?

PETER. Well, first thing we decided on was to give my restaurant a chance. It's an upscale high-end Japanese restaurant with a very diverse menu. And from there, if the restaurant does well, we may give other things a chance.

TERRANCE. I see. Your restaurant has a few locations, I hear. We do have a big list of Japanese tourists and high-end gamblers that come to Vegas frequently.

FELIZE. Exactly. Our research show that the Asian population is growing out here in the last ten years, and that's why we believe Peter's restaurant would be a good fit out here.

PETER. And on top of that, there is a big percentage of Asian entertainers and exotic dancers out here also, so our firm believes that we can capitalize on that.

TERRANCE. You know, the thing is, being straight up with you, guys, I looked at your numbers and you guys have done quite an impressive job your first three years, a very fast start for your investment firm. You guys have nailed some huge million-dollar deals in your first three years, and looking at your real estate and stock portfolio, it's pretty amazing. Hell, I'm impressed.

PETER. Well, I appreciate that. We're just getting the wheels turning though.

TERRANCE. Yeah, the wheels are spinning pretty fast, I say. You guys have stretched outside of the tristate area. You're accumulating a lot of land down south and in Florida. I also noticed your trucking business is growing bigger and bigger every year.

PETER. Thank you. I see you've done your homework like a real investor and businessman. I like that.

FELIZE. Without throwing shade on anything, I had a huge part in the real estate sector, and these cocksuckers still don't give me my credit, Terrance. You believe that?

Terrance grins as he leans back in his seat. He smiles at Felize and looks at Peter, pointing back at Felize. He nods his head and leans up in his chair. He stands up and looks out the glass window overlooking Vegas. Peter looks at Felize, and Felize looks back at him. Felize is showing a confident face and nodding his head back at Peter.

TERRANCE. I'm gonna be real with you, guys. I'd seen enough to know serious earning potential when I see it. My uncle is old-school, and the old-timers always have been leery of new money. Especially from the East Coast area, you guys have a reputation of being to flashy and not budgeting for the long-term. Plus, you, over the years, always bring heat with you, but you guys are all legit, which is great, something uncle likes.

Terrance walks around his desk with a deep-thinking look on his face. Felize and Peter are listening and looking Terrance straight in the eye. Terrance looks at the folder that Peter gave him earlier. He leans on his desk and takes a sip of his afternoon drink from his bar inside his office.

TERRANCE. Uncle believes in loyalty. He spoke of knowing your father when he used to come out here with his business partners. He knows about Steven's dad's close friends who were good friends with my uncle. Even Haseem's dad worked hard to get some of uncle's associates in New York acquitted. That's why I believe he will make it happen for you guys. He looks at it as a favor.
PETER. So you think we got a good chance of reaching a deal? I mean, you really think so?
TERRANCE. Yes, I pretty much know so because I see your firm's vision, and I like what I see from you guys, all four of y'all. I just wanna make sure if we do this, it's got to work, the location got to be right. That's why I'm thinking inside a stadium

instead of a casino. That way, the space won't be an issue, and the atmosphere would be perfect for it.

FELIZE. I see what you're saying, targeting more of the sports world instead of the drunks and gamblers who ain't thinking about eating because they're trying to recoup the money they're losing.

TERRANCE. Exactly, exactly. There is only one thing, Peter. I lobbied and talked my uncle pretty much into this, but you know, these old-timers believe in paying your dues and kick up percentages. Uncle's dues and percentages are normally high, but he hasn't given me the green light yet, but he's gonna want 10 percent off the top of your earnings for the first three years. Can you live with that?

Peter takes a deep breath and raises his eyebrows. His facial expression is a little shocked, but he nods his head in agreement.

FELIZE. Bro, his uncle and all those old-timers freaking hit you in the gut hard for kickups and dues. I mean, 30 to 40 percent is normal to them, so if he's asking for only 10 percent, you're getting a sweet deal, bro. A sweet deal!

TERRANCE. He is right. They don't give a heck who you are. They look at everybody as visitors on their playground. Even I don't believe in cutting people breaks. Believe me, I don't care who you are. I'm about money, period. But Uncle values his old connections and friends and family of his people he likes. So you think you can handle that? I mean, are we close to making this deal work for the both of us?

PETER. Very, very close. Let me just run it by the guys real quick, Terrance, but I'm pretty certain we got a deal.

All three men stand up and shake hands and give one another small hugs. Terrance walks over to the bar and brings over two glasses for Felize and Peter. He pours them a drink, and they share a toast. All three men smile at one another as they drink their shots. End of scene seven.

Scene eight. Carleena is driving Darren to the airport for his flight to Vegas. Darren is on the phone, talking recklessly about some girl he was dealing with the other night. Carleena is very upset, and her facial expression is angry. Darren hangs up the phone and starts to look out the window with a mad facial expression also.

CARLEENA. You know, I think it's really disrespectful how you degrade women like that right in front of me.

DARREN. Fuck you. I say what the fuck I want when I want.

CARLEENA. You have no respect for women. Look how you're acting.

DARREN. Correction, I have respect for real classy women, not stuck-up arrogant bitches.

CARLEENA. You are a complete asshole. I can't stand your punk ass.

DARREN. I can't stand your prissy ass either. I hate that I'm even in the car with you.

CARLEENA. Believe me, the feeling is mutual. Steven told me to bring your low-life ass to the airport and to book the flight.

DARREN. So do it and shut the fuck up. I don't wanna hear shit you got to say.

Carleena is so angry that she starts to drive faster; she is furious at the way Darren is talking to her. Darren looks at her with a very mean look on his face as she starts to drive faster.

CARLEENA. You don't know me yo. You don't know me. Keep on thinking you can disrespect me.

DARREN. You ain't gonna do nothing. What you gonna do? Beg Steven to ban me from the sports bar? Bitch, please! You don't know me and how I get down. You're lucky for Steven because I would have been gotten you hit, chick.

CARLEENA. Same here, trust me. Same here. What, you think you the only person who knows hitters?

DARREN. Yo, shut up and just drive. I don't like you, you don't like me, so don't talk to me.

Carleena looks at him very angrily and shakes her head. She rolls her eyes and twists her mouth up to the left. Darren pulls out a cigarette and gets ready to light it when Carleena notices what he is doing. She looks at Darren like he is crazy.

CARLEENA. Yo, I don't smoke in my car. Don't play with me.

Darren looks at Carleena and frowns his face at her. He puts the cigarette back in his pack and puts them back in his pocket. He then shakes his head and looks out the window. Carleena looks at Darren as if she is surprised that he actually listened to her command.

CARLEENA. You actually listened and gave me some respect. Wow!

Darren just looks at her and twists his mouth up as if he is trying to ignore her. Carleena arrives at the airport. She is approaching the terminal to drop Darren off. She looks back at Darren and shakes her head in disgust.

CARLEENA. I really hope you understand one day that I'm not going anywhere. I'm here to manage Steven's place and make it a huge success. Steven trusts in me and I will not let him down, so hate it or love it, asshole. I'm not going anywhere.

DARREN. I'm glad you're so confident in yourself, but let me make something clear to you once again. Blood is thicker than water, Ms. Airhead.

CARLEENA. So what are you saying, Mr. Wannabe Kingpin?

DARREN. Figure it out, birdbrain. You think you know Steven so well? You think after only a few months that he will listen and do whatever you say? Keep on walking around with your head in the clouds. Keep on sleeping on my and Steven's relationship. You're gonna be back waiting tables and collecting tips again before you know it.

CARLEENA. Whatever! You swear you got so much control. You really believe you're a shot caller? Get out of the fantasy world you're living.

Carleena pulls up to the curb to let Darren out. She doesn't even look at him as she checks her phone to see if she got any messages. Darren gets out the car and gets his carry-on bag out of the back seat. He closes the back door and glances back at Carleena before he closes the front door. Carleena cuts her eyes back toward Darren, as if she waiting on his closing remark.

DARREN. Hmm. I wonder, Ms. Know-It-All, why you weren't invited since Steven really cares and trusts you so much. You know who is there? Evelyn, the one that the whole firm believes in and really trusts, the one who has a corner office next to Peter. And look at you! You don't even have a fucking desk.

Darren broke Carleena with that one as she is staring at him with an evil look on her face. Darren gives her a very evil, cruel look back. He taps the car and blows her a kiss as he turns and walks away. Carleena watches him walk into the airport. She looks away and looks a little bothered by what Darren just said to her. End of scene eight.

Scene nine. Haseem and Steven are walking with Mr. Fernandez in one of the weed dispensaries in Nevada. Mr. Fernandez is showing them around and explaining things to them. Haseem and Steven are impressed with everything they are hearing and really like the different varieties that are there. Mr. Fernandez walks them out to the massive land for growing. All three of them are strolling around the land.

MR. FERNANDEZ. So, Haseem, it's really that simple. We are growing fast out here and are looking to further expand our land purchasing for growing. This whole industry is just in the first inning, and the time is now to get in before you lose out on huge paydays.

HASEEM. I'm with you on that, Mr. Fernandez. That is why I have been tracking the industry for sometime now and recently got invested in down in the Carolinas.

MR. FERNANDEZ. I was told that and told lots of good things about you and your investment firm. I am impressed with your firm's body of work. You, in particular, have stood out to me because of your ability and expertise in the software industry. We can really use some updated and advanced network systems around here.

HASEEM. Well, I would be honored to help your company improve its network capability and computer software, sir.

STEVEN. Mr. Fernandez, let me get this right. You're saying that eventually every state is gonna be looking for land and space to build their dispensaries and grow weed?

MR. FERNANDEZ. They'd been looking, Steven. You see, as this industry gains more traction and leverage from politicians, lawmakers, celebrities, the land is gonna be in so much demand that companies will pay millions on top of millions for the technology to become successful. It's gonna be a battle for number one, but believe me, there will be enough money for everyone who invested wisely.

Haseem and Steven look at each other and give an impressed facial expression to each other; they both are sold on the investment. Mr. Fernandez excuses himself to take a phone call that came on his phone.

STEVEN. I want in on this. He is dead-on about the direction this industry is going in the next five years. This industry, I believe, is gonna be bigger than the internet explosion years ago. We got to get in on this. It's too good to pass up.

HASEEM. Yeah, I know why you think. I've been trying to convince Peter to give me a bigger budget for spending and to focus more on this industry so we can grow with it.

STEVEN. You know how Peter is, conservative sometimes, but he starting to see it and I'm glad he sees it. Hey, why don't you try to one-hand wash another with this guy, offer to build and expand his network issues and improve his software issues. We probably can win over this deal.

HASEEM. Yeah, I was thinking the same thing. I'm gonna throw it out there and see if he bites.

STEVEN. Heck, I might be able one day to help out with the construction too. Anything to get our feet in out here, bro. Vegas is a gold mine, and we got to get in somehow.

HASEEM. Nah, you're right. We got the resources to secure the deal with him. I just hope he will give us a chance.

Mr. Fernandez finishes up his phone call and walks back over to Haseem and Steven. Haseem and Steven notices him walking back over and quiet their conversation.

MR. FERNANDEZ. So what do you think, Haseem? Are you interested in becoming involved with our global expansion?

HASEEM. I was thinking, Mr. Fernandez, about what you said. How about we help each other out?

MR. FERNANDEZ. What exactly do you have in mind?

HASEEM. I will improve your software and build a better network system for your company and also work on building your mobile application for better communication. You see, I truly believe that your company and our firm can work together and become partners. As you know, we can offer engineering and construction services as well.

Mr. Fernandez nods his head as if he is in deep thought to what Haseem is telling him. He looks at Steven and Haseem and looks around the land where they are standing. Steven notices that he is considering their offer, and his facial expression switches to attack mode.

STEVEN. We both can help each other in a huge tremendous way, and both of us can benefit and gain exposure with big profits together.

MR. FERNANDEZ. Your firm has a good amount of land already, especially back east and some in the south. You're right, this could work well for both of us, son. I'm so glad your aunt brought us together. She said you were a bright young man with a strong vision. You guys got a deal. We can dominate this market working together.

HASEEM. I'm glad you see my vision and thankful you are giving us an opportunity to get involved in this growing industry, sir.

STEVEN. Yes, this is amazing, and I am extremely excited to be part of this as well, Mr. Fernandez. This is a big day for us, and this calls for a toast or smoke out. Whatever choice you make, I'm fine with either.

Mr. Fernandez smiles at Steven and laughs to himself as Haseem laughs also at Steven. Steven is looking back at them, wondering why they're laughing at him, but he gets it and grins also.

MR. FERNANDEZ. When are you guys leaving? Haseem, I will try to get a contract drawn up as soon as possible.

HASEEM. No rush. We're gonna be here for a few more days, but if not, you can send us the contract and we will work out the specifics at a later time.

MR. FERNANDEZ. That sounds like a plan. Come, Steven, let's go have our toast together.

STEVEN. Damn, I was hoping you said smoke. With all this good bud I see, I'm feening to try some.

End of scene nine.

Scene ten. Peter and Mohan are back at their penthouse suite and talking business while Haseem, Steven, and Felize are in their penthouse suite, discussing their plans for the night. Meanwhile, Evelyn and her friend Tanasha are relaxing down at the swimming pool, enjoying some wine and swimming. Scene ten is focused on Haseem's phone conversation he has with his fiancée, Nadia.

MOHAN. What is more important, Peter, expanding out here in Vegas or building a stronger foundation back east? You guys are acting like Vegas is closing its doors and won't be accepting any more money. What is the rush for where we haven't even gotten the Florida project going or any of the new projects yet either?

PETER. Believe me, Mohan, I get where you're coming from. We are kinda spreading our wings a little too far, but this is a once-in-a-lifetime opportunity that doesn't come around too often. I just think if we budget right and cut back on a few things or maybe just delay a few projects, we can do this and nothing will skip a beat.

MOHAN. Cut back, cut back! You think Haseem or Steven are going to want to hear cut back? Both of them live life fast, and you know they're not okay with taking a pay cut. Me, it doesn't really matter to me. I can make do, and I know you can too. I don't know about putting projects on hold either.

PETER. I'm not talking a big pay cut or putting major projects aside. I'm talking smaller ones like Steven's sports bar down in AC. Is that really profitable with online gambling getting bigger? I'm not really sold on people really flocking back down to AC like that. I'm just saying we need to really consider what make dollars and what really makes sense.

Mohan looks at Peter with a serious face and walks a few steps away from the conversation. He looks at his phone and sees Natalie calling him, and he texts her back that he is in a meeting, then he looks back at Peter and raises his eyebrows.

PETER. Think about it. All the different connections we can build out here, how we can network and build relations with shot callers and big dogs out in LA. You know Vegas is their backyard. This could lead to all kinds of different revenue streams. I mean, we can really plant our flag out here, especially now while we are still young.

MOHAN. I don't know, Peter. I see what you're saying. Why not get started early in life, take a small bite now, and gobble up a mouthful later? I feel you. I mean, LA and West Coast expansion is something we envisioned in the future. I just didn't think this soon.

PETER. Look at it like this. Jersey is only gonna get us so big. If we really wanna grow this firm, we got to start swimming with the big fish sooner or later. Felize boy and his family can position us where we need to be. They got the power and the leverage to help us build this firm bigger than we could by ourselves.

MOHAN. Yeah, but, Peter, can we really fully trust these people? Can we really put our faith in them and feel confident that they got our best interest?

PETER. Now you know I'm the first one not to trust, but these old-timers live by the old-school rules. They live and die by sticking to their roots of what built organized wealth. Loyalty is everything to them, and the reason they wanna do business with us is because of our deeply rooted families that they trust and believe in. Mohan, the stage is set for us. The lights are on and are very bright. All we got to do is perform and do what we do.

Mohan looks at Peter and nods his head and looks back at Haseem on the balcony, talking on the phone. He looks back at Peter and shakes his hand. Peter grabs his friend and gives him a hug and looks back at him as he releases his grip on him.

PETER. Let's do it the right way and discuss it with the team and make sure we're all on the same page.

End of scene ten.

Scene eleven. Nadia and her girlfriend Kia are out at a rooftop party in New York. They are dressed in tight designer name dresses and look like they are about to hit the red carpet. They are being watched by quite a few men from afar. They have their drinks in hand and are dancing to the mellow jazz music being played in the background. Nadia doesn't notice her phone has been ringing a few times as Haseem is trying to reach her. Nadia and her friend Kia are loving the attention as they glance at some of the men who are looking at them.

NADIA. You know, I haven't been out in so long, girl. This is really a nice place you took me to. I guess you were sort of right about me getting out a little more.

KIA. I'd been trying to tell you for how long now. You're too young to be acting like some old grandma who doesn't even have any kids yet. I mean, at least when you have a kid or two, a girl can understand you falling back a little.

Both girls chuckle and laugh as they make their way back to their table. Nadia tells Kia she's going to the bathroom, and Kia sits down and orders them another drink. Kia looks at Nadia's phone as she notices it ringing. She looks at it and picks it up in her hand. She frowns and presses the Decline button on it. She then takes it a step further and erases the missed calls from Haseem. As she is doing that, Nadia is making her way back to the table.

NADIA. That line is too long. I will wait. Did you order us something to drink?

KIA. You know I did. The night is young, so one or two more won't hurt. (*Kia looks at her girlfriend and looks around the party as she takes a sip from her glass.*) Now you're reminding me of the old chick that I used to run with, who made heads turn and put ballers into bankrupt.

NADIA. Yeah, well, I used to put in some work, I guess, you can say, but I was only as good as my team was. They ran the show. I was just a role player.

Kia and Nadia both laugh as they give each other handclaps as the waitress brings over their drinks.

KIA. On the real, girl, this is what you need to be doing. You're young, full of good positive energy, educated, and intellectual. Your smile lights up the room. Real talk, you always had that glow.

NADIA. Ahh, come on now, girl. Got me all blushing and emotional.

KIA. Nah, for real, getting married to a good man has always been the dream for us, and I believe you found that, but at the same time, I just feel Haseem wants to switch up your flow, wipe off your sauce a little. He wants you to be in his spotlight and not creating your own, if you feel what I'm saying.

Nadia looks at Kia with a listening facial expression. She is nodding her head as she acknowledges what her friend is saying.

KIA. Haseem is that dude. He's getting his bags and making real moves, but he gets his me time in with his business partners also. They are powerful rich men who attract a bunch of thirsty chicks. You know how this game is, girl, and I'm not gonna see you turn into some housewife sitting in some mansion in the woods somewhere, wondering what time he's coming back.

Nadia's phone rings again, and she looks at it. It's Haseem, and she contemplates picking it up to answer. She looks at Kia and has a curious look on her face.

NADIA. I got to answer this.

KIA. Girl, he doesn't want nothing but just checking to make sure you're home. You know how we play sometimes. You gotta make their mind wonder a little bit. It keeps them off-balance.

NADIA. You're right. This is only the first time he called since he's been away. If it's important, he'll call back.

KIA. Exactly.

Both ladies give each other that look as they chuckle and tap their wine glasses together. As they are busy grinning, two well-dressed men walk over to their table and introduce themselves. Kia is all in on the well-dressed men; she is smiling and flirting back with them. Nadia is a little guarded as the guy reaches his hand out to her and asks if he can have a dance with her. Nadia smiles and looks and notices Kia is already making her way to the dance floor. She stands up, and her eyebrows are raised as she starts to walk to the dance floor with the handsome guy. End of scene eleven.

Scene twelve. The pool scene is lit. Steven and Felize have taken over the whole pool area. Champagne bottles are everywhere. The girls they partied with the night before have brought their girlfriends for round two. The DJ is spinning music, and the whole pool area is rocking. Steven is smoking a cigar with his shirt off, and his shorts are falling down his waist as he dances with the ladies. Darren has made his way to the pool area and has brought some more ladies with him to enjoy his first night out in Vegas. Mohan and Peter are also relaxing by the poolside with a couple of sexy ladies. Haseem is on the balcony, looking down at his friends with a worried look on his face, phone in his hand.

DARREN. Yo, let's get it popping. I'm fucking here Vegas, baby! I'm ready to fire up, drink up, and definitely fuck something up!

Darren hugs Steven and walks over and gives Felize, Mohan, and Peter hugs also. He looks around at all the beautiful ladies in the pool and around the pool area and smiles.

STEVEN. I see you brought a few friends with you. My man, it doesn't take you long to find entertainment wherever you go, I see.
DARREN. Shit, soon as I walked off the plane, they were on me, cuz. They were feeling me. I guess it's that Jersey swag, you know. You can't tell me I ain't fly, supafly, that is.
STEVEN. I see your work, playboy. I see how you get down. Damn, they're looking official too. Yo, we got this whole thing on smash, cigars, and champagne over on the table. Some exotic trees are in the bag by the chair, and some exotic asses are all around us. Can't ask for too much more.

Darren and Steven laugh as they give each other handclaps and hugs again. They are smiling from ear to ear. Darren pulls out a big wad of cash from his pocket and tells the waitress to bring over five more bottles of champagne, then he grabs a cigar and begins to light one up.

DARREN. Where the hell is Haseem?

Steven points up at the balcony where Haseem is. Darren looks to find what Steven is pointing at; he notices Haseem and just shakes his head.

DARREN. What the fuck's the matter with him? I know he not in Sin City with all this ass walking around here, stressing about Nadia.

STEVEN. I don't know. He's been acting weird since we got back, pacing back and forth on his phone, staring at the sky. Hey, that's on him. Hopefully he'll snap out of it.

DARREN. Yo, Jamal's on his way here. Maybe he will spark a match to him. He's cold as ice right now. Damn, she got my boy in some panties. Even Mohan and Peter are enjoying themselves.

STEVEN. Yo, our first few days out here been lovely. I smashed shorty over there last night, and she brought some fresh meat over for me. You should know by now, cuz.

DARREN. Well, I'm here now and I'm not holding nothing back. No holds barred for me, fam. Everything is on the table for me to grab on.

The waitress brings Darren his five champagne bottles, along with glasses. He hands the ladies he came with each a bottle. They start to pop the corks as the DJ turns up the music. Haseem hears the doorbell, and he walks in to see who it is at the door. He opens the door and sees his boy Jamal, Maracella, and Natalie on the other side. His face starts to smile.

JAMAL. Let's burn up the sky, my gee. Your boy made it!

HASEEM. So glad to see you, bro. What's up, girls? Y'all ready for some action?

NATALIE. *Action* ain't the word, Haseem. *Popping* is more like it.

Natalie smiles at Haseem as all three of them walk into the penthouse suite; they look around at how nice the suite is, then they make their way out to the balcony. Jamal puts his arm around Haseem and looks at him with a devilish grin on his face as he stares at Natalie's and Maracella's lovely hips as they walk in front of them.

JAMAL. Yo, you good, bro? Why you by yourself? Where is everybody at?

HASEEM. There they go. Steven and Felize haven't slowed down since we got here. They got the whole poolside on smash, bro.

JAMAL. Shit, that's what I'm talking about. What I'm trying to figure out is why you the hell up here by yourself. The action—and I do mean action—is down there. Damn, look at the chicks they got with them. Those are my boys right there. Damn, they turned up!

Haseem pours some champagne for Jamal, Natalie, and Maracella, then he pours him a glass also. They all start dancing to the music playing and bopping their heads to the music. They are feeling the whole vibe, and finally, Haseem is turning back to his old self now that Jamal is here.

NATALIE. Damn, girl, we made it. Vegas, girl, we here!

MARACELLA. I don't see myself going to sleep for like the next forty-eight hours. Wow, I can't believe how your brother and them got the whole pool section locked down.

NATALIE. Believe me, that ain't Mohan getting it lit. That's Darren's and Steven's crazy asses, I bet.

MARACELLA. Seems like Haseem need some flame. He was looking a little down when he answered the door.

NATALIE. Yeah, something ain't right with him. I will try to spark it up for him, get him back right.

Felize notices Haseem and everyone on the balcony. He gets Darren's and Steven's attention. They look up and smile. Darren puts his hands in the air as two ladies twerk for him. Steven also has a few ladies twerking for him also. They put their champagne bottles in the air and take a toke on their cigars. They point their bottles toward Jamal and Haseem and smile. They acknowledge them and point back to them with bigger smiles as Natalie and Maracella dance with them on the balcony. End of episode eleven.

Episode 12 (Season Finale)

Scene one. The firm is having a lunch meeting to discuss what investments they need to prioritize for next year. Peter is strong on the Vegas and Florida investments opportunities while Steven feels his Atlantic City expansion is being overlooked. Haseem is not happy about the marijuana expansion being put on hold; he feels the firm is not looking at the money that can be made.

PETER. Well, fellas, we have been enjoying ourselves out here in Vegas, but as our time out here is running out, we need to discuss our projects for next year—what direction the firm should be heading, critical investments we need to focus on, and what are the firm priorities for next year.

Peter walks over to the screen in the conference room and looks at it while looking over at the guys with a serious face. The guys are looking over the papers in front of them and looking up at the screen; they all are looking at Peter with a curious look on their faces.

MOHAN. We also have to discuss the possibility of expanding the firm to a fifth member. If we do expand out to Vegas and with the Florida project happening, we need assistance on that.

STEVEN. Whoa, wait a minute, wait one damn minute. We just added Evelyn to manage the firm's future. We gave her a good salary to lure her in. I didn't really like taking a cut on that, but I understood somewhat. Now we got to add another person for Vegas and Florida. I don't think that's necessary right away.

HASEEM. Listen, Steven got a point here. What the hell is Evelyn supposed to be doing? What is her job? She's getting paid to grow and manage the firm, so if she has to take trips to Vegas and Florida throughout the year, she's getting paid good money for it. Second of all, this whole Vegas expansion needs to be discussed and voted on, so let's just figure out is this even good for us right now.

PETER. Look, I think Vegas is something we should highly consider doing. The connections we have out here and the market out here for the restaurant business is big. When you add in the deal with Mr. Fernandez and the construction and software business that you and Steven's companies will handle, it's a no-brainer to me.

MOHAN. Yeah, man, just from the construction side of things, Mr. Fernandez's land expansion will bring in seven digits every year alone.

STEVEN. I haven't zeroed in on the numbers yet, but the way he's talking, it can bring in eight digits in the next few years.

MOHAN. And, Haseem, your company can grow significantly out here, taking in big profits as well. That's why I agree that Vegas is our chance right now to take the firm to higher levels.

PETER. This is an opportunity where all our companies can see major growth, all four of our companies can see million-dollar profits in the next few years. Plus, the networking and relationships we can build out here can develop the firm's West Coast presence, something we all dreamed of back in college.

HASEEM. Yeah, Peter, something we all wanted, but to what cost? I mean, something gonna has to take a back seat unless we take loans out to finance all these investments.

Peter walks around the conference room and clicks on his laptop to change the screen on the TV monitor. He then walks toward it very slowly, as if he is wondering how to explain his thoughts. Mohan looks at Steven and Haseem as if he knows how they are going to respond to what Peter's plans are.

PETER. What I am thinking is if we tone things down a little to free up some of our revenue in the first two quarters of next year, liquidate some of our stocks, sell off a portion of our real estate, and take a small pay cut, we should be good according to my research.

HASEEM. Take a pay cut? I knew that was something you were gonna say. Peter, your lifestyle is different from me and Steven. You're basic and plain and we like to live and look good. So a pay cut is something I don't agree with. Besides, the income from the new deals should help get things off the ground in the beginning.

MOHAN. You're probably right on that, Haseem, but some of our other projects we got planned might have to be pushed off for a little while to make sure we are not overspending.

STEVEN. Here we go. Now we're fucking talking. Let's get to it, Peter. You wanna hold back on me and Haseem's business investments but still push your restaurant expansion. See, that's bullshit to me because Haseem just got the green light from his aunt, and AC is back on track to jump into right now.

HASEEM. Yeah, bro, I ain't feeling that. It seems a little selfish to me. Our income projections for me and Steven investments are positive and impressive. Meanwhile, your restaurant expansion back home is limited growth. No disrespect but it only caters to your nationality and the profits aren't that overwhelming.

PETER. Look, I feel what you guys are saying. I understand where you're coming from, but let's keep things real here. My restaurants got things going for us. We were able to take the profits and pour them into real estate and Wall Street, and it helped jumpstart other business ventures. Did I act selfish back then? Did I complain about it? Heck, no, I did for the firm. Let's not forget that!

STEVEN. Look, we all know what you did for us to get the firm rolling, but tables have turned, my friend, and me and Haseem's companies are pulling in more dividends than your restaurants. So no disrespect, bro, but it's time you acknowledge what we bring into this firm.

HASEEM. You're damn right!

MOHAN. All right, hold up, hold up. Listen, this is not the time to start ego-tripping. I understand how everyone feels, but let's not forget what the golden rule is. If it doesn't make dollars, it doesn't make sense. Now to Peter's defense, we made him the boss. We put him in charge because we trust his vision. We trust his leadership and his business savvy. Steven, Haseem, we all know the potential of your business plans and how high the ceiling is, but we also all know how Vegas is, something that everyone can benefit from.

Haseem and Steven look at each other, and both stare off, looking around the conference room. They are in heavy consideration to what Mohan has said. Mohan is looking both at Haseem and Steven with a compassionate but serious look on his face. Peter sits back down in the chair and looks at the monitor and then clicks his laptop to pull up another screen on the monitor.

PETER. Haseem, I know how hard you and your aunt worked to get the marijuana dispensary license, and, Steven, I know how bad you wanna expand down to AC. Trust me, if I got to take a pay cut by myself, sell off a few things. Whatever it takes, we will get it done. All I'm asking is we just put it off for a little while longer so the funding for the Vegas expansion won't hurt our finances. I'm against borrowing money to fund our projects, but if it means that much to you, guys, then I will do it.

HASEEM. Look, Peter, I'm willing to sacrifice if I have to. I'm all about the firm achieving new levels and becoming what we dreamed of. I might just cut back on some things on my end to get the dispensary up and running.

STEVEN. To be real about it, my hands are tied up with the construction deals popping off back in Jersey, and it's getting bigger than I expected so early. Maybe it wouldn't hurt putting the AC project on hold for a little bit.

MOHAN. In my heart, I think we're doing the right thing. We're already fully extended in our work schedule back home, and the last thing we wanna do is get involved with these loan-sharking banks.

Haseem and Steven look at each other, and they look at Peter and Mohan. They shake their heads, understanding the brotherhood and commitment that they have in building up the firm. Peter has a happy look on his face as he is glad that everyone sees his point.

HASEEM. Who do you have in mind to handle our out of state projects? (*Mohan and Peter look at each other as Peter stands up and walks around the room.*)

PETER. I'm leaning toward giving that responsibility to Felize. He has good relations with people out here in Vegas. Plus, he did bring us a gold-mine deal with the Florida project. Felize is a go-getter. He's a straight-up hustler, and he has done a lot for us so far.

MOHAN. I agree. He has worked on some key real estate deals for us, and he always has the firm's best interest in mind. He cares about us.

HASEEM. He's a good dude and he knows the game. I don't see nothing wrong with him representing us out here.

STEVEN. Hey, man, I can't complain with that one. I know he's gonna always have some nice entertainment for me when I come out here. He's a ladies' man, and having him around is a plus for our entertainment nights.

All four men laugh at Steven and look at one another as scene one comes to an end.

Scene two. Darren is chilling out in his bed with a couple of lady friends he met out there last night. He is watching TV while the ladies are passing a blunt to each other. Darren is checking his phone and texting a couple of people back. Although he is into his phone, he makes sure he is massaging his lady friend's booty.

DARREN. Young boys don't listen yo. They just don't freaking listen. Exactly why I'm not messing with cats. This game ain't for me anymore.

LADY FRIEND 1. Yo, don't worry about that right now. Just blow and let things naturally flow.

LADY FRIEND 2. Hell yeah, I'm tired of the BS too. It's your friends and people you swing with be knowing what buttons to push.

Darren's phone rings again as he is receiving a text page. He reads it and has a mean smirk on his face. Meanwhile, the girls give each other a look in the eye; they both are reading each other's mind as they pass the blunt to each other. Darren shakes his head in disgust as he continues to answer his text back. He flips his phone down and glances at the TV. The girls notice his feelings has changed.

LADY FRIEND 2. Yo, real talk, Dee. We just met last night and all, but you're one hundred with the way you've been treating me and my girl. You move around like a real G who's doing his numbers, with a no bullshit East Coast swag.

LADY FRIEND 1. Yeah, and your man Jamal. Yo, you can tell he's definitely 'bout that life. I wanna fuck with dude heavy he can get it, but shorty he mess with ain't sharing that. She ain't letting that go.

DARREN. Don't get it twisted. He feeling her, but he will still beat that thing up for you. I'm gonna get at him later on and see if I can arrange that for you.

LADY FRIEND 1. Yeah, see what's up with that.

DARREN. I like you, Florida girls. Y'all know how to swing with the kid. We might build together or something down the road.

LADY FRIEND 2. I didn't wanna come at you fast and have you thinking I'm on one, but I see you're 'bout that paper and you're getting it. But my people, they move heavy, heavy work down there, and I can plug you in.

Darren looks at her with a serious interested look on his face as he takes the blunt from the other lady and contemplates what he just heard. He takes a pull of the blunt and stares off at the TV and then looks look back at her and nods his head.

DARREN. I'm trying to clean my money up and go more straight, but I can't turn down something that can be good for me.

LADY FRIEND 2. You trying to come up big, or you just wanna keep a steady pace?

DARREN. Real talk, I got almost half of Jersey on lock. That's why I wanna start going straight so I can slowly scale back. I'm tired of the game and the risks out there.

LADY FRIEND 1. Real dudes know when they're ahead and know how to protect their lead and not let them boys catch up on them.

DARREN. Yeah, and we also know when it's enough talk and no action. Ladies, I need some affection. I feel so alone by myself, care for me, an embrace my hurt and pain.

Darren pulls the ladies in closely as he starts to rub and kiss on both of them. The ladies are going hard back on Darren as they seem to be too much for him to handle as he bangs his head back in the pillow and looks at the ceiling with a smile on his face. End of scene two.

Scene three. Jamal and Maracella are walking down the strip in Vegas; both are smiling and enjoying themselves. Jamal is hugging her and whispering things in her ear, and they are doing some shopping in and out of a few stores.

JAMAL. I'm really glad you came out here to Vegas with me. For some reason, I thought you were gonna bail out on me on some corny stuff. But you're starting to really show me you're not so geeked out after all.

MARACELLA. If you're just getting the real me by now, then you're slacking, bro. Anyway, what's the estimated departure time for you? I mean, how long is this love parade gonna carry on?

JAMAL. Love parade, I like that. I mean, carnivals, parades. You're right, don't stay around too long. But by now, I would have thought you would see that I'm trying to lock down a long-term contract if the terms is right. (*Jamal puts his arm around her and gives her a kiss on the cheek. Maracella is smiling as she looks at Jamal.*)

MARACELLA. Look, I see your worth, Jamal, and I know you're a play-boy like I said before, but as long as I don't see or start to sense sneaky or fake, we should be aight unless something better than you comes along.

Maracella gives Jamal that playful joking look, but Jamal is not feeling that comment. He stares back at her with a smirk on his face.

JAMAL. What's up with your girl Natalie? I get a feeling that she's up to something with my homey. Don't act like you don't see what I see.

MARACELLA. I mean, you know I think that she cares about him a little too much. I think she underestimates Haseem and how on point he is. She got a big heart, and she hates to see people she cares about get played out. She used to be on me about every dude I dated. She fell back a little.

JAMAL. What you mean she hates to see people she cares about get played? She knows something on Nadia and she not telling my man?

MARACELLA. Now I don't know about all that. Natalie will always keep it real and give you the truth. All I'm saying is she got her feelings about Nadia, and she doesn't believe she's the one for Haseem. I think she's just caught up on how to approach him about it.

Jamal looks at Maracella with a curious look on his face. He lights up a cigar and takes a few pulls. He exhales on his cigar and stares off at people around him. He then looks back at Maracella.

JAMAL. You know, I never been one to try to convince someone if and when the time is right for them to get married. I just let people follow their heart 'cause only they know what they can deal with. Hass, my man, and I know him better than anybody. If Nadia's moving foul, he gonna peep it. Believe me, he's gonna see her bullshit.

Scene four. Haseem is relaxing in the Jacuzzi by himself. He is looking at the TV and chilling when his phone goes off. He takes a few seconds before he reaches for it and notices it's Nadia that is calling for him. His face turns to an upset, annoyed facial expression. He thinks he is alone but doesn't know that Natalie is getting ready to walk in to get in the Jacuzzi also. He doesn't notice her and answers the phone.

HASEEM. Well, I'm glad you finally decided to return my calls. What's going on with you?

NADIA. Calls? You called me a little while ago and I was in the shower. What you talking about?

HASEEM. Nadia, I called you three times last night. You trying to tell me you didn't get them?

NADIA. If I did, why wouldn't I answer the phone? What kind of silly childish shit you take me as?

HASEEM. Listen, I know I called you and it kept going to voice mail. Matter of fact, you sent me to voice mail on one of the times I called you because it only rang like two times.

NADIA. Yo, I don't know what you were drinking last night, or maybe you were trying to call someone else, but it damn sure wasn't me you were calling.

HASEEM. So now I'm on some drunk stupid I-can't-remember-who-I'm-calling mess. Yo, you're really on one for real.

NADIA. I'm not calling you that, but all I know is you didn't call me because I would have answered you. I don't play games, especially when my man is across the country, and anything could be happening.

HASEEM. Yeah, well, look, I don't get it. I don't like how you're moving, Nadia. Where were you at last night? I bet it wasn't home.

NADIA. How I'm moving what? Whatever that's supposed to mean? Anyway, yeah, I did go out last night for a few. But that doesn't have nothing to do with me not answering your call.

HASEEM. Well, at least you're admitting to that because nobody answered the house phone either, so I guess I'm not as crazy as you're making me seem.

283

Both Nadia and Haseem are looking very frustrated over the phone conversation. They both are upset with the way they are being talked to. Meanwhile, Natalie is looking at her phone and looking at pictures that Nadia's friend Kia posted last night. She is shaking her head as she looks at the pictures.

HASEEM. So let me guess. You were out with your gold digger friend Kia, and she had you up in all kind of dudes' faces last night. I mean, let's be real here. We both know how she gets down.

NADIA. I was out enjoying myself. Nothing much really. She was doing her, and you should believe in me to know that I wouldn't disrespect you or me like that.

HASEEM. I thought by now, Nadia, you would know me better than you do, but obviously you don't. Trust is not one of my strongest qualities.

NADIA. Same here, but you don't see me coming at you like that. Hell, you're all the way out in Vegas with whoever doing whatever, and I don't doubt your firm manager Evelyn is there. Am I on point with that because I know how it's so important for her to be there, how she is so critical to the firm?

Haseem pauses for a second and looks around the room and shakes his head. Nadia is waiting for a response from Haseem. She is not happy and her facial expression is very serious. Natalie is looking at Haseem, and her eyebrows are raised as she looks surprised by the way Haseem is looking.

NADIA. Anytime now. I mean, it's a very simple question, bro. She there or not?

HASEEM. She wasn't supposed to be here. She flew out here because Peter forgot some important papers that he needed for our meeting. He didn't even know she was coming out here.

NADIA. See, that's my point exactly. Every time it's supposed to be a *business trip* or *guy trip*, she somehow slithers her way to be around you. I don't trust her, Haseem, but I'm gonna believe and listen to you.

HASEEM. Yeah, and I damn sure don't trust Kia, that's for sure. It's just funny to me how you didn't answer my calls on a night you were hanging with her. Real strange to me. But it is what it is. Time always reveals what's real and what's not.

NADIA. Yes, it does, my love, yes, it does.

HASEEM. Well, listen, let me forewarn you since your phone is having technical issues nowadays that I will give you a call tomorrow before I fly back. I'm going to need a ride from the airport. Hopefully Kia doesn't have you tied up somewhere.

NADIA. Well, if, by chance, she does, I'm pretty sure Evelyn will give you a nice, safe, cushy ride.

HASEEM. I'm not doing this with you, but I know one thing. Your tone of voice is getting real confrontational, so I'm gonna talk to you later, sweetheart.

Both Haseem and Nadia hang up the phone. Nadia's facial expression is still upset, and Haseem is very serious and straight, with no frown of smirk on his face at all. Natalie notices that Haseem is upset as she watches him for a few seconds, then she unwraps her towel and walks into the room.

Scene five. Haseem is still upset and puts his head up toward the ceiling as he looks frustrated by the conversation he just had with Nadia. Natalie catches him off guard as she walks in and says hello to him. She is putting her hair in a bun, and Haseem can't believe how gorgeous she looks in her two-piece.

NATALIE. You okay, Haseem? You look a little stressed or upset about something.

HASEEM. Yeah, I'm aight. I'm a little confused about a few things, but I'm not gonna let it slow me down.

NATALIE. Well, you definitely can't let it slow you down. Life is gonna always throw distractions and negativity at you, but as you already know, better days are ahead if you stay focused on what really matters.

Natalie gets in the Jacuzzi very slowly and continues to play around with her hair. She decides to undo it and let it hang out as the water is making her look so sexy and erotic. Haseem is looking at her with a seduced look on his face but tries to stay calm as he straightens up in the Jacuzzi.

HASEEM. You were dropping and shaking hard last night. I see you letting the Vegas nightlife open you up a little.

NATALIE. Vegas is so electrifying, and the energy out here gives me a buzz for real. I couldn't wait to get here to see what it's all about. This is a very stimulating few days for me. I'm feeling this whole vibe out here.

HASEEM. Yeah, I am, too, for the most part. So far, from a business standpoint, things are looking up and I'm happy about that. But I'm just having a little struggle really enjoying things out here the way I should.

NATALIE. I've noticed that. You didn't really seem like yourself last night. It seems like something's bothering you. You okay?

Haseem looks at Natalie as if he's unsure he should open up about his issues with Nadia. He takes a sip of his drink and ponders on for a second. Natalie is looking at Haseem with a concerned look on her face, but she knows Haseem is private on his personal life.

NATALIE. If you don't want to talk about it, I understand. I just know that you're not yourself and everything is up for you right now.

HASEEM. I just sometimes don't get women sometimes. Seeing the things I'd seen in relationships growing up, you think I would have seen this coming.

NATALIE. Seen it coming, what you ain't see because I know you and you don't miss nothing. Your senses be dead-on.

HASEEM. I mean, don't get it twisted. I know how some of her girl-friends are. They're sliding off with the highest bidder. They would sacrifice everything for a taste of the lifestyle. Nadia's supposed to be better than that. It's like she doesn't listen to what I am telling her sometimes.

NATALIE. I had a feeling it had something to do with Nadia. Haseem, look, I love seeing true, solid, real, and authentic love. No ulterior motives, no agenda, a real connection that is felt every day that you with them.

HASEEM. That's all I need. Exactly that right there. I mean, she's sweet and I know she loves me. It's her selfishness that gets me.

NATALIE. Haseem, you know you're my dude. You're like a brother to me. I rock with you heavy all day every day. But there's a reason I wasn't at the engagement party or her surprise birthday party. I wanted to be there out of love for you, but I just couldn't do it.

Haseem looks at Natalie with a confused, wondering look as he reaches for his drink. Natalie looks away for a second and stares off into the water of the Jacuzzi like she's wondering if she should go there with Haseem.

NATALIE. When I went with her house shopping, she just came across like it's all about her, how she wants this, how this has to be to her liking, how the house has to be a certain location or size. She just seemed selfish and spoiled. To me, a lady that isn't really bringing a whole lot to the table shouldn't be overly concerned about that kind of stuff. She should be happy that she found a man that is giving her the good life.

Haseem nods his head as he thinks about what Natalie has said. He sits up on the edge of the Jacuzzi and takes another sip of his drink. Natalie comes closer to him and looks up at Haseem as he is staring back at her.

NATALIE. Love is mysterious and baffling sometimes. People go through life opening and giving their heart to someone who doesn't recognize the goodness and the purity of a real good person. Sometimes, love is closer than you realize you know. Sometimes, we're not able to see what's right for us because our attention and focus is not in tune.

HASEEM. Natalie, I know you're educated and all, but yo, you should have been a marriage counselor or relationship therapist or something. You're deep as hell and dead-on too.

NATALIE. (*Laughing.*)

HASEEM. Real talk, you good with it. Got me like, damn, you know what, I'm going back to the single life. (*Laughing.*)

NATALIE. I just know, for me, that when I get lucky and the right man comes into my life, I'm gonna give him all I can give him and let him see that he's appreciated.

Haseem slides back in the Jacuzzi and comes closer to Natalie. Haseem is a little tipsy from his drinking, and he slides his hand through Natalie's beautiful hair. Natalie looks at Haseem and smiles a little as she stands up near his chest, and they both are looking deeply in each other's eyes.

NATALIE. I want you to know, Haseem, that I have love for you and I got your back always. I know you're a good man who deserves to be treated like a king. Take your time on getting married, make sure that she is the one for you, make sure you don't miss out on something special.

HASEEM. Trust me, I'm on it. I'd been doing a lot of thinking about it, and I feel like I need to reconsider some things. I wanna make sure I'm doing the right thing and not missing out on a real diamond, not miss out on something precious.

Both of them look in each other's eyes as they hug. Natalie enjoys the hug from Haseem as she closes her eyes and has a smile on her face. Haseem is rubbing her hair with his hand and slowly rubs her shoulders and back. Without them knowing or watching, Evelyn and her friend are walking by and notice them from the other room. Evelyn's face is shocked as she can't believe what she is seeing. She tells her friend to be quiet so they don't hear them. She takes out her phone and starts recording Haseem and Natalie. She has an evil grin on her face. End of scene five.

Scene six. Darren is chilling outside of the casino. He is walking back and forth, waiting for Jamal to show up. He looks at his phone and texts Jamal to see where he is at. Jamal walks up on Darren from behind and yokes him up from behind playfully. Darren breaks free and throws a couple of punches back at Jamal; both are shadowboxing, laughing at each other.

JAMAL. What's good with you? This better be good, man. I was about to get my smash on with Maracella.

DARREN. Man, listen to you. All you wanna do lately is be with her. Maracella is a bad one, but I know my boy and I know she ain't got you whipped up.

JAMAL. Whipped up? Come on now. Picture that one, but I'm definitely locking that down before she ends up with somebody like you.

DARREN. Somebody like me? What the heck is that supposed to mean? Anyway, yo, check it out. I think I just plugged in with a big connect. Remember the chicks from the other night that I was with?

JAMAL. Yeah, you were all over them all night, but they're bad though. What's up with them?

DARREN. Turns out they got family in Florida that's 'bout that life, and they got serious work that they're moving around. So you know how I'm thinking. The price is right. We can open up shop with them.

Jamal looks Darren in the face as he walks down the strip with him. He looks around as if he's considering what Darren just told him.

JAMAL. Dee, we're supposed to be going clean, bro. Haseem and Steven are looking us out with our business plans. They got our back, and this is what we been wanting for how long?

DARREN. I know that, and we're still rolling with that. Legit businesses is number one, of course, but this is something that we can have our boys handle and we still cash in.

JAMAL. I don't know if I'm with that. I mean, we made some good money over the years, Darren. We touched some big bags. Crazy thing is we never really did any serious time or caught any heavy charges. Real talk is we've been blessed not to get caught up. I know for me this is a perfect time to get out of the game, and I really think it's best for you to do the same.

DARREN. We are getting out the game. I'm not going against the plan because you and I know clean money is the best money. But feel what I'm saying. If we can tie up this connect and let our boys handle it, we can be on the sidelines handling business, doing the legit thing, and still pocket some cash a little bit longer before we bail out all the way.

JAMAL. Steven and Haseem are risking a lot on us. They're taking a chance on us because they believe in us. They're trusting us to do the right thing. If we do this and something goes wrong, do you know the heat it's gonna bring on their firm? They could lose everything, bro.

DARREN. Jamal, you don't think I know that? That's why I'm not gonna touch nothing or be involved. All we're gonna do is plug in our team to the connect. That's all we're gonna do.

JAMAL. How much do you know about these girls? I mean, for all we know they could be put on to us. We don't have no history or nothing with them.

DARREN. That's why I arranged a little sit-down, a little meeting with them so you can feel them out. I think they're one hundred, but I want you to meet them and see if you smell BS.

Darren and Jamal walk into the casino, and both are looking around the casino as if they are looking for someone. Darren texts the girls to let them know they are both here for their lunch meeting. Jamal's facial expression is unsure and hesitant about what he and Darren are doing.

JAMAL. Yeah, listen, I will meet with them, but I'm telling you right now, I am not making any quick decisions on nothing, and I'm getting out the game no matter what.

DARREN. Just hear things out and let's see what's good. You and I know businesses don't profit much in the beginning, so we're both gonna be taking a big hit in our pockets. That's why this right here can get us over the slow transition period. I'm telling you I got a good feeling about this.

Jamal's eyes are fixed on Darren's lady friends as they walk across the casino toward them. Darren notices them also, and he gives them a slight smile as they approach him and Jamal.

DARREN. What's up, ladies? Looking good and smelling good, so soft. You already met Jamal, I believe. Everything aight with y'all?
LADY FRIEND. Yeah, we're good. We've been up early shopping, checking out the strip a little. What do you wanna do for lunch? It doesn't really matter to us.
DARREN. We can eat over there. They look like their food's good. I want some steak and potatoes or ribs. I'm starving.

Darren and Jamal walk with the ladies over to the restaurant as Jamal is locking eyes in on Darren's lady friends. He can't deny how beautiful they are, but he's not budging on how he feels either. The ladies are checking Jamal out too as they smile at him with their sexy facial expressions. End of scene six.

Scene seven. Peter and Steven are chilling out by the pool. Steven is having a piña colada drink and watching everything with his Versace shades on. Peter is also enjoying a drink but is paying attention to a few ladies that have caught his eye; he has made eye contact with one of them, and she seems to be interested in Peter.

PETER. Hey, you ordered some food yet? You got me drinking early in the day. Now I'm hungry.
STEVEN. Nah, I didn't order nothing yet, but you shouldn't be thinking about food. You should be flirting with them chicks. How about you go over there and just say something?
PETER. What you mean?

STEVEN. What I mean, you and shorty over there have been giving each other googly eyes for the last twenty minutes. She's probably wondering why you're so stiff and scared to come say hi. I keep telling you to stop looking and just go talk. You're always shortchanging yourself.

PETER. And I keep telling you that I don't got time for games either. When the time is right for me to find that special lady, I will find her.

STEVEN. Nobody said nothing about finding a special lady. How about just finding a one-night fling, a weekend fling, somebody you can chill with on a Tuesday night watching the Yankees game? Peter, it's called socializing, mingling. You don't know what you missing out on, bro. For instance, she could be an actress in China, over here shooting a movie or something.

PETER. She isn't Chinese. She's from Japan.

STEVEN. Who gives a shit? Point is, she's looking at you, flirting with you, and you're ignoring her. Stop being dull, bro, and learn to open doors sometimes. Go say something or you want me to go spark it off for you?

Peter thinks about what Steven is saying. He sips on his drink and continues to look over at the nice-looking lady hanging with her friends. He is giving thought and decides to prove to Steven that he's not scared to socialize with random woman. He gets up and starts to walk over to the bar. He orders two drinks of what he thinks the young lady is drinking. Steven is smiling as he watches Peter finally show some heart. He is grinning to himself as Peter walks over to her.

PETER. I don't know you and I'm not one to come up to people that I don't know, but I couldn't ignore how beautiful you are. I know you had to see me looking at you for the last fifteen minutes. What's your name?

AKIRA. I'm Akira, and yes, I was starting to think either you're gay or just too nervous to come say hello. Either way, you were turning me off by your shyness.

PETER. Nice to meet you, Akira. I'm Peter, and no, I'm not gay, but I am shy. I will admit to that. I just believe in mental connection and not so much in physical connection, so I was trying to figure you out before I come introduce myself.

AKIRA. Mental connection, huh? Okay, well, Peter how will you ever establish that without coming into my space and seeing if our energy corresponds well with each other?

PETER. True. You're right about that. How long have you been here in the US?

AKIRA. I'm back and forth from time to time. I got some businesses here that requires my time. Plus, I am finishing up a movie over here.

PETER. I knew you had to be an actress or model or something. You're very beautiful with amazing curves. I can't deny it. That's the first thing I noticed about you. But beauty is only skin-deep to me. Educated minds are what strikes me.

AKIRA. You don't come off as one that will just talk to anyone. You seem very private and distant, someone who carefully plans out his every move.

PETER. Yeah, you're pretty much on point. I just know for me to achieve my goals that being focused is top priority.

AKIRA What are your goals?

PETER. I run an investment firm, partners really, but my partners trust in me to make the day-to-day decisions and lead the firm. We set our rules and guidelines while we were in college. We're on course to reaching our dream, but I just don't wanna have any distractions that will disable me from letting my partners down.

AKIRA. So basically you're shortchanging your happiness and life for a while?

PETER. Well, life is what you make it. Happiness is what you want it to be at the end of the day.

AKIRA. So your personal life, how you deal with the loneliness or being so secluded?

Peter looks at Akira in admiration, like he can't believe how she is interested in him. He is taken in by her. Akira sips on her drink and is paying attention to Peter. She finds him interesting also. Meanwhile, Steven is checking out his boy from afar. He gets a text from Carleena that she needs to talk to him.

PETER. I'm not alone. My mother is close, and I spend time with her. My father stays in Japan most of the time, overseeing his companies. Me, the firm is my personal life. I believe you're not supposed to look for love. Love will find you, and when it does, I wanna be ready for it.

AKIRA. We got some things in common, especially with our parents' situations. Our fathers sound alike, that's for sure, and we both share the same ideology as far as love is concerned.

PETER. With that said, Akira, we should get to know each other better. I mean, we both got busy schedules, but I definitely will find a way to see you again.

AKIRA. Destiny is something you can never figure out sometimes, but yeah, maybe this spark can lead to something. You're intriguing enough for me wanting to know more.

End of scene seven.

Scene eight. Steven is walking back to his penthouse suite to get his Bluetooth speaker when he remembers he has to call Carleena back. He walks back in his suite and calls her back. He notices that his suite is being cleaned by a few nice-looking housekeepers who are smiling at him, so he walks out on the balcony to have a private conversation.

STEVEN. Hey, sorry about that. There was so much noise down there by the pool, so I waited till I got somewhere where I can talk. Everything okay?

CARLEENA. Well, I didn't wanna disturb you out there 'cause I know how important the meetings are, but I think we have some issues that's gonna have to be dealt with when you get back.

STEVEN. Issues? What do you mean? I told you whenever you ready for the renovations go ahead and get started.

CARLEENA. No, Steven, it's not that. Look, I'm not gonna cut any corners with you. You hired me to manage and assist you and be straight up with you.

STEVEN. Exactly. That's what I want you to do. What happened?

CARLEENA. Darren's boys, his thug friends, are doing some dealing around here, I believe. I've been looking at our surveillance tapes, and they are meeting up with customers inside and outside your bar. And it's been going on for a while, Steven.

STEVEN. Really? Is Darren in any of the clips?

CARLEENA. Surprisingly, he isn't in the clips, which makes me believe that he doesn't know what they are doing. But the way he's been acting lately, I mean, he went ham on me driving him to the airport. And he's so against me and everything I'm trying to do here, it's like he feels I'm going to disrupt his plans or actions he got going on here.

Steven is on the balcony, looking down at the pool area. He is watching Peter and his new friend Akira talk. He glances over the Vegas strip and takes a few steps away from the balcony railing. He scratches his head as if he is confused by what Carleena just told him.

STEVEN. Well, I'm gonna have a talk with Darren today, and this is gonna have to stop. His boys can't be dealing at my spot. I don't give a shit where they do things, how they do things, what they do, but I don't want no parts of it.

CARLEENA. The thing is, Steven, it looks like they're already being investigated. I've been noticing a few detectives in unmarked cars riding through here the last few days. The other morning, when I was closing up, two guys were watching me as I walked to the car. I didn't really trip because it was a cop car and an unmarked car. They could have just been talking or something.

STEVEN. Shit, they were watching you? How long were they there? Why are you just telling me this?

CARLEENA. They were out there about twenty minutes before I closed up. None of Darren's friends were here. That's why I thought it was a little strange. Steven, I didn't wanna worry you. I know how important this trip is for you and the firm. I should have just waited till you got back home.

STEVEN. Nah, you did the right thing. You did the right thing. Always call me and keep me aware of what's going on. Fuck, damn it, I'm going to make an example out of those little punks when I get back, and if I find out that Darren knew about this, then I'm finished with him. It's over with me and him!

CARLEENA. I will review more tapes further back to when I started managing here, and I will have everything ready for you when you get home. I know you are angry, but calm down and enjoy Vegas. This is what happens, Steven, when too many friends are riding the money train. They eventually slow the ride down.

STEVEN. Yeah, I can't believe this. You got the beaches and all the other bars up the street, and you're doing dumb shit at my place. Nah, this will cease one way or another, I promise you that!

CARLEENA. Steven, let me go. I will call you later.

Steven and Carleena hang up the phones as Steven is pissed; he is so angry he throws his drink down on the floor. Peter, who is now at the bar, still talking to his new friend Akira, looks up and notices Steven very angry on the balcony. Carleena hangs up the phone and notices one of the men that was watching them in Atlantic City just came in and is observing things going on at the sports bar.

Scene nine. Evelyn, Natalie, Maracella, and Evelyn's friend Tanasha are all walking down the Vegas strip and are enjoying some time together. They are doing some shopping and flirting with a few guys who are checking them out. Natalie and Evelyn are in conversation about things while their friends are trying on some clothes.

NATALIE. Girl, I have really been enjoying this Vegas getaway. I can see myself buying a little spot out here one day. There's so much to do out here.

EVELYN. Yeah, I was saying the same thing, girl. This is where I need to be at. Don't get me wrong. I'm an East Coast girl and everything, but I'm loving this whole vibe out here. So many different connections and things you can invest in, and with Cali a few hours away, I'm with you on moving out here.

NATALIE. That's why going back to what we talked about on the boat trip, we're in with the right crew, girl. They're doing it up, and we can capitalize off that. I did some real thinking on it, and Mohan would love for me to help out, and Peter backs you 100 percent.

EVELYN. Only thing is Haseem. I don't know if he would back me out of our plan for us to start our own firm.

NATALIE. Ahh, don't worry about Haseem. I got him. I mean, he won't be any problem for us. He won't have any issues with what we're doing. He's not like that.

Evelyn notices how confident Natalie seems to have Haseem figured out. She raises her eyebrow to her "I got him" comment, but she plays it off like she doesn't know anything or didn't see their heated Jacuzzi session. She stands up and looks at her shoes and hat she is thinking about buying.

EVELYN. I guess you're right. One thing about Haseem, it's about winning and getting his cut, so he will flow with it, I believe. We have to zero in on what industries to go after first. I think we should follow their blueprint on Wall Street and real estate first.

NATALIE. Yes, I agree with that. Following their footsteps is a smart idea.

EVELYN. Besides, I think it's smart that we do it now while we're young, no kids, no husbands. This is our best life right now. There isn't anyone or anything that can slow us down. We can dedicate all our time to developing our firm.

NATALIE. How do you feel about Carleena's ideas? I think she has great ambition and very focused on her work.

EVELYN. I feel the same way. I like how she is locked in on Steven's bar. She is locked in on growing it. She is ambitious too, and she is perfect for us. The three of us can really inspire and motivate young girls in our neighborhoods, empower them to become leaders.

NATALIE. Yes, yes, that's how I feel too. We can build them up, and I even wanna recruit some up-and-coming creative minds on our firm one day, create a big conglomerate of successful woman from all different backgrounds and cultures.

EVELYN. My plan is to expand, just like Peter and them, but I want them to see that they can trust in me by showing them I can build their firm up bigger and better. Once they see my work and my worth to the firm, then it's gonna open up the door for us, girl.

NATALIE. Let's get it. I'm definitely with it all the way.

Evelyn and Natalie give each other a handclap as they smile at each other. Maracella and Tanasha are walking over toward them with some bags. They are both wondering what Evelyn and Natalie are so happy about.

MARACELLA. Ya been sitting here grinning and smiling hard. What the heck is so funny, chick?

NATALIE. Girl, nothing. We're just building on some thoughts.

EVELYN. Damn, Tanasha, I thought you said you just wanna find some shoes. You found more than that, I see.

TANASHA. You over here laughing and giggling, chick. I found some nice deals over there. I guess I'm gonna be late on rent next month.

All four girls are laughing out loud to what Tanasha said about being late on rent; they are laughing so hard that others have noticed them 'cause they are loud. End of scene eight.

Scene nine. Felize is back with the contract proposal from Terrance and his uncle. He is smiling and in a good mood as he walks into the conference room where Mohan and Peter are waiting on him. They both notice how happy Felize seems as he enters the conference room.

MOHAN. Well, somebody is really happy, smiling and walking with that confident strut.

PETER. Man, either you just scored again with a dime piece or you did right on these contracts.

FELIZE. Fellas, what's going on? You know all I'm going to say is when we open up shop out here and if I'm the one representing the firm, we're in really good hands.

PETER. Somebody's feeling real cocky today. What happened? Did they agree to our terms?

Felize smiles and looks at Mohan and Peter with a look of confidence and opens up his folder and gives them copies of the contract proposals from Terrance and Mr. Fernandez. Peter and Mohan look at the contracts, and Felize is watching them, waiting for their reaction.

MOHAN. Wow, 60/40? How in the hell did you swing that? They went for that?

PETER. Wait a minute. Three restaurants? We agreed to one, bro.

FELIZE. One restaurant to start off with, but that's the thing. They want a long-term commitment from the firm. They want to see that you're dedicated and committed to building a serious business relationship with them. One restaurant to them is like you're rolling the dice and hoping you hit. They're gonna secure us prime locations for all three.

MOHAN. I see they expect the first restaurant to be completed within one year. That's a stiff deadline. That's gonna be a little tight for us to do.

FELIZE. Listen, they're talking locations around the stadium or possibly inside the stadium. The 60/40 is because they want to make sure there isn't any complaints on operating costs or construction costs. Terrance's uncle understands your investment firm is young and just getting off the ground. That's why he willing to bend and be flexible.

PETER. I like it, and we can meet that one-year deadline. Don't worry, Mohan. Felize, I know this is possible mainly because of your relationship with Terrance. We are really grateful and appreciate what you have done for us.

MOHAN. Yeah, I'm nitpicking. You did your thing for us. You negotiated a good deal for us, good-looking bro.

Felize gives Peter and Mohan a hug and handshake; they embrace one another with hugs and smiles. Felize hands them the other contracts from Mr. Fernandez, and Peter and Mohan start looking at the contracts.

FELIZE. Now this deal with Mr. Fernandez is simple. He agrees to let Haseem's software company rework his network system. He also needs Steven's construction company to break ground on his new development sites early spring. I told him that may be difficult because we have Mohan's work that is also slated to start around the same time.

PETER. I don't know if that's possible. Mohan's deal with that real estate mogul is number one priority.

MOHAN. Heck, that's our biggest deal on the table for next year, numbers wise. We can't put him on the back burner.

FELIZE. You think Steven can talk to his father and see if he can chip in with some of the construction?

Peter and Mohan look at each other, then look at Felize. They then glance back at the contracts with a frown on their faces. Felize looks at both of them curiously as to why they are looking so gloomy.

PETER. Ahhh, I don't know about that one. Steven's still a little salty because we're putting his sports bar expansion on hold.

MOHAN. You know Steven, and that might be hard. We'll talk to him about it.

PETER. Overall, everything is a green light. Terms are reasonable for us to match. Financially we can swing it. Just got to hire a little bit, but that's a small issue.

FELIZE. So did I come through or what! Did I nail it like I said I would? If I haven't earned enough credit and respect yet to be partners, then I don't know what else I can do.

MOHAN. You definitely put enough work in to us. You earned your stripes to me and Peter. We just got to vote on it, that's all.

PETER. I've seen your worth. Me and Mohan see your value to this firm.

FELIZE. A vote? It's got to be voted on?

PETER. Yeah, everything pretty much got to be voted on. That's the way Cultural Dividends works. But don't worry, you're good. Even if the vote is split, I got an ace in my back pocket that will push you in.

Peter smiles at Felize with an evil smirk on his face. Mohan is grinning also as he looks at Felize. Felize sees that Peter and Mohan are confident that everything is gonna be okay, so he relaxes and cracks a little smile. All three of them embrace one another again with hugs and handshakes. End of scene nine.

Scene ten. Carleena is in her office, doing some paperwork and checking out things on her laptop. She glances at the camera monitors on the big-screen TV. She notices that the same guy from Atlantic City is still hanging out, watching TV; she also notices two of Darren's associates just walked in. She seems a little tense as she grabs her cell phone, then puts it back down. She stands up and walks out to the bar area to check things out. She is watching things closely as she stands behind the bar.

CARLEENA. What is this guy doing? Is he drinking or eating? What's he been up to?

WAITRESS. He's just watching people. Kind of spooky. He ordered some wings and a few beers, but that's it.

CARLEENA. Has he paid his tab yet?

WAITRESS. Every time I ask him, he keep saying he might order something else. He's a weirdo.

Carleena starts to walk over there toward him. She is watching him very closely as she makes her way around the bar. She sees that the mystery man is paying close attention to what Darren's associates are doing.

CARLEENA. Will you be having anything else?
MYSTERY MAN. Nah, I'm okay.
CARLEENA. Here you go then.

The mystery man looks up at Carleena after she hands him his bill. He then looks at the bill and puts the money inside to pay for it. Carleena is watching him closely, and he notices her sharp stare that she is giving him.

MYSTERY MAN. Well, you're a fine-looking lady. You must be the manager or wife of the owner.
CARLEENA. Thank you for the compliment.
MYSTERY MAN. So this is what keeps all the fancy cars and the big ballers around. You and the lady waitresses are gorgeous. Now I see why this place stay packed.
CARLEENA. Excuse me, I don't know, you who are you?
MYSTERY MAN. Excuse my manners. So sorry. I apologize about that. I'm Detective Mitchell. I work this area from time to time and been meaning to stop in here and check out all the food. I've heard the wings are good, and they sure are. Matter of fact, if you don't mind, can I have some to go?

Carleena motions for the waitress and tells her to get another order of wings for the gentleman; she then brings back his change for his tab.

CARLEENA. Here you go, sir, and the wings will be up in a few. Nice meeting you.
DETECTIVE MITCHELL. Hey, ahh, I haven't seen Darren come in here tonight. He normally hangs out here from time to time.

CARLEENA. Who, sir?

DETECTIVE MITCHELL. Darren. You should know who I'm talking about. You gotta know who I'm talking about. Matter of fact, wasn't you the one who drove him to the airport the other day, and you were hanging out with him down in AC a few weeks ago, right?

CARLEENA. Look here, Detective. I don't owe you any answers on who I hang with or who comes in and eats here. Your wings will be up soon.

DETECTIVE MITCHELL. Well, I didn't mean to offend you or make you upset, Carleena.

CARLEENA. Nah, I'm not upset at all, sir, and I don't know how you know me or whatever, but I'm glad you like the food here, and I hope you come back again. Spread the word to your friends and family.

Detective Mitchell gives Carleena a look of joy on his face; he has a smirk on his face that Carleena can tell is no good. Detective Mitchell looks at some of the customers in the sports bar. He glances at the TV and looks back at her.

DETECTIVE MITCHELL. Yeah, I definitely think I will be back. This seems like a place I may want to check out from time to time, especially if my boy Darren and his comrades are hanging out. Them some slick boys there, who always got some kind of action going on.

The waitress brings Carleena the wings, and she hands them to Detective Mitchell. He takes them from her and smiles at the waitress and Carleena.

CARLEENA. Well, you drive safe, and these are on the house since you really like our wings so much. It's the least I can do.

DETECTIVE MITCHELL. Thank you. Thank you so much. I really appreciate that. Take care, and, ahhh, see you again down the road.

Detective Mitchell smiles as he heads out the door with his wings. Carleena smiles all the way till he walks out the door. Then her smile turns into a frown as she curls her lips in anger. End of scene ten.

Scene eleven. Darren and Jamal are walking through the door of Darren's suite at the casino. Jamal is listening to what Darren is telling him. As they walk in, they are greeted by a big surprise. Steven is sitting in the chair, watching them both. Jamal notices him first and taps Darren on the arm.

DARREN. Yo, what the
STEVEN. Surprise to see me, huh?
DARREN. How the hell you get in here, cuz?
STEVEN. You act like you saw the devil standing here. You guys been
gone for a while. Out sightseeing?

Darren looks at Jamal with a strange worried look on his face, Steven stands up and walks toward the both of them, staring right at Darren as he approaches.

STEVEN. Jamal, if you don't mind, I need to talk to my hardheaded
cousin.
JAMAL. No problem. I'll get up with y'all later on.

Steven glances at Jamal and nods his head in agreement. Jamal leaves out the suite. Steven is giving Darren a cold serious look on his face. Darren is standing, still not knowing what is going on.

DARREN. What's up, man? Everything aight?
STEVEN. You're no dummy. I'm sure you can read the look on my
face. You got a lot of nerve to think you can deal shit at my bar.
DARREN. Whoa, whoa, you know I would never do no shit like that.
STEVEN. Yeah, maybe you won't. I know you ain't that stupid to take
my kindness for weakness. You know better than that. You got
something you need to tell me, something you need to put me
on to?

DARREN. I don't know what you're talking about, Steven.

Steven raises his voice and starts pointing in Darren's face. Darren is nervous and unsure of what Steven is trying to get at.

STEVEN. You don't know what I'm talking about? You don't know what your crew is doing at my bar? You don't know they've been wheeling and dealing around my bar?

DARREN. This is the first time I'm hearing this. They know not to do anything at your spot. I told them to never fuck around there. Its off-limits.

STEVEN. Well, obviously, they're not listening to you, or maybe they just don't respect you anymore, cuz. You tell me because they've been meeting customers at my bar for over a month, outside in the parking lot. They're even bold enough to have them come inside and handle their business inside.

DARREN. Those little sons of bitches. They're fucking dead, I swear to you. I will bash their heads in when I get back home! Don't worry, Steven, I—

STEVEN. Don't worry. Don't freaking worry. Do you know they will shut me down and take away my liquor license if they catch them dealing up there? You know the money I would lose trying to reopen? Everything that I have will be over, fucking over!

Steven kicks the chair over in Darren's room; he then pushes the same chair and yells out loud. Darren is nervous and has a scared look on his face. He can't believe how angry Steven is, but he understands as he shakes his head and looks down to the ground, with his hands folded in front of him.

DARREN. Steven, I knew nothing about this. I would never order them to sell at your bar. You know how much I care about you. You know how thankful I am for what you have done for me. I would never do this to you. I would never see you lose every-thing behind me. Never I would ever, Steven.

STEVEN. If they got my bar under investigation, I swear I will unleash fury on them like they've never seen before. Who the hell do they think they are to have the balls to sell shit at my bar?

DARREN. Only idiot to be dumb enough is Edgar or maybe Davey. Whoever it is, I guarantee you I will handle their ass as soon as I get home. I promise you, Steven, I would never tell them to do any shady business at your bar. I would never. I know how hard you worked and how hard you and the firm are working to expand and do everything legal. I want you to succeed and win. You know that.

Steven is walking in around the room with a very angry face. He is shaking his head and is very upset. His phone goes off and he receives a text from Mohan that they are waiting on him. He reads it and looks at Darren.

DARREN. Listen, Steven, I promise you I knew nothing about these assholes doing this. I preached and preached to them about staying clear of the sports bar. They know better. They're getting sloppy and lazy, and I will straighten their asses out.

STEVEN. If Peter finds out about this, I will never get the approval for expanding. They would shut me down and never let me expand. Darren, we're family, but I will not let you bring me down. I will not let you ruin me and the firm's hopes and dreams.

Darren nods his head and looks at Steven with a very sad facial expression. He knows he is in deep shit with Steven and feels terrible about what has happened.

DARREN. I know. I just can't wait to see them little assholes. I'm going to fuck their dumb asses up! How stupid can you be? How freaking stupid can you be? They are done. I'm cutting them off. I'm done with them!

STEVEN. I want you to start showing Carleena respect and stop giving her attitude.

DARREN. Yes, I will. I promise you I will, Steven. I will show her respect, but she can be a little snappy toward me.

STEVEN. Show her respect. I don't give a shit. She is doing good things for the firm and me. She is doing a lot of legwork that I don't have time to do anymore. Be patient with her and understand she's trying hard to prove herself to me. Carleena's the type that will bend over backward to help you and will help your landscaping business grow. She is a good girl, Darren.

DARREN. I understand. You got it. I will listen to her.

STEVEN. I want you to call those little fucks and tell them to stay out of my bar, at least till we get back home, then we will deal with them. Tell them don't even be in the parking lot, the street, nowhere near there. My bar is off-limits until I say it's okay for them to come back.

DARREN. I'm on it. Trust me, I'm on it!

STEVEN. You better handle this. You better make them understand at any means, whatever it takes! I got to go to this meeting. I just hope they don't know. That fucking Peter can smell shit miles away.

Steven gives Darren a serious look in his eye Darren looks him back kinda cowardly and nods his head to Steven. Steven walks away and leaves out the suite. Darren slams his fist on the counter in anger and frustration. End of scene eleven.

Scene twelve. Darren's lady friends are walking out of an elevator and are heading down the hallway. They are looking for a certain room number. They have a serious look on their faces as they are looking at the room numbers on the doors. They have found the room they are looking for and start knocking on the door. They look at each other as they wait for someone to answer the door. A tall gray-haired man answers the door. He looks at both ladies and invite them in. The girls enter the room, and the guy makes sure they haven't been followed.

GRAY-HAIRED MAN. Ladies, so good to see you. Did everything go according to plan?

LADY FRIEND 1. No issues. Everything went okay. Darren is completely all in on it. Jamal is not gonna be easy, but I believe Abigail will win him over.

ABIGAIL. First off, before we go into details, do you have what you promised us, Detective Johnson?

DETECTIVE JOHNSON. All I see is what this is. You girls want to be compensated for all your handwork you put in. I know how tiring it is getting drunk and high for the last few days can be. There is much more work to do. I want the both of you to stick to them hard. Detective Johnson hands the ladies separate envelopes of cash. The ladies look through the envelopes and pluck the money with smiles on their faces.

DETECTIVE JOHNSON. Nancy, do you have what I need?

NANCY. Of course, he wants to see me again before he leaves tomorrow.

DETECTIVE JOHNSON. Hmm, seems like you got him wide-open. That's exactly what we need. Make him feel comfortable and relaxed. Open up to him about personal things in your life. I want him to feel connected to you mentally.

NANCY. I got this, don't worry. Darren ain't the first and damn sure won't be the last, I turn out.

ABIGAIL. You want me to fall back and let her do her tomorrow?

DETECTIVE JOHNSON. Yeah, I want him to build just with Nancy. He's leaving, so I want him to turn into a little droopy puppy-eyed bitch when he knows he's not gonna see her for a while. Then you know what to do. Reel him in and try to get him to come see you down in Miami to meet your people.

NANCY. Got you. What about fat boy?

DETECTIVE JOHNSON. Fat boy, I'm not concerned about right now. Darren will connect the dots for us in due time. Don't even bring fat boy up.

ABIGAIL. Damn, I guess I ain't gonna get my shot at Jamal. I wanna ride that thing so bad. He's so sexy.

DETECTIVE JOHNSON. In time, you will get yours, believe me. Darren will make sure his boy stays in touch with you because he's thirsty and desperate. Listen, it's important you record this last little rendezvous you have tomorrow with him. I will listen to what we have so far and talk to y'all tomorrow night when they are gone.

Detective Johnson walks out of the room and walks out on the balcony. He picks up his phone and calls Detective Mitchell. Detective Mitchell picks up the phone.

DETECTIVE JOHNSON. They did it. They got to him.
DETECTIVE MITCHELL. Yes, I was a little unsure if they could get to him. Yes, we're in there.
DETECTIVE JOHNSON. I will go over everything and forward it to you tomorrow.
DETECTIVE MITCHELL. You just made my day. We're gonna walk slow with this one before we run with it. Talk to you tomorrow.

Detective Mitchell hangs up the phone and smiles as he nods his head. Detective Johnson also is smiling as he looks down at the beautiful Vegas strip. End of scene twelve.

Scene thirteen. Peter, Mohan, Haseem, and Evelyn are sitting in the conference room of a nightclub. Felize is standing up and talking to Haseem when Steven walks in to the room. Everybody looks at Steven as he enters.

STEVEN. It would have been nice if we could have some steaks or something. Y'all ate already?
MOHAN. Don't worry, we got plenty of food and drinks waiting on us.
STEVEN. Waiting? Hell, send some in now. I'm hungry. Where the waitress at?
PETER. Damn, bro, can we take care of business first?

HASEEM. I mean, he does got a point. Every meeting we had out here there hasn't been no food. I mean, a bagel or dinner rolls, doughnuts something.

MOHAN. All right already, I got it. Your dude is greedy, man.

Mohan gets on the speakerphone and tells the waitress to bring in the food. Then he stands up and walks over to open the door for her to bring in the food. Steven shakes his head as they bring in the food. Evelyn is laughing at Steven and Haseem as they are the first ones grabbing some food.

PETER. Everybody good now?

STEVEN. I'm straight now.

PETER. Look, we know what we already discussed last meeting. I just wanna say this has been a great business trip for us. We locked down some exclusive deals. We established ourselves out here with the help of Felize. He connected us with the right people, and he negotiated some good contracts for us.

MOHAN. All our companies will profit and gain exposure out here working, so nobody's company is gonna be left out. Everybody is gonna eat real good. We are living out what we originally talked about back in school, and if living our dream out isn't number one priority, then what is?

PETER. This has been our biggest year so far. We have expanded down into the Carolinas and Florida, and our trucks are delivering all over the country. We are only at the tip of the iceberg, fellas, and it's only gonna get better down the road.

Haseem, Steven, Evelyn, and Felize are listening closely to everything that is being said. They are showing no emotion on their faces, only nodding their heads in agreement.

PETER. We all know by now what the forecast is for next year, and I ensure all of you that everybody's needs, wants, and desires will happen within the year. Everything is sequenced in order, and

if needed, we will vote on all adjustments. If there are any con-
cerns, now is the time to speak before we vote.

HASEEM. The budget for all our projects next year. What effect will
that have on our annual salary?

MOHAN. Peter assures us that our salary will not take a hit next year.

STEVEN. How are we gonna deal with these new projects back home
and take on projects out here in Vegas?

PETER. Evelyn and Felize will oversee things out here in Vegas as far
as the hiring of the new employees. We already have looked into
the numbers with our accountant, and we will be fine. Plus,
Terrance and Mr. Fernandez will offer assistance on supplying
manpower if needed.

FELIZE. They both are very eager on working with us. Mr. Fernandez,
especially, can't wait for you Haseem to fix his software and
network issues.

*Peter looks around the room at everyone. Mohan, Haseem, Steven,
and Evelyn are all looking at one another. Felize and Peter look at each
other and nod their heads. The room is quiet and a little tense.*

PETER. So if all is good and understood and we all are in agreement
with everything, then let's vote and start enjoying our last night
here in Vegas. All in favor in agreement with the contracts for
the Las Vegas projects?

*All four partners of the firm raise their hands in agreement. Felize
and Evelyn look on with joy on their faces. Mohan is clapping his hands,
and everyone else starts to clap. Peter walks to the front of the table.*

PETER. Great! This is wonderful. I'm glad we are all in on this. All
in favor of making our Vegas projects our top priority for next
year?

*Peter and Mohan raise their hands and look at Steven and Haseem.
Steven and Haseem look at Mohan and Peter and then look at each*

other. They both shake their heads, and Mohan looks frustrated at their response.

STEVEN. Listen, I love what we're doing out here. I really do, but I just don't think it's fair that my and Haseem's projects get pushed back like our shit don't matter.

HASEEM. I'm with him on that. We work just as hard as everyone here, and our goals and aspirations shouldn't be taken for granted. I think we should reconsider our sequence here.

PETER. Fellas, look, I understand how you may feel, and I get it may even look like we're pushing your projects back, but this is our breadwinner right here. Please look at the big picture here and how we all are gonna grow our companies' brands out here. No telling where the exposure we build out here is gonna take us.

STEVEN. I hear you, Peter, but we don't need to jump the gun either. We got a lot of stuff to get done, and if we don't take care of home, then everything will crumble.

MOHAN. Come on now. There is no way we will allow that to happen, and you guys know that. What, you guys don't believe in Peter's vision anymore? You don't trust him or something?

HASEEM. That doesn't a have a damn thing to do with it, Mohan. It's about not stuffing our mouth full and end up choking because we're fucking greedy!

PETER. Guys, you are aware of the clause that's in Evelyn's contract when she signed on as executive manager of the firm, right?

HASEEM. Don't even fucking try to go there, Peter. She's been with the firm for a few weeks literally, and you're gonna give her the power to vote!

STEVEN. Yeah, that's bullshit. No offense, Evelyn, but you haven't even made us a dime yet basically, and she gets to decide the tiebreaker? Hell no!

FELIZE. Guys, calm down and let's talk this out peacefully. Relax. We will come to a—

Steven interrupts Felize and takes a few steps to the back of the room. Haseem walks to the side of the room and shrugs his shoulders. He looks at Evelyn with an evil look. She stares back at him with the same evil look.

STEVEN. You know what, as for me, yeah, go ahead, Peter, pull your leverage political bullshit on us. You make the call, bro.

PETER. Guys, look, I knew one day we were gonna have a tough, difficult time agreeing on our business investments. That's the main reason I wanted that fifth person to be able to help us when we're stuck on something. We always agreed on everything together since we started the firm. I hate to see this happen.

All the men look at one another in frustration. The room is quiet as everyone is in deep thought. Felize and Evelyn look at each other with sad looks on their faces.

PETER. Evelyn, you are the executive manager of the firm. You know all the details of what's going on, right? Is there anything you're not sure about?

EVELYN. No, I'm aware of everything, Peter.

PETER. Well then, Evelyn, how do you vote on this?

EVELYN. I vote for the Vegas projects to be top priority for the firm investments next year. (*Haseem looks at Evelyn with anger. He looks at Steven, and they both are upset.*)

PETER. Well, there it is. Final vote is three for yes, two for no. Let's party and enjoy our night, fellas.

Mohan pops some champagne and music starts to play. Haseem is upset but joins in on the toast that the firm always has when deals are reached.

PETER. Next year is gonna be bigger than this year. Let's get it!

Everyone share hugs and handshakes. They all are happy except for Haseem and Steven, but they are not gonna disrupt the fun and the excitement that everyone else is having. Haseem gives everyone a hug and whispers something to Evelyn before he leaves the room. Steven grabs Haseem before he leaves the room.

STEVEN. Hey, bro, it's all good. Let's get it in tonight, our last night out here. We'll deal with this crap when we get back home. We will make Peter give in to us one way or another.

HASEEM. No doubt. Let me get some air for a minute.

Haseem's phone rings as he leaves. It's Nadia calling him, but he does not answer. Music is blasting through the club as Haseem is leaving. Natalie sees Haseem leaving and notices he looks upset. Haseem goes up to his room and closes the door. Nadia sends him a text that reads, "What happened to you calling me back? Now you're not answering the phone either. WTF." The doorbell rings, and Haseem is furious somebody followed him back to his room.

HASEEM. Yo, I don't wanna be bothered. I will be down in a few. (*The doorbell rings again, and Haseem shakes his head in frustration.*)

HASEEM. Yo, come on, give me some space. What the hell yo! Can I breathe a little!

Haseem stands up and walks toward the door; he is angry and whispers to himself, "Yo, Jamal, you're my dude but not right now. I'm pissed, bro." He opens up the door, and to his surprise, it's Natalie. His facial expression is shocked, and he looks surprised.

NATALIE. Haseem, is everything okay? I was worried about you.

End of episode twelve.

Main Characters

Cultural Dividends

Mohan is a twenty-four-year-old Native American from Edison, New Jersey, who went to school at Rutgers University. His childhood was good; he grew up with both parents in the home. His father was a heart surgeon, and his mother also was in the medical industry; she was a dentist. Mohan has one sister named Natalie, who is twenty-one years old. Mohan was dedicated to his education and becoming successful in life. He wants to become an engineer very bad, but college life has distracted him just a little bit.

Haseem is also twenty-four-years old. He is an African American from Montclair, New Jersey. Haseem also went to school at Rutgers University and majored in computer science. His childhood was good, and he also grew up with both parents in the home. His father was big-time criminal attorney who represented big-time criminals and high-profile celebrities. Haseem's mother was a former model who also did a little acting in her earlier years. She now runs a modeling agency. He is the only child and was a true daddy's boy growing up. He is very active on creating mobile apps for up-and-coming businesses. With the help of his father, he started his own computer software business. He is engaged to his college sweetheart, Nadia, who majored in journalism.

Peter is twenty-three years old. He is from Japan but moved to America when he was eight years old. He grew up in Ewing, New Jersey, and also went to Rutgers University, where he majored in business management. Peter's childhood was great; he was very advanced in school and even graduated high school early. He grew up with both of his parents, but he was closer to his mom because his father ran a major shipping business back in Japan. Peter's father was back and forth from Japan to America. He was a little to overwhelmed with his million-dollar shipping business. Peter's mother was a stay-at-home mom who took care of her children. With the help of his father, Peter has opened a few high-end Japanese restaurants in the Philadelphia area. But his wild temper and hurt from his father ignoring him is causing problems for him.

Steven is twenty-four years old. He is an Italian from Belmar, New Jersey, and the shore life has been very exciting for him so far. He started out at Monmouth University, but being close to home got Steven into a whole lot of problems. His parents forced him to go to Rutgers to get a little farther away from friends to finish college, and that is where his life changed for the better. He met Peter, Haseem, and Mohan. He went on to major in world economics and became very knowledgeable of the stock market in America and oversees. Steven grew up with both of his parents also; his father owned a huge construction company, and his mother runs a fancy beauty salon and is thinking about retiring. His energy and motivation is starting to really help him blossom.

All four guys met during their freshman year, but Peter and Steven knew each other from their childhood days playing baseball together. They met at baseball camp and got closer when they got to college while Mohan and Haseem lived in the same dorms on campus. They all hung out together in their spare time and talked about starting businesses together when they graduated. Mohan convinced everyone to start investing in some tech companies, and they wanted to save the earnings to make larger investments by their senior year of college. During their college years, they all made a bond with one another to become partners for life and to build a conglomerate of successful businesses. All four friends have similar traits; they love sports and enjoy working hard to accomplish their goals. They all have a problem with trusting people and don't believe in doing business outside the family unless they all approve.

Cultural Dividends' side characters and costars Felize Munoz, a real estate developer; his strength is in commercial property. He has become very successful in developing open land and turning them into strip malls and hotels and high-end franchises like Walmart, Says Club, BJ's, etc. He graduated from Ryder University and knew Peter from high school. He brings key real estate opportunity's to the firm and has gotten them huge deals recently. He has secured huge profits for them from finding great deals around the United States. He also has some knowledge in the Silicon Valley tech world also and a very multilayered guy who is very loyal to Peter.

Haseem's Aunt Pelynda is an assemblywoman from the Eighteenth Legislative District in New Jersey. She loves Haseem so much and has spoiled him with everything he wants since childhood. He is her only nephew and does everything she can to help him succeed even if that means using her political influence to get things done. She's very powerful black woman who has a huge network of powerful friends. Pelynda isn't that close to her brother, Darryl, Haseem's father,; she doesn't agree with his lifestyle and his clients he represents.

Steven cousin Darren, a very big mover and shaker down in the Jersey shore, living a crazy wild life in the underworld. Drugs, alcohol, women, and expensive clothes and cars are Darren's lifestyle. Ocean City, Wildwood, Seaside, and Belmar are his playgrounds where he gets his money from all kind of illegal schemes, but he tries his best from keeping his cousin Steven blind to what he is doing; he doesn't want him to get in any kind of trouble. Darren is a good-hearted guy who loves and cares so much about his little cousin Steven.

Mohan's sister, Natalie, has three urgent care centers that her parents put in her name; she followed her parents in the medical world, unlike Mohan who chose differently. Mohan's parents cater to Natalie because she is the youngest and daddy's little girl. Plus, she is obedient to her parents, where Mohan is a loose cannon sometimes. Natalie is the jewel of the family, and her parents want to make sure they give her all the tools she needs to be successful in life. Only thing is her parents don't know she is very loyal to Mohan and kinda envy all the fun he and his friends have and how she dabs in the nightlife a little bit herself. Natalie loves her brother dearly and believes in him, and she will never betray or turn her back on him no matter what.

Haseem's childhood friend Jamal has known Haseem since fifth grade when they used to play basketball for recreation. Jamal used to stand up to anybody who didn't like or had a problem with Haseem. He stopped kids from Newark that used to tease and mess with Haseem because he wasn't like them; he was a suburban kid. Only problem with Jamal is he is living in the criminal world, hanging with the wrong people who are street thugs. Jamal grew up in the streets and cool with everybody from gangbangers to drug dealers; he also loves the ladies, and that has always tempted Haseem to hang with him. He also is in a relationship with a beautiful model who works for Haseem's mother. Jamal's charm and charisma, plus being street-smart, make Haseem feel he shouldn't cut ties with him. Haseem's loyalty to Jamal is tight, and he loves him like a brother.

About the Author

Jonathan Palmer was born and raised in the city of New Brunswick, a small city in central New Jersey. Growing up in New Brunswick was rough, and he learned at an early age that only the strong will survive when faced with the harsh reality of life. He was fortunate and lucky to have both parents in his life; they were married, and they raised him and his brother to never quit and work hard to achieve their goals. Both of his parents were strict and disciplined him hard when he did bad in school. His father was his mentor and he inspired him to be tough and never be weak and to never make excuses for his mistakes.

By the time he was thirty-five, he lost both of his parents; his mother died in 2001, and his dad died in 2012. His father's death really affected him hard, and it lead to him being depressed, but at the same time, it made him determined to make him proud of him. Being a father of two at an early stage in his life helped him stay motivated and focused on living right and not doing anything wrong because he knew they needed their father in their life. He worked at Coca-Cola for twenty years, and even though it was a good-paying job, he knew he wanted more in life. You see, he always envisioned himself being an entrepreneur and owning my businesses. Yes, he didn't want to stop at one. He wanted multiple sources of income.

After being wrongfully terminated from Coke in 2018, he decided that it was time to put his future in his own hands and to never again let another company or person control his destiny.

In 2019, he changed everything; he started working out at the gym five days a week. He started having a Bible study and drew closer to God; with prayer and devotion, his life did a complete 360. He started writing *Cultural Dividends* which is loosely based off his life and people that he know. Then he started investing in stocks and built a strong portfolio. From there, he started his own dump truck and landscaping business. After that, he went working on his favorite business endeavor, Mobil-Lize, a mobile advertising platform which will launch late fall season of 2021.

Inspiration for writing *Cultural Dividends* was basically him wanting to show the younger generation that you can become successful outside of crime and violence. You can live life right and build a bright future for yourself, without doing anything illegal or living a life of crime. He sacrificed the early part of life to raise his kids and be there for them. He put off his dreams and goals to try to give them everything they needed. He always, since a child, wanted to be an entrepreneur and own multiple businesses. Real estate, Wall Street, and ownership is something he always believed in, and being determined and driven with strong discipline, you will achieve it. Organized success is something he always wanted. Multiple minds working together is better than one doing it by himself. Working together as a team, trusting and believing in one another, regardless of race, gender, or color, is the true essence of what the America dream is.

About the Coauthor

Johnnie Brown is a native of New Brunswick, New Jersey, where he was raised by his mother, Mary, and sister, Tina Brown. Johnnie has three other siblings: two sisters—Moniuqe Gray and Dominique Brown—and one brother—Darren "Aciec" Shivers. Together they moved around the city several times before settling on Delavan Street. New Brunswick in the '80s still resonates with Johnnie today. Families would sit out on their porches while kids played together. As a kid, Johnnie enjoyed playing basketball and riding his bike. The neighborhood had its ups and downs, but you learned how to survive. By fourth grade, Johnnie's mom decided to send him to live with his father, who lived in the suburbs—CULTURE SHOCK. There were Italians, Indians, and Chinese kids everywhere, but Johnnie embraced the opportunity to meet new friends. Johnnie's father worked mostly throughout his time living there, so Johnnie would enjoy spending time with these other families. Each family owned businesses that one day would be passed down to their kids—GENERATIONAL WEALTH! After Johnnie's son, Jave, was born, he knew he wanted better for himself and for his family. Today, after reuniting with some of his childhood friends, Johnnie is now an entrepreneur in several ventures including his first book, *Cultural Dividends*! This book is to inspire, motivate, and energize anyone who has big dreams. If you can envision it, you can achieve it.

CPSIA information can be obtained
at www.ICGtesting.com
Printed in the USA
BVHW071224200122
626624BV00003B/246

9 781662 455551